WALKING IN THE SHADOW OF THE VETERAN

The Heart of the Veteran

By
Linda L. Leary, BA, BS

Published by
Paradise Copies, Inc
21 Conz St.
Northampton, MA 01060

August, 2014

ISBN: 978-0-9836716-2-6

TABLE OF CONTENTS

Preface

Having recently retired from the Veterans Administration Medical Center, I am very proud of having served and dedicated thirty-four years of my life to the care of our men and women who placed their lives in combat to protect and preserve our freedoms. I encountered and cared for Veterans whose service time spanned from the Spanish-American War to Operation Iraqi Freedom. My major goal and belief was to work for the Veteran, the Veteran was not there to work for me.

Many Veterans of various backgrounds have crossed over the threshold of the VA. There were White Americans, Afro-Americans, full-blooded Native Americans, Hispanics, Orientals, as well as Catholics, Protestants, Muslims, Jehovah's Witnesses, Born-Again Christians, Jewish, Mormons, and Atheists. I have always fostered a tremendous respect for our Veterans. Having been born into an actively-patriotic family and being the second youngest of six children born to my parents, I believe that my strong love of country and the respect of our military men and women had been instilled in me from birth.

My great grandfather was a Veteran of the Civil War serving in the Union Army and representing the State of New York. I had five Leary's (four uncles and an aunt) who proudly served during World War II. My Aunt June was a Lieutenant in the Army Nurse Corps, my uncles Phil and Jack also served in the Army and both were at the rank of Sergeants. My Uncle Jack saw combat in the South Pacific, while my Uncle Phil was involved in the European Theater. My Uncle Bud (Martin) was in the Marines, but I am not sure where he was stationed during the war because not much was ever discussed about his time. The last, but not the least, of the Leary's who served in WWII was my Uncle Bob. He enlisted into the U.S. Navy and being a college graduate was lifted to the rank of Lieutenant, junior grade (Ltig). This uncle saw heavy action in the South Pacific. Each of these five Leary's all had their pictures on the front page of the Holyoke Transcript. Uncle Bob was the image of his mother and he followed well in his mother's footsteps. He was a teacher as was his mother. I was never aware that I was born on my uncle's birthday until I had to attend a family funeral. After the funeral, I went over to his grave to say a prayer when I noticed his date of birth on his gravestone. He had passed away in 1958 from a myocardial infarction at the age of 48.

I have four brothers and three out of the four served in the military. David served in the Army, but was never involved in any combat because he served between wars, Korean and Vietnam. Bill and Kevin both served in the Navy. Bill was aboard ship and was involved in the Cuban Missile Crisis. Kevin was a Seabee and served eighteen months in Vietnam. This is the brother that it seemed to take me forever to convince him to seek assistance from the VA. It seemed that everyone else could see that his behavior was not "normal" and that it was screaming Post-Traumatic Stress Disorder (PTSD), but he would only comment,

"Leave me alone, I'm alright!"

My godson and nephew, Patrick, is a Veteran of Operation Iraqi Freedom. His brother Daniel was involved in Operation Enduring Freedom. Both these brothers were Veterans of the United States Air Force. Another nephew, Scott, served in Operation Desert Storm in the Air Force. He was indirectly involved in the war because he was an airplane mechanic and was utilized in repairing many of the aircrafts that were involved in fighting and transportation of soldiers and equipment back and forth to the Middle East. I would also like to acknowledge my neighbor, Thomas Chirgwin, for proudly serving thirteen months in Vietnam in the United States Coast Guard.

As I have stated at the beginning, I have a very extensive background dealing with and caring for Veterans, both through my family and in the VA system. All names have been changed and if there is any similarity or duplicate of a given name, it is without my knowledge or intent.

Dedication

This book is written and dedicated to all the Veterans of the Leary and Desnoyers families, with special recognition to my brothers David, William, and Kevin, for proudly serving and dedicating their lives in the military of the United States of America.

CHAPTER ONE

It was still dark at 7 a.m. as I drove along Route 5 on my way to my first day of employment at the Veterans Administration (VA) Hospital in Northampton. I felt nervous and apprehensive because I had never worked outside the city limits of my hometown of Holyoke. Although it is only twelve miles from my home to the VA, I found myself gripping the steering wheel and praying to God that he deliver me safe and sound to the VA. We had a huge snowstorm the day before and I was very scared of sliding on packed snow or ice. January and February are the worst winter months in New England and the weather is so unpredictable. I've seen beautiful sunrises where the ground was clear and the sky looked like it belonged in some tropical setting. Then by 11 a.m., the snow was falling and there was a good two inches of snow on the ground with the expectation of 9 – 11 inches by 8 p.m. Weather changes very fast in New England and there is an old saying, " If you don't like the weather in New England…just wait a minute, it will change!"

Arriving at the entrance to the VA (Veterans Administration), I slowly drove up to the front of Building 1 and parked in one of the empty spaces. My instructions were to enter the front door and sit in one of the chairs in the lobby and that someone would assist me momentarily. As I took a seat, I noticed two other individuals sitting there as well, one was a male and the other was a female. After introductions on a first-name basis and conversing with each other, we realized that we were all there for the same reason. We were all new employees in the VA and we were all in the same class of CNA's (Certified Nursing Assistants). Within ten minutes the lobby was filled with about thirteen new employees and we were all in the same nursing assistant class. At approximately 7:50a.m., a very pleasant nursing instructor entered the lobby, introduced herself as Olive Crane and explained to us the processes we would be going through for that day.

Ms. Crane instructed us to follow her down the hallway. I had to snicker to myself because we looked like ducklings following the mother duck down a hallway that appeared to go on forever. I looked all around me at the surroundings of the edifice I was walking through and noticed the painted white steam pipes exposed on the ceiling, the cream colored walls that stretched from one end to the other, along with the water fountains that appeared to be specifically inserted in the walls along this corridor. We then exited this hallway and climbed the stairs to the second floor. I was the last one to come through the second floor door and was surprised to see everyone lined up in single file. My curiosity was getting the best of me so I inquired to the individual in front of me, "What's going on here?" He responded, "It's the laboratory and we all have to have a blood test!"

At this point, I just leaned against the wall and waited for my turn to come.

After the lab we all went back down to the first floor and were directed to a small conference room where we were going to meet the Chief of Personnel Service. He would instruct us in the rules and regulations of working for the Federal Government and he would also swear us in by reciting the Oath of Allegiance to uphold and defend the Constitution of the United States. The rest of the first day was just to make sure that we were fully prepared to begin our ten weeks of CNA training. We were issued three sets of VA uniforms, keys, and ID tags. There was a lunch break and a coffee break, but they seemed to have been dissolved in the chaos of this first day of federal employment on January 24, 1977.

During the next three weeks, we stayed in the classroom setting learning how to be a Nursing Assistant according to the Federal Government's rules and regulations. In the fourth week, we received assignments to different wards and we were usually paired off with another classmate. My first assignment was to Ward B in Bldg.1 which was an acute medical unit. I was assigned there with Betty Koske who was perpetually smiling and clung to me like glue. Betty was new to the working field and new to the VA. She lived nearby and was married and the mother of two daughters. Betty stated the reason she applied at the VA is because her husband was working there. It made it easier for both of them to work at the same facility being that they only had one vehicle. Three days after we were assigned together Betty confided in me and stated, "I apologize for staying near you asking you a flood of questions, but I have never done this kind of job before and I don't want to make any mistakes. It is very obvious that you have done this care before because you are so relaxed and you talk to everybody like you've known them for years."

I couldn't help but smile at Betty and I responded with, "I don't mind, you can ask me any question you want, after all that's how we learn by inquiring about things we do not understand".

Ward B had a little different setup than the other wards. This was probably due to the fact that it was a medical ward and even though the patients were primarily psychiatric patients, they were on this ward for a medical condition. There were several private rooms and two bedrooms in which pneumonia, terminally ill, or contagious disease patients were treated and observed. These critically-ill patients were never assigned a nursing assistant because they required the care of the doctor or RN (Registered Nurse), who were licensed to distribute medications, oxygen, IV's and catheters and any other professional need that the patient required.

During the training period all nursing assistants (NA) are assigned to another NA on the wards that they are receiving their training on. I remember that there was an LPN (Licensed Practical

Nurse) named Tilly and also a NA named Tilly. In my training on Ward B, I was assigned to NA Tilly. She had been working there for several years and she was excellent in her duties. She was very conscientious and cared for every patient she was assigned to on any given day. She was even kind and caring to patients she wasn't assigned by getting them something to drink, an extra blanket or to clean them if they had an accident. Tilly was a middle-aged woman, small-framed and wore her streaked silver-gray hair in a French twist. She referred to everyone, patients and employees alike, as "dear" or "hon". About a week into my clinical practice on the medical ward I was in the break room with Tilly and I asked her, "How long have you been employed at this hospital?"

She had a comical side to her because she gave me a stream of answers. She stated, "Too long!" or "Seventeen years and I should have left yesterday!" and she would finish it off by saying, "Ah, I've got nothing better to do, so I think I'll stay!"

Tilly was a hands-on person, excellent, conscientious and I appreciated working with her for the three weeks I was assigned on Ward B.

On the second rotation of my training I was assigned to Ward 2. This was a chronic psychiatric unit and the setting was very different from the medical unit. As I entered this locked unit, I turned a sharp left and entered a large dayroom and viewed several patients doing some weird various behaviors. This was my first experience on a psychiatric unit as I stood there with my mouth gaped open and the only part of my body that was moving were my eyes as they surveyed the dayroom. There were patients sitting in chairs screaming at some character on the TV, some others were walking in circles and still others that appeared calm and collected carrying on a conversation to an unoccupied chair next to them. I proceeded to the nurse's station to introduce myself to the head nurse and to hear what my assigned duties would be on this unit. As a new recruit and the first time assigned to this unit I was assigned to strip and remake beds in the dormitories. Upon entering the dormitories it reminded me of barracks in the military. There were two huge rooms and all the beds jutted out from the four walls with enough space between each bed for a bed-stand and wheelchair to fit through. All the wardrobes were back- to- back and side-by-side in the center of the dormitory. There was about four feet of space between the bottom of the beds and the ward-robes for patients to walk around freely or for patients with wheel-chairs and walkers to get to their beds. As I was making beds, other nursing assistants were doing other details such as bringing some patients to appointments in building 1, giving patients that were assigned a tub-bath or a shower, or just passing out snacks or cigarettes in the dayroom and observing the clientele for possible events of choking or starting a fire with a cigarette. Patients were never allowed to have matches or a lighter on their person because many psychiatric patients have a fascination with fire and have no concept of its dangers or even their own mortality.

One of the seasoned male NA's approached me and pointed to the slight-statured patient who was rocking gently back and forth while standing against the wall near the nurse's station. He appeared to be very quiet and shy. Max, the seasoned NA stated, "Hey Linda, go and ask him what his name is?" My first reaction was to say, "Why? Doesn't he know his own name?" Max was emphatic and stated, "Just go and ask him!"

So I approached this timid, soft-spoken patient and inquired about his name. Without missing one step in his back and forth rocking, he responded with "Mickey Mouse!"

I turned my head to look at Max who was grinning from ear to ear in the doorway of the shower room. I grinned back and shook my head. I figured this was some form of initiation for new employees assigned to the ward. The rest of the three weeks that I was assigned to Ward 2 involved a variation of assignments that nursing assistants were qualified to do.

Chapter Two

The last day of classes had finally arrived and we were all anxious to find out if we were going to be assigned a medical or a psychiatric ward. It seemed like all of the males in this class were assigned a psychiatric ward, while all the females were assigned a medical or a geriatric psychiatry (psych) unit. I was assigned to a geriatric psych unit which was Ward B annex (BX). I was accompanied by another female classmate, Marsha Jedowicz, who was likewise assigned to BX. All the nursing assistants were instructed to go to their assigned wards as soon as everyone received their designated wards. Classes were held in building 12 and Marsha and I had to trek across a few parking lots, passed a few buildings, so we could arrive at the far East side of building 1. Ward BX is on the second floor and Marsha and I arrived at the head nurse's office to introduce ourselves and to let the head nurse know that we were the new assignees to her unit. I arrived at the dutch-door to the office and saw two nurses sitting there in some kind of conference. I learned later on that it wasn't a conference. It was the night shift giving the day shift a report. With a smile on my face I stated, "Excuse me for any interruption, but my name is Linda Leary and this is Marsha Jedowicz and we were assigned to this ward by our instructor, Miss Crane."

The nurse that was closest to the door responded, "I am Gwen Berlin, I am the Head Nurse on this unit and I am very pleased to have you both aboard."

Ms. Berlin instructed us to go to the break room at the end of the hallway and that she would be with us shortly. There was about seven or eight staff members that were in the break room waiting to receive their work detail for the day.

I noticed an entire wall of lockers at one end of this break room and some were empty with the keys in the doors of the lockers. We were told by staff members that we could select any locker that was open as our own. I chose locker number 39; it was in the second row third from the left. I placed my locker key on the same ring as my MN key.

Around 8 a.m. Ms. Berlin entered the break-room and appointed all staff members to a team assignment. There were three teams which consisted of one RN or LPN and two to three Nursing Assistants. Team 1 involved showering/bathing their assigned patients first and after they were finished with the showers, the NA's proceeded to making the beds in the dorms. Team II had bathroom detail. This detail consisted of toileting all the Veterans, washing their hands and face and combing their hair and then placing the patients in the hallway. When the bathroom detail was completed by this team, they would shower the assigned patient from their team. Every patient was showered every other day or at least three times a week. Team III had the dayroom detail which consisted of shaving every veteran in the dayroom and picking them up from the hallway and placing them in the dayroom. The staff assigned to the dayroom would also be responsible for passing out snacks, drinks and cigarettes. I was assigned with Shirley Larson, who was working on BX for about four years. She was around forty years old, married and had three children. She was also a grandmother being that her son was married and had a little boy, but she found it difficult to see them on a regular basis because he lived in Tennessee. Shirley gave me the impression that she just couldn't be bothered with training anyone and also displayed a "better than thou" attitude. After working with her for one day, I realized that she was more an observer of new people rather than a conversationalist. She would observe if the newcomer was capable of doing the duties that they were assigned or incompetent. Either way, she always managed to make it to the head nurses office at the end of the shift to report her findings. Shirley was also a chronic complainer, but I learned to ignore it because she possessed a very generous and giving heart.

Kip Michalski was another fairly new employee being that he was in the previous nursing assistant class and had been working on BX for six months. Kip was an excellent worker and was always there for the patients and their needs. Every week the Recreation Department would show movies on the ward for wheelchair patients. Kip and I had set up all the wheelchairs to face the movie screen that was mounted above the door in the dayroom. When everybody was all set, the recreation worker started the film and stated that he would return shortly from a meeting that he had to attend for about an hour. Gwen, the Head Nurse was also away at a mandatory meeting in Nursing Service. Kip was leaning up against the wall in front of the head nurses office and I was across the hallway with my back up against the medication room wall. As the movie started to roll it appeared to be a western, but after about ten minutes into the movie it appeared to be very close to an X-rated movie because the characters were engaged in deep breathing exercises and consensual sexual positions. This made the staff believe that the film was never reviewed before it was shown. I could hear Kip starting to laugh so I looked across the hallway and stated, "Now, what are you laughing at?"

As he continued to giggle, his face red as a beet, he turned and said, "If Gwen ever walks on this ward and sees this, she will shit!"

I couldn't help starting to laugh because I could just picture that whole scenario. Within five minutes Kip and I heard, "JESUS, MARY and JOSEPH…What is going on here!"

We turned to see Gwen standing there with her hands on her hips staring at the movie screen. Needless to say, Kip and I ended up laughing like crazy because we didn't expect her early return to the ward from her meeting. She instructed the film to be shut off and she immediately called Mr. Murphy, the head of the Recreation Department to inquire why that film was shown on a chronic psychiatric ward with 80% of the patients in wheelchairs and had catheters. We could hear her telling Mr. Murphy not to ever send another film like that to her unit because it was going to get these patients excited and resulting in clogged catheters. When she got off the phone she stood in the doorway of her office and said, "Boy, the afternoon shift will be earning their pay tonight! They'll be busy changing catheters all evening!"

I enjoyed the idea of having assignments on teams. This broke the monotony and no one was ever assigned to one team in succession. This rotation of teams enabled every staff member to know every patient on that ward. I specifically liked being assigned to the dayroom because this assignment gave any staff member time to talk to every patient on a personal basis, if and only if they were in the mood to talk. Andre was a little Frenchman who was basically very quiet and didn't make much conversation with anyone. One day I approached Andre and pulled up a chair next to him and introduced myself. Andre turned to me with squinting eyes and asked to shake my hand. When he held my hand he stated, "You're a girl! I can't see too well!"

I inquired with other staff about glasses for him and I was told that he had glasses in the medication room drawer. I retrieved his glasses and I wasn't surprised that they were as thick as coke bottles. When I put them on him he appeared pleased, but still stated that he had difficulty seeing. After ten minutes Andre took his glasses off and put them on the tray of his chair. Andre did inform me through our conversation that he was the youngest of fifteen children and that he used to belong to a barbershop quartet with his brothers. I was intrigued with the statement that he was part of a barbershop quartet. After all, Andre was a quiet, nonverbal, uncomplaining patient who just sat in his chair and went with the flow of things on Ward BX. I diplomatically asked Andre if

13

he would entertain me with a song. With his eyes still squinting, Andre slowly turned his face in my direction and stated, "You pick the song!"

I sat back for about ten seconds to try and think of a barbershop song and settled on "DOWN BY THE OLD MILL STREAM". I sang the first line of the song. When I started the second line Andre came in perfect harmony and continued to the end of the song. When he reached the end of his song, he ended it with "HOOO!" Andre didn't forget anything about his barbershop quartet days and my initial opening of this tiny window of his life resulted in his emergence as a completely different individual who surprised the entire staff. When Andre was singing staff heads were popping out of every doorway in total disbelief that he was singing when they never even heard him talk. From that day on, whenever Andre heard my voice he would call out, "Honey... let's sing a song!"

There were several other veterans who decided that singing, whistling or humming was better than just sitting in a chair and watching TV. Flynn was a well-dressed schizophrenic who would walk around the ward from one end to the other waiting for the ward door to open so that he could go down to the canteen to get a large coffee. Flynn walked with his left hand in his dress pants pocket and his lips pursed as if he were whistling, but there was never a sound that came out of his lips. On one particular occasion, Flynn happened to be doing his typical routine of walking when he passed in front of Vinnie who was in his chair and screaming that he wanted a cigarette. As Flynn passed Vinnie he turned around and stated, "Give the veteran a cookie for Christ sake! Poor little veteran is crying!"

Vinnie was another schizophrenic who was elderly and he had one lone tooth in his bottom lower gum. He reminded me a lot of a "Humpty-Dumpty" type and screaming out was a rare happening for him. Usually, Vinnie would sit in his chair and just wait for snacks, cigarettes, or his meals. It seemed like once a week Vinnie would be in a singing mood and he would sing the same song each week. He would jump into his rendition of "By the Sea" and would sing it great for the first two lines of the song. When he couldn't remember the words, he would fill the rest of the song in with "OOOOH OOOH's". He gently hummed the rest of it and then would repeat this same song for about an hour and a half.

As the months went by and the assignment teams changed daily, I realized that I was extremely satisfied and pleased working for the Federal Government. I had previously been employed in a State Veterans Home where I had worked for six and a half years, so if one was to add up the State Veterans Home years with the VA years, it would bring me to over forty years working with Veterans. It is difficult for me to imagine that all those years are behind me because the faces and personalities of those unique and marvelous veterans remain like a sculpture that has been chiseled into my memory.

When I would hear a statement like, "There's a full moon coming on!" from other co-workers, I never said anything at the beginning, but as time went on I inquired about that expression and was told to just stand back and watch. I couldn't believe what I was seeing and hearing.....patients were banging their tray tables , refusing medications and showers , screaming for no particular reason, knocking meal trays off the chairs, tables etc. etc. etc. It was on these days that I realized that this was not just any hospital, but rather a psychiatric VA hospital. These "full-moon" occurrences not only affected the day shift, but rather all shifts, not for one day, but for two to three days and sometimes on occasion , it would slip into the fourth day. I learned very fast that the moon has a definite effect on psychiatric patients, as well as witnessing its' effect on some employees.

The VA in Northampton looks like a double-shelled egg from an aerial view. The body of the egg is called the Oval and the double shells are the two roads that go around the Oval. Between the two roads are all the buildings (wards) that go from number 1-25.

Building 1 was the Admissions Building and also housed administrative offices and the Blind Unit which were all on the first floor. The second floor was comprised of two geriatric psych. Units (DX & BX) and two medical units (B & D). Wards 2, 3, 4, 6, 7, 8 and 10 were general psych units. The one exception was Ward 4 which was the Admission Unit for acute psych. This unit was referred to as the "bull pen" because it housed the "toughest of the toughest" patients. These patients were acutely psychotic and assaultive with destructive behaviors and sometimes had homicidal and suicidal ideations. Many employees would walk or run around the oval on their break times and I even witnessed a past hospital director who would rollerblade around the oval. He would transfer from the inner oval road to the outer oval road and pleasantly greeted anyone he met as he leisurely glided along the route. In 1977, the middle of the oval was a beautiful plush green lawn, where patients would play softball, lawn bowling and horseshoes. There were also about five good-size trees that provided shade for wheelchair patients on hot summer afternoons. Sadly, about eighteen years ago, this plush area was converted into a large parking lot so that there would be ample space for outpatient visits and for new employees.

I was always one that would welcome "change". I always felt that change was best for both patients and employees alike. Most people like and deal very well with change, but you always get the certain few who like to stay in their monotonous lifestyles. On August 15, 1977, this was the first day that I had called in sick to work. I had been working for seven months and was proud of the fact that I never missed one day of work. I had the weekend off and was scheduled to report to work on Monday, but instead, through my parent's insistence, I reported to my primary care physician. I had experienced right upper quadrant pain that was literally taking my breath away because I felt like I was being run through with a sword. I arrived at the doctor's office at about 1:30 p.m. and he told me to take everything off from the waist up. After an extremely quick exam, the doctor told me to get dressed and meet him in his office. I continued to experience pain and after getting dressed, I opened the exam-room door and entered the doctor's office and gingerly sat in the chair in the front of his desk. The doctor looked at me and stated, "Linda, I'm going to give you two choices, Holyoke or Providence!!"

I must have looked at him in shock because I answered with, "I can't go into the hospital! I've got to get back to work!"

He looked at me and stated, "The only place you are going is to the hospital!! You are in serious trouble GIRL!!"

I knew that I was not able to bail out of this so I told the doctor that I would go into Holyoke Hospital. He was so adamant that he didn't even want me to go home to pack a bag. He wanted me to go directly from his office and I was admitted to the hospital at 2:30 p.m. on August 15, 1977. While I was in the hospital and after receiving a Demerol injection to relieve the pain, I asked the staff if I could use the payphone to call work to inform them of this hospital admission. I phoned Ward BX and talked to Gwen Berlin, the Head Nurse and I told her that I was in Holyoke Hospital for testing on gallbladder problems.

She stated," You're not fair, fat and forty!" I hesitantly said, "No! I'm fair, fat and 28!"

She further stated that she would inform nursing service to let them know that I would be out for an indefinite period of time. On August 16, 1977, I was reading the newspaper and had my TV on in my room when there was a news flash announcing that Elvis Presley had passed away in his Graceland mansion. With so many spontaneous events that were occurring, it made it very difficult to roll with the changes. I realize that I have stated that I like change, but change that is abrupt and spontaneous is difficult for even the best to deal with because it leaves no room for thought, only reactions.

I returned to work on October 15, 1977 after having been out for two months recuperating from gallbladder surgery. When I walked onto the ward, I was greeted by co-workers who informed me of the patients who were constantly calling for me…most particular, Andre, whom they stated went back into a slump as a result of my two-month absence.

Two weeks after my return to work, I was informed that my name came up for rotation and that I was scheduled for the Midnight to 8 a.m. shift for two weeks to cover one of the CNA's who was on annual leave (vacation). I had been working the 7:30 a.m. to 4 p.m. shift since I had started working there last January. It was now the beginning of November and I was scheduled to work two weeks on the midnight shift. Having never worked a grave-yard shift, I found it to be interesting and frightening at the same time. Interesting, because this was my initial debut at working on the midnight shift and frightful because I would be driving my car in the pitch black of night and if anything went wrong I had no way or means of contacting anyone. Cell phones were not in existence at this time and payphones were not that available. If one was on a desolate road pay phones didn't exist at all. It was Friday and I was scheduled to have the weekend off and would be reporting for work on Monday to start my two weeks on the midnight shift. About five minutes before I was scheduled to be off duty I was summoned to Gwen's office. When I entered her office she told me that she wanted to remind me that I was to report to work at midnight for Monday. I stated, "Gwen, everything has been explained to me and I understand everything!" Gwen sighed and said," Are you aware that you have to come in on Sunday night because at midnight, it becomes Monday?"

I was very pleased that she explained that to me because I was already gung-ho to have a nice long weekend off and to start work on Monday night, which would have been Tuesday, after her explanation.

I was a little tense driving to work in such bleak darkness. Route 5 from the old Mountain Park entrance in Holyoke to the bowling alley in Northampton can be very lonesome and quiet. It follows the Connecticut River on a parallel course all the way up to Canada. I sincerely believe that centuries ago Rte.5 was an old Indian trail that they just paved over and made a road. I was pleased to enter the road to the VA and surprised to see many employees parking their cars and entering the different wards. Everything was lit up….doorways, parking lots, tunnels and the hallways in every building. It was so bright that I thought I was working the day shift. When I entered BX, the only other female employee on the midnight shift was the nurse. I felt a little out-of-place because I had just entered a male domain of nursing assistants. I was told by Gwen after I had worked two days that the crew on the midnight shift appreciated having me work with them and that they wouldn't mind me coming back. I was puzzled and wondered why she was giving me this information. Gwen stated, "The midnight crew is a tough bunch of guys! I don't send just anyone to work with them! I usually will send a male from days, but I knew you would carry your own weight and do your job. I also knew that they would accept you unconditionally."

At this point, Gwen's phone rang and this conversation ended. Bella Androv was the R.N. that worked the midnight shift. As a matter of fact, Bella was the other nurse that was in the office giving report to Gwen on that first day that I reported to Ward BX. Bella was a very pleasant, sociable and caring nurse. She also had the bluest eyes I have ever seen. I enjoyed working with Bella and the midnight male gang. It seemed like the two weeks of being off-tour just flew by.

Last September Gwen put a holiday list up so that all staff members could choose which holidays they wanted to sign up for a designated day off. This list consisted solely of Thanksgiving, Christmas Eve, Christmas Day, New Year's Eve and New Year's Day. Considering the fact that my name was at the bottom of the list and I would have the last choice of the holidays never seemed to disturb me. My parents were all packed and were going to spend three months in Florida and planned to leave the Saturday after

Thanksgiving, so the only holiday I was interested in was Thanksgiving. When the time was posted, I saw that I was scheduled to have not only Thanksgiving off, but also Friday and the weekend after. In 1977, Thanksgiving was on November 24th. On November 22nd tragedy hit my family like a bomb. I was summoned out of work by my brother, Kevin, who had called to inform me that our father had a heart attack and was rushed by ambulance to Holyoke Hospital. Gwen was in the conference room which is where all the lockers for the employees were kept. She was instructing a group of nursing students and specified to the staff that she wanted no interruptions at all. I was confused and a little disoriented because I didn't want to go in that conference room and I was in shock from the information that my brother just gave me. I was walking in circles near the conference room door when Brian Robbins, a ward R.N. came up to me stating, "LINDA, you have to knock on that door and tell Gwen that you have to leave! THIS IS AN EMERGENCY!!"

I lightly knocked on the door and beckoned Gwen with my hand to come into the hallway. She must have seen the distress on my face because she bolted to the door and asked me what was wrong. When I informed her of the phone call I had just received, she told me to leave immediately and that she would inform Nursing Service of my situation. On November 23, 1977, my dear father passed away and his funeral was on November 26, 1977, which was the day that my parents planned to leave for Florida for the winter.

I returned to work on November 29, 1977 and resumed my tasks of caring for the Veterans. I was in the shower room drying a veteran with a towel when the shower curtain opened and standing there was Mr. Donaldson, the Chief of Nursing Service. He was on his usual rounds and I greeted him with a gentle "Hello"!

He returned the greeting with, "How is your father doing?"

Feeling a bit perplexed by this question, I slowly turned my head in his direction and stated, "I buried him last Saturday!"

He quickly exited the doorway and bolted for the exit door of the ward. I somehow felt that he was extremely embarrassed by his question and had no idea that my father had passed away. When I had completed dressing the patient that I was caring for in the shower room and returned him to the dayroom, I approached Gwen and informed her of the question that Mr. Donaldson had asked me. Gwen bolted from her chair and ranted, "THAT COLD-HEARTED, UNFEELING, SON OF A BITCH!!!! Linda, I informed everyone in Nursing Service and staff on this ward of your father's passing."

I looked at Gwen and told her that I wasn't blaming anyone. I just could not understand why he would ask me that question if he knew that my father had died.

As the weeks went on, I was slowly overcoming the heartbreak of losing my father and was back to giving 100% to the patients when I was on the job. Andre started singing again and participated in the question-and- answer games which appeared to mentally stimulate these unmotivated, stagnant veterans. I began by asking about cartoon characters such as, "What was the name of Donald Duck's girlfriend?"

Without any hesitation and from the other side of the room came the response, "DAISY DUCK!!"

I then inquired about Mickey Mouse's girlfriend's name and again someone else responded with, "MINNIE MOUSE!"

After going through every cartoon character I could remember, I switched to giving simple word problems. I told a little story to these Veterans and asked them to listen and try to understand completely. My story was as follows, "Why can't a man living in Winston-Salem N.C. be buried in Lexington, Kentucky?"

The facial and eye expressions that were coming in my direction were priceless. Some had no idea of what I just said. While others were trying to make some sense out of it, the answer was revealed by a Veteran who rarely spoke because of a huge mass on his neck. He slowly turned his whole body and stated, "Because he is still living! You can't bury living people."

These games also caught the attention of the staff as well and many office members along with the doctor, who likewise joined in the fun. On this one particular occasion, I was assigned to the dayroom and was in the process of collecting the patients that were in the hallway and transporting them to the dayroom. I noticed that there were several employees in Gwen's office, along with Gwen, who were reading the "BEAR HILL NEWS". The Bear Hill News was a news bulletin that was published every month and distributed to the wards and offices. This little bulletin gave information about any new employees, retired employees and also gave a complete list of happenings for that month. As I was headed back down the hallway to gather another Veteran, I was beckoned into the office by Gwen. She had been reading the back cover and she stated that there were several mental puzzles that everyone had figured out, but there were also a chosen few that they just couldn't understand or figure what the answer could be. Gwen looked at me and stated, "Linda, maybe you might have the answer to this puzzle because it isn't making any sense to any of us."

She read me the problem puzzle.

"You have two coins in your hand that add up to 55 cents, one of these coins is not a half dollar, what two coins do you have in your hand?"

I noticed that all eyes were on me and I stated, "You seriously cannot figure that out! It's very obvious to me!"

The secretary, whose name was Emma, quietly asked me, "What was the answer to the puzzle?"

I looked at Gwen and said, "One is a nickel, the OTHER one is a half dollar!!!"

I then turned and exited the office and continued to do the assignment I was assigned to for that day. Dr. Wolfgang Weinstein was the Ward Physician and he was usually writing medications or renewing medications for the patients on Ward BX every Wednesday. There was one Wednesday that the staff was asking each other several trivia questions that involved one word answers. I asked the question, "Who invented dynamite?"

I was sitting in the dayroom when I asked this question and it wasn't getting answered too quickly. I started to think that I had everybody stumped when all of a sudden I could hear Dr. Weinstein blurt out from his office, "I know, I know, it was Alfred Nobel!"

I told him that he was absolutely correct and we continued to ask questions of each other in the dayroom. When the afternoon arrived and the doctor was gone, it is the nurse's responsibility to review the medication orders that were written that morning. Gwen was reviewing the medications and suddenly everyone could hear her laughing in her office. She got up from her desk and came out and told me that she knew when Dr. Weinstein answered my trivia question about Alfred Nobel because she noticed that Theo Harris's chart had a new medication order…it was 15mgs. TNT!

Christmas was approaching very quickly and other employees were awaiting their selected holiday time. It was a complete surprise to me when I looked at the time sheet to view what days I would have off and saw that I was off on Christmas Eve and Christmas Day. I approached Gwen and told her that there was a mistake with my time because I did not request Christmas Day off. She turned to me and stated, "Linda, you are not leaving your mother alone on Christmas! I am the one that scheduled that time and you are taking it off!"

I was feeling guilty because I didn't request it and that it was unfair to the ones that did request it for their first choice. Gwen further stated, "Everything is all settled and there will be enough coverage on the ward over the holiday and no one is going to change that time!"

She made that statement with a stone-cold definitive expression on her face and I knew that the time was written in stone. I enjoyed the Christmas holidays, but the guilt I was feeling didn't decrease because I didn't want to be categorized as "favorite", which is a common occurrence in a hospital setting. There are always certain employees that stand out on every ward and they are given special assignments, time schedules and specific days off. These situations happened more among the staff nurses and older nursing assistants. I remember a Staff Nurse named Yvette Malley who shared the same birthday with an older nursing assistant and no matter what request he made, she gave it to him if she was the nurse–in-charge on that day. Gwen never worked the weekends, so if there was anything that was changed over the weekend Gwen would change it back on Monday. She would inquire, "Who changed this schedule? NO ONE IS TO TOUCH THE TIME!!!!"

Sometimes the culprit would admit to being the guilty party, but most of the time they would just listen because they were fearful of Gwen's direct-eye-contact and her ability of knowing, just by looking at them who the guilty party was.

I never was disappointed with any of the assignments I received because I fully enjoyed and looked forward to caring for these Veterans. Some cases were difficult as a result of a stroke, Lou Gehrig's disease or Huntington's chorea which resulted in muscle atrophy and stiffness of the joints. One had to be extremely careful in bathing and feeding these patients because they could choke on their food and drown in a tub. Therefore, the plan for these Veterans was to shower them and to have their food pureed and given in small portions on teaspoons to prevent any possibility of choking.

Otis was a slender Black American who would sit in a geriatric chair in the dayroom and loved to be facing the hallway so that he could see everything there. Otis was schizophrenic and no one had ever heard him talk and his family was very dedicated in visiting him on a biweekly basis. On this particular day, I was assigned to give Otis a shower. He was never a problem and he cooperated with everything that was done for him. Otis enjoyed the shower and upon finishing the shower and drying him off with a blanket towel, I rolled him out to the general shower room and wrapped the blanket around him while I went to get his clothing. When I arrived back with his clothing, Otis had gotten hold of a container of baby powder and had dumped it all over his body. He was white from head to toe! I stood there holding his clothes and uttered, "OH NO"! A coworker had entered the shower room just behind me and smiled and said, "I should have warned you about Otis! You never leave him near any powder because he always empties the contents on his body because he doesn't want to be Black. He stated years before that he is White not Black and he will not talk to anyone who is Black!"

That comment bothered me because I knew that his family was arriving this afternoon to visit with him and his brother was an ordained Baptist minister. My coworker told me to observe Otis when his family comes because he will ignore them totally. I observed in total disbelief at what I was seeing. If his family stood at the right side of his chair, he turned his head to the left and vice versa. There were four family members who came to visit and Otis acted and behaved like they didn't exist. They even brought him ice cream which he loves. Because they brought it, he wouldn't touch it, so they turned to me and asked if I would put it in the freezer so that he could have it after. I felt very badly for his family and wondered what it was that had traumatized him to think that he was White instead of Black. Otis was a handsome black man that did not look his truthful age of 66 years. When I first met him, I thought that he was 35 years old. My jaw dropped when I heard his actual age. He was a gentle schizophrenic who strongly felt that he was born White and then something happened that turned him Black. He would never look in the mirror because he wanted nothing to do with the Black man that was looking back at him. His behaviors strongly displayed that he was traumatized at some point in his life, but it was not known when or where or what age that this trauma occurred.

Chapter Three

With the holidays over I was settling into a new year with the hopes that 1978 would be a much better year than 1977 had been. It was at this same time that Gwen took me into her confidence and told me that she would be transferring to Loma Linda VA in California. She stated that the hospital was in the process of being built and that she probably wouldn't be leaving for about a year. I remember just sitting there and listening to her as she spoke of this dream change to the West Coast. I asked her, "Why are you telling me this?"

Gwen looked at me and stated, "Linda, I have complete trust in you. I know you will not say anything to anybody because I asked you not to say anything to anybody! I have been working here for twenty-five years and I feel that I need a change. During my twenty-five years I had entrusted others with some plans that I had and they ended up getting told all over this hill and resulted in my losing out. I'm putting my trust in you to let me make this announcement when the time comes!"

Months passed and I locked that secret in my memory. Around the month of February or March I was doing my usual assignment on Ward BX when Kip approached me and said, "Gwen wants you in her office, right now!"

I entered her office along with Kip and Marsha and was extremely surprised when Gwen handed each of us a promotion and followed it up with "Congratulations!" Even though I had the paper in my hand I was in disbelief and felt like I was walking on cloud nine. When someone receives a promotion, the promotion is never finalized until the chief of the department that you received it in signs it. Each of us met individually with Mr. Donaldson in which he inquired of us the reasons we felt we deserved this promotion. Mr. Donaldson was twisting a timecard around in his hand and after I gave him the reasons that I thought I was promoted, he suddenly stopped twisting the card and said to me, "You didn't mention anything about your time!" "My time"? "Yes, you have two long periods of missed time on your card!"

I sat back in my chair, looked him right in his eyes and stated, "Mr. Donaldson, I was in the hospital having my gallbladder removed and recovering from 8/15/77 – 10/15/77 and I didn't ask for gallbladder problems, then I was out again from 11/22/77 – 11/29/77 for my father's funeral and believe me.....I didn't ask for my father to die!!"

He casually signed the paper and I noticed that my pay increased the following pay period.

In October 1978, I began to hear a rumor that Gwen was going to be transferred to Ward 3 which was a chronic psychiatric unit. Gwen was going to Ward 3 to straighten it out because she did such a good job in organizing Ward BX according to the rumor. I pulled Gwen aside when she returned from a head nurses meeting and informed her about this rumor that was going around. After telling me to stay right where I was, she made an about-face and exited the ward through the same door she had just entered through upon returning from her meeting. In about fifteen minutes time, Gwen had returned to the ward and announced that she wanted all available staff to meet in the conference room. She walked to the bathroom and when she emerged from the bathroom, she quietly came up to me and said, "Today is the day!"

I sauntered along to the conference room with the other staff members and sat in a chair in the back of the room. Everybody was inquiring with each other about why we had to gather in the conference room and wondered what was going on! Gwen entered and sat at the head of the table and visually scanned the room to see if all available staff was present. She patiently waited for all the inquisitive chatter to cease and when she knew that she had everyone's attention, she proceeded with this announcement, "I have just returned from Mr. Donaldson's office because I was informed that there was a rumor going around that I was going to be transferred to Ward 3. I told Mr. Donaldson that he was half right! It is true that I am going to be transferred, but I am transferring to California……not Ward 3. Now that I have informed him, I stressed the need of immediately returning to my ward to inform my staff of this transfer. I believe that you people should know before anybody else on this hill!"

As everyone sat there with shocked expressions on their faces Gwen was open to answer any questions that her staff inquired of her. Several were wondering when this transfer was going to take place and she calmly answered that she would be working at the Loma Linda VA on January 15, 1979. We all realized that we only had three months left to work with Gwen Berlin and I was particularly satisfied knowing that I kept her secret and allowed her to announce her long-planned transition from New England to California.

Floyd Jenks was a colorful character as many of the veterans were, but he was a severe schizophrenic who displayed mild, friendly mannerisms as long as you went along with him. Floyd liked to smoke cigars and his cigars were stored in the medication room drawer and he would always approach Gwen and ask her for a cigar. She had made an agreement with him a long while back in which she told him that he would only get a cigar if he dressed properly. Floyd had a habit of putting his pants over his pajama bottoms and his shirt over his pajama top. Well, this particular morning Floyd approached Gwen for a cigar and she noticed his pajamas covering the tops of his shoes jutting out from under his pants and she instructed him to go back to his room to take his pajamas off and put underwear on. As Floyd slowly turned he looked at Gwen with a squinted eye, like Popeye and a finger pointed in her direction and he proceeded to emit a flood of nasty statements, "BASH HER HEAD RIGHT OFF!!! DON'T BE SCARED TO RIP HER, MARGARET!! GIVE HER EVERY DISEASE KNOWN TO MAN, SEYMOUR!!!! STAB HER IN THE HEART, MARK!!! Etc. Etc."

He made these statements all the way down the hallway. By the time he returned to get his cigar, he had settled down and Gwen gladly gave him his cigar along with complimenting him on his proper attire.

Gwen was also a colorful person. She was well-respected by her staff and I noticed that no matter what team I was assigned to, I would always see her enter the dorm room at the end of the hallway every morning. I thought that she was probably making sure that the dorm was clear and that there were no patients in or on their beds. On one particular occasion, I was in the shower room and I had to retrieve some clothes for a showered patient. Upon entering the dorm, I looked way down at the far end and noticed that Gwen was stripping and making beds. She was all by herself so I approached her and said, "Gwen you're the Head Nurse…you shouldn't be in here making beds!"

While she put a pillow in a pillowcase she looked at me and asked me this question, "Linda, Head Nurse, Graduate Nurse, Registered Nurse, Licensed Practical Nurse, and Nursing Assistant…What is the common word in these titles?"

I answered, "Nurse"

She looked very seriously at me and said, "Always a Nurse"!!!

With her point being made, I exited the dorm room and never made any more statements about who had the responsibility of any menial job on the ward. The one big lesson that I learned was that it was everyone's job to care for the Veterans and it didn't matter how great or how small your title. Everyone from the hospital director to the janitor was working for the Veterans.

I believe it was around July 1979 that I requested to transfer to the 12 midnight – 8 a.m. shift because I was starting to attend Nursing School and all the classes were held during the day. The guys on the night shift were glad to see me as a regular and for one month I worked alongside them on Ward BX. The regular night nurse was Bella Andros whom I spoke of earlier. The night shift was also responsible for Ward A annex which was directly below Ward BX on the first floor. AX (A Annex) was also the Blind Unit and it held twelve patients when it was full. I was assigned to Ward AX on a full-time basis on the night shift.

Each Veteran on the Blind Unit was assigned their own individual room. This was well-planned because it allowed the blind to acclimate themselves to their personal surroundings, as well as the placements of their beds, lockers and the identification of their clothes along with explanations of what clothes were placed in each drawer or shelf. When a patient was admitted to the blind ward, they were given a full tour, explained where the bathroom, dayroom, and nurses' station were located. Patients were guided by hand and told to count the steps from their rooms to each one of these important places on the unit. On each shift, there was a nursing assistant assigned to this unit for the full eight hours. An RN would come down, sporadically, to pass out medications or if there was a problem, but for the most part, it was to pass out medications. When I started to work on the Blind Unit on the midnight to eight shift, I was surprised to see so many patients awake and sitting in the dayroom. I approached Bella and inquired if she knew the reason for these Veterans still being awake at such a late hour. With her crystal blue eyes and a smile on her face, Bella stated, "Linda, these gentlemen are in darkness twenty-four hours a day. They have no idea what time of day it is, other than them inquiring about the time. Many of them have braille watches and their names and numbers/letters of their rooms are also written in braille on their doors. Late evenings and night time are their down times. They can converse with one another and staff at that time and then will retire to their rooms around 1 a.m. to 2 a.m. and sleep until 6 a.m. when they are awakened for their medications and to get ready for breakfast."

Being that there were only twelve veterans on this blind unit I became familiar with each one of them fairly quickly. Likewise, they became familiar with me and we shared many laughs, stories and jokes with each other. I learned not to take any of my senses for granted when I worked on this unit. These Veterans ranged in ages from 20 years old to well into their seventies. There was also a variety of reasons that resulted in their blindness; some were blinded by diabetes or multiple sclerosis, while others were in-volved in traffic accidents, fights or falls from a high place causing damage to the occipital lobe of the brain. I recall one particular patient whose blindness resulted when he scratched his own eyes with a piece of broken glass when he had a psychotic breakdown while attending college in Worcester, MA. This patient was very intelligent and enjoyed hearing poetry and classical novels. He was very much a loner and would rarely participate in the group dis-cussions in the dayroom with the others. He would slouch down in the chair, his eyes closed and his lips pursed as if he were suck-ing on a lemon. I approached him and inquired if there was any-thing bothering him and he stated, "No, I'm okay, I'm just listening to the others and I find some of their conversation interesting!!"

It didn't take me long to acclimate myself to these blind Vet-erans. They were amazing because there was never any time for self-pity or to dwell on feelings that they were extremely limited because of their blindness. These men had already passed that hur-dle several years past and were willing and able to conquer their handicap in very big ways. They would reject any sympathy and on a rare occasion would excuse themselves from any conversations or event where they overheard sympathetic comments directed at them. I remember one night getting involved in a conversation with four of these Veterans and discussing when they became blind and the cause of their blindness. After everyone stated what it was that led to their blindness and the ages that it occurred at, I calmly said, "Boy, it's a heck of a handicap!"

I was proud of each one of these Veterans, but I felt at a loss for words that the admiration I held for them could not have been expressed in a better statement. These Veterans respected me and looked forward to my coming on duty. Raoul came to this blind unit from Puerto Rico and his blindness was caused from diabetes. He was a married man and held a very good job at the airport in San Juan. As Raoul was sitting comfortably in the chair, he slowly turned his head toward my direction and commented on the word "handicapped". He said, "Linda, nothing against you, but I have a problem with that word! There was a time that I was handicapped by my blindness because I allowed myself to be handicapped. I was angry and depressed and felt that life was not worth living as a result of my loss of vision. I lost my job, couldn't drive anymore and lost my independence and self- esteem. I would sit and mope around the house and was wading in a big pool of self-pity. I didn't eat or drink anything and came very close to losing my family. One day out of the blue, my wife angrily approached me and stated to me, "Big deal, you're blind, but you're not dead, so stop acting like you are!!!" "Upon hearing that statement from her, she walked out the door and was gone for about six hours. It made me think that she was absolutely right! I started to go outside in the yard and neighbors would see me and come over to talk about sports or current events. I was successful in retrieving some of my independence back. So you see why I have a problem with the word "handicap", one is handicapped only if one chooses to be handicapped!"

The three other veterans that were also present and heard Raoul's explanation appeared to agree with his statement. I could only smile and I looked at these four non-handicapped, non-debilitating men and told them that I will never voice that word again in reference to them and with humility, apologized for mentioning the word," handicap". I realized that they taught me more about blindness than what I could ever teach them. I would wonder who was really blind, the sighted individual who rolls his eyes and takes everything for granted or the blind individual who sees everything through their senses of touch, hearing and smell.

Yvette Malley was assigned the Head Nurses position on Ward BX upon Gwen's transfer to California. She showed a great deal of favoritism among the staff. This favoritism didn't bother me or affect me because I was permanently on the 12 midnight to 8 a.m. tour of duty. At change of shift in the morning, I would hear a few of the aides complaining about their assignments. They felt that it wasn't fair because they had the same assignment for a week and some had it for a two-week stretch of time. The assignments weren't being rotated as they were when Gwen was there. The favorites were getting what they wanted like having a steady shift from 6 a.m. to 2 p.m. and were having fewer duties to perform. Amazingly, these favorites were at the highest level of the pay scale for CNA's and to be at that level you had to function and perform the duties of that level which did not include folding towels and putting them away. These were the duties of a CNA at a much lower level. Another fact that I overheard from these disgruntled employees was that these favorites were getting more weekends off than anyone else as well. I felt bad that employees were not being treated fairly on the day shift, but I never uttered a word because it was none of my business…I was a night-shift employee.

I enjoyed the night-shift and after a few weeks my body adjusted well to it. I had set days off during the week and worked every weekend. I was working on Ward AX on Easter weekend and I remember I was waiting to be relieved by the day shift CNA who was Wendy Nawicki. Wendy was married and had three sons and she lived in Greenfield, MA. She appeared to be running late, but I didn't mind because it was Easter and she was probably letting her boys have an Easter egg hunt before she came to work.

At 9 a.m. the nurse from BX came downstairs and asked me if I could stay until 11 a.m. because Wendy would not be coming into work because she perished in a house fire with two of her three sons early that morning. I couldn't believe what I was hearing. My heart seemed to have dropped down somewhere in my intestines and I just sat there in shock. I was recalling the day before when Wendy had relieved me and she was so excited about the preparations she was making for her family for the Easter Holiday. She told me about the beautiful ham dinner, the Easter baskets for the boys, buying everyone new clothes, going to church and then an egg-hunt for the boys. Everything sounded like it was going to be the best Easter she had ever had. Sadly, she never was able to enjoy these preparations. It was reported that Wendy managed to throw the baby out the second-floor window to the firemen, then collapsed by that window with her other two boys and died in the conflagration. One never knows, here today, gone tomorrow! There is nothing guaranteed in life and the expression, "Live every day like it's your last" makes a great deal of sense to me now!

In June Yvette Malley approached me and stated, "They need help on Ward 8 on the night shift, so I am transferring you to that ward and you will start there next week."

Yvette was great at dropping bombs like that and then just walking away. She never gave anyone a chance to respond.

CHAPTER FOUR

Ward 8 was an acute psychiatric admission ward and patients were admitted to this unit on all shifts. The procedures were entirely different in dealing with these admissions as well. Patients that were admitted intoxicated or high on drugs had to be escorted to the ward, their pockets were emptied and the contents were placed on the counter to be recorded. All cigarettes, cigars and pipes were put in the medication room along with any lighters and matches. All money above the amount of $5.00 was placed in Patient Funds in Building 1. After the completion of these tasks, the Veteran was handed a pair of hospital pajamas and escorted by a male aide into the shower room. While the Veteran was showering, the aide would put latex gloves on and would then bag the clothes that were discarded on the shower room floor. The aide explained to the Veteran that his dirty clothes had to go to the laundry and that he would have them returned to him in a few days. In the meantime, he had to remain on the ward and in pajamas. Upon completion of his shower and given something to eat, the Veteran had an intake done by the nurse and was assigned a bed and administered any medications that were prescribed by the admitting doctor.

When I first arrived on Ward 8, it was an acute psychiatric admission ward that was slowly transitioning to a behavior modification ward. When the ward was completely behavior modification, I transferred to the 4 p.m.–12 Midnight tour which was much better for my physical and mental health. I had to get myself back on a more normal schedule in which I was sleeping less during the day hours and more at the night hours. Changing your sleep patterns and waking hours is not an easy task, especially when you've been conditioned to a certain routine for six and a half years. I found the time on the 4 p.m.-12 Midnight shift to pass very quickly because all the patients were there and involved in various activities on the ward. Some veterans were reading newspapers, some were watching TV, some playing cards or pool and many were on the porch smoking cigarettes. This ward had veterans with a variety of diagnoses on it and all the patients were capable of attending to their Activities of Daily Living skills, feeding and dressing themselves, as well as knowing the times that they would receive their medications in which they respectfully approached the medication nurse requesting their meds at these appropriate times.

The year was 1980 and it was on Ward 8 that I first heard the diagnosis of Post-Traumatic Stress Disorder or more commonly referred to as PTSD. Prior to this diagnosis, all Vietnam Veterans were tagged with the diagnosis, "Vietnam Syndrome" for lack of a better description given to all the returning Vietnam Veterans who were trying to find out where they fit in in the American society. We also had schizophrenics, manic-depressives, substance-abusers, personality-disorders, sexual-abusers and victims of abuse and a small sprinkling of sociopaths. This psychiatric setting was a far-cry from the complacent ward that I was very familiar with on BX. These patients basically cared for themselves and needed reminders for certain things, but more appropriately, they were reminded that they were in the VA hospital and that there were rules and regulations that they were obligated to follow. I found that the alcoholic or drug-abuser was the most problematic patient to treat because they had no memory of getting to the VA, let alone being admitted to it. After a 24-hour period, the substance-abusers would request discharge because they no longer wished to be there. The ward doctor would grant their request and discharge them in the morning, only to have them re-admitted by late afternoon, stoned or inebriated out of their minds. This cycle would occur so often that some staff would feel that it was a waste of time doing all the admission paperwork and care just to have the patient stay to sleep and eat and then be discharged within twelve hours of their admission. Even I felt that it was a waste of time. But, as the years went on, I realized that a Veteran is never a waste of time for anyone who is employed in the VA. Veterans did not come to the VA with hang nails, they came with a truck-load of problems that they wanted straightened out.

Ward 8 had a few employees that I had worked with on Ward BX. Shirley Larson, the "complainer" from BX was working the day shift. She had taken a leave of absence to care for her ailing mother who had passed away just before Christmas. Shirley returned to work after the New Year and was stationed on Ward 8. There were several others whom I knew from their floating over to Ward BX when we were short-staffed. The doctor was Kermit Mindsky, M.D., and although I never saw him because I was working the 12 Midnight – 8 a.m. or 4 p.m. -12 Midnight shifts, I figured that he had to be a very colorful character because his office walls, desk and file cabinets were all painted purple. It was a sight that I will never forget, because I absolutely abhor the color purple. I never liked purple or any shade or hue. I know and realize that purple is the color of royalty, but it always reminded me of death. It seemed every funeral home that I went into always had these deep-purple curtains draping a window above a coffin. As a result of this exposure, I find purple to be a very morbid color. I was informed by a day-staff member that Dr. Mindsky painted his office purple because it was his daughter's favorite color and he wanted to please her. I often wondered what effect this office would have on the patients when they were brought in to talk to the doctor.

The Head Nurse was Frieda Nyland. Frieda was very familiar to me because I would deliver the weekend report to her on Monday mornings when I was working the midnight shift on B annex. She was a very pleasant woman who maintained hospital tradition. Hospital styles were changing to colors and printed uniforms or the wearing of the surgical blues and greens. Frieda continued to wear the traditional nursing "whites". She maintained control of patients and staff on Ward 8. I remember one particular instance on the 4 p.m.-12 midnight shift when about four of the aides were joking around with each other and they had decided to put one of the aides in "cuff and belt" and then place them in a laundry cart and park the cart on the porch. This occurrence happened during the summer. I knew that the staff was just having fun with each other and I witnessed this as I was taking blood pressures of some veterans in the dayroom. The following day when I reported for duty, I was instructed to report to Ms. Nyland's office. When I rounded the nurse's station and entered Frieda's office, I was surprised to see the whole staff that I had worked with the evening before present in the office. Mentally, I was wondering what was going on. Frieda stated, "As soon as the last individual that worked last evening gets here, we will proceed."

Two minutes later, the evening nurse entered the office. Everyone was standing because the office was small and seven people crammed into a small office makes one feel like a sardine, but the cramped quarters didn't eliminate our curiosities of why we were there. Frieda began by holding up a white paper in her right hand and directly stated, "I received an incident report from the front office telling me that a staff member on this unit was put in cuff and belt last evening. I want to know who the employee was that was put in cuff and belt? Who were the ones who put this employee in cuff and belt? Cuff and belt requires a doctor's order and what you thought was a joke is a SERIOUS MATTER!!"

The evening nurse, Nora, was surprised to hear this because she had been in the medication room and was not aware that this so-called little joke was taking place. Frieda then turned towards me and asked, "Linda, do you know anything about this incident?"

I looked around the room at all the faces that were looking in my direction and replied, "Yes, I saw the incident, but I wasn't involved in it. I was taking blood pressures in the dayroom."

"Could you tell me which of the staff members were involved?"

I remarked, "I don't feel that this is my place to be an informant! I believe that through the process of elimination you will be able to figure it out. There are seven people that worked last evening and these same seven are here in your office. You heard from the nurse and you heard from me, that leaves five people left and four out of those five were involved and the one remaining is innocent."

When I concluded my statement, I excused myself so that there would be a staff member attending to the patients in the dayroom because it was change of shift and the day-shift had gone home.

In every job that I have worked I explained to supervisors and team-leaders that if I had done something wrong, I would admit to it without hesitation and I would accept any punitive measure for that wrongdoing, but on another note, "NEVER accuse me of something I didn't do, because I will never accept that!"

This is also the basic reason that I cannot and will not be an informant or rather a "squealer" for anyone. I feel that honesty is the best policy, but after this incident with the cuff and belt, the culprit who started the whole venture, never opened his mouth or admitted to any guilt. I learned over the years that this employee was the first in a long line of non-admitting guilty parties. This line included some supervisors, some service-line managers and in one isolated case, the hospital director.

Ward 8 had established some female rooms on the first floor. There were two rooms and one room had two beds and the larger room had three beds in it. Most of the time the female beds were always full. Most of the women that were admitted usually had a diagnosis of Alcohol or Substance Abuse and after about three weeks, they acquired secondary diagnoses such as, Borderline Personality Disorder, Manic-Depressive Disorder, Schizo-Affective Disorder and just a few of straight Schizophrenia.

Sergio Ranchetti had to be the most colorful character on Ward 8. He reminded me of a paunchy "Liberace" who walked around with his arms folded and smiled continuously. He was also adamant about stating that he was a homosexual and "schizophrenic paranoid". Most of the patients on Ward 8 received $5.00/day for spending money and most would purchase cigarettes in the canteen. Sergio would purchase 5 packs of cigarettes every day and by 4 p.m. he didn't have a cigarette to his name because other patients were borrowing cigarettes from him. This borrowing situation resulted in a community meeting and the Psychologist, Dr. Lionel Pelc, strongly stated that this borrowing was going to cease and desist immediately. He told all the patients that if anyone borrows money, cigarettes, snacks etc. they will not receive their $5.00 the following day. Sergio always bought five packs of Pall Mall cigarettes. When he returned to the ward the same afternoon as the big speech was given that morning he again had no cigarettes. Sergio was a 100% service-connected Veteran and the few predators that would nail him for cigarettes didn't have any money at all. But, they always had cigarettes so it wasn't too difficult to figure out how they got them. I was sitting at the desk in the nurse's station when Sergio entered the ward. There were about ten patients sitting in the dayroom at this time. I noticed that Sergio approached one of these individuals and asked him for a cigarette. This Veteran bolted to his feet and yelled at Sergio, "YOU'RE NOT SUPPOSED TO BE BORROWING ANYTHING! YOU HEARD WHAT DR. PELC SAID THIS MORNING!"

Upon hearing this Sergio gently retreated and went upstairs. The patient that had just yelled at him withdrew a pack of Pall Mall cigarettes from his breast pocket, took out a cigarette and went to smoke it on the porch. Mentally, I thought and realized that Sergio was only asking for one of his own cigarettes back.

Patients started to mill around the dayroom waiting to go to the dining hall for supper.

A regular occurrence for the Veterans on Ward 8 was to return to the ward and watch the 6 p.m. news on the TV. Sergio climbed the stairs to his room and after about a half-hour returned to the dayroom in his pajamas and robe. It was obvious that he had showered and washed his hair and had combed his thick grey hair into a bouffant. I was sitting behind the counter in the nurse's station and fixed my eyes on Sergio who was walking in a large circle in the dayroom. I sensed that something was going to happen, so I dropped the pen which I was using to record blood pressures and focused my full attention on the dayroom. It wasn't long before Sergio stood smack-dab in the middle of the dayroom with his arms folded and blurted out, "I am a woman! Who wants to fuck me for a cigarette?"

I bolted from the chair I was sitting in and responded, "SERGIO! Come over here, right now!"

He slowly sauntered over to the counter and I explained to him that this behavior was not acceptable. Sergio just smiled and lowered his head. I further told him that he was in a state of frenzy over nicotine depravation. I inquired of him when he had his last cigarette. Sergio told me that he had his last smoke in the middle of the morning around 10 a.m. Being a smoker myself, I handed Sergio my half of a pack of cigarettes, told him to take the filter off and it would seem like he was smoking Pall Malls. Before departing the counter, Sergio took the cigarettes, smiled at me and said, "Thank you Miss Linda!!" and proceeded to the porch to smoke.

On another occasion, Sergio decided to comically speak up in the community meeting. Everyone was present, both staff and patients gathered in the dayroom to vocalize any problems that existed on the ward. For about ten minutes no one raised their hand to utter a complaint about anything. Everybody was looking at each other wondering when someone was going to break the silence. Sergio was sitting with his arms folded and nonchalantly started pointing at various other vets and saying, "He's a homosexual!" and surprisingly, he was pointing to the Vietnam Veterans on the ward and referring to them as homosexuals. He then turned his attention to Dr. Benedicto and stated that he was a "closet homosexual!" With that, the entire dayroom was in an uproar of laughter. Dr. Benedicto remarked as he ran his finger over his eyebrow, "Sergio! You shouldn't have let our secret out!"

The laughter was highly therapeutic for all and it was just the right thing that broke the silence barrier.

The afternoon shift had more action and occurrences than any of the other shifts because all the Veterans were using their downtime. Some went for walks, some played cards or pool or read the paper and still others would be talking to staff about current events or sports. It was again at this time that Sergio approached me with another of his many statements. He was doing his usual walking around with his arms folded and the ward was fairly quiet when he approached me at the counter.

"Miss Linda, you know who makes me weak here?"

I lifted my head and visually surveyed the eight people that were in the dayroom. I then looked at Sergio and stated, "Sergio, I have no idea who makes you weak here!"

Still smiling, he started, "See baldy over there, well he doesn't!" See that short fat one there, he doesn't either!"

At this point, I interrupted Sergio and stated, "I thought you were going to tell me who makes you weak, here."

Clark Douglass was sitting way down the dayroom right next to the TV. Clark was a two-tour Vietnam Veteran who sported shoulder-length red hair and a full red beard. He was sitting in the chair with both his legs nervously twitching up and down. Sergio never could remember any names of the other patients and referred to Clark as "RED". Quietly Sergio said to me, "You see Red way down there, Ah! He makes me very weak!"

He made this statement with a slight lisp in his soft voice. I looked across the room at Clark and then turned my eyes to Sergio and told him, "You don't want to mess around with Red, he is the meanest SOB the east side of the Mississippi River!"

Sergio backed up one step and said, "Thank you Miss Linda… he doesn't make me weak anymore!"

The regular evening nurse was Lester Authier and I believe Lester had some form of scoliosis because he walked with a mild limp as a result of one leg being a little longer than the other which caused his hip to pull a little towards the right. Sergio was sitting in the dayroom close to the side exit door. All staff parked their vehicles in the side parking lot so they always entered and exited the ward by that door. As Lester was heading out the side door for supper, Sergio looked at him and stated, "Don't sachet by me because it doesn't do a thing for me!"

Lester quickly responded with, "I didn't know I was sacheting!"

On another occasion, I was assigned to take the ward to the dining hall for supper and there were two patients that were going to be sitting at the isolation table. The isolation table was for newly admitted patients or patients that committed a rule infraction. There was a new female Veteran that was admitted that day who was sitting at that table along with Sergio who happened to be an hour late returning to the ward. Both of these Veterans sat on one side of the table and I sat on the other with my back up against the wall. The female Veteran got in line and returned to the table with a full tray. Sergio went to the iced water fountain and returned to the table with two glasses of water. I didn't say anything to him because several patients would eat something in the Canteen and there was a good possibility that he wasn't hungry. Everyone was doing well when suddenly I noticed Sergio start to snicker to himself. I asked him, "What are you laughing at?"

He remarked, "I am pretending that I am in a bar and I'm cruising!"

He continued to pretend for a minute more when all of a sudden he stated to me, "You know Miss Linda; I believe I know when all my troubles started! It was in 1956 in New York City when I got fucked up the ass with a 12 inch dick!"

Immediately upon hearing this and almost choking on her food, the female patient turned her head to Sergio and crudely remarked, "Yeah and I bet you loved every foot of it, you SOB!"

I immediately told both of them to stop and told Sergio to go and get a tray of food which he readily did. Things calmed down and the rest of the evening was uneventful. Usually when Sergio gets on a roll it is very difficult to get him back on track, short of medicating him. It's as if he gets into a homosexual frenzy and labels everything and everyone gay or homosexual. Like the time he told me that Proctor and Gamble were homosexuals and that Johnson and Johnson were Siamese twin homosexuals. Another time he approached me and stated, "Miss Linda, I am a homosexual! I like the men; women don't do a thing for me!"

My return statement was, "Well Sergio, I must be homosexual too because women don't do a thing for me either!"

He smiled back at me and said, "Yeth, I understand!"

In May 1982, I transferred to the day shift upon completion of my schooling and graduated with a Bachelor of Science in Nursing. Like the 4 p.m.-12 Midnight shift, the 7:30 a.m. – 4 p.m. shift was entirely different from the other shifts. On the day shift, there were requirements for all patients to attend two and sometimes three groups a day. Dr. Pelc had established various groups to meet the needs of the clientele he was treating. He had an ADL group (Activities of Daily Living) in which many schizophrenics attended, as well as anyone else who had any trouble caring for themselves or difficulty doing any household tasks, such as cooking, laundry and cleaning. There was a PTSD group which was only attended by Vietnam Veterans and a sprinkling of Korean War Veterans. The Vietnam War had just ended in 1975. All the

VA's were receiving such an influx of these war Veterans who were looking for answers for their rapid mood swings, mistrust of everyone, but more particularly ,mistrust of their government. There was an interpersonal group which was divided into three separate groups. The reason for the three separate groups was that all the clients had to attend one of these interpersonal groups which were facilitated by a psychologist, a social worker or the interns of psychology or social work.

When I was working the Midnight to 8 a.m. shift, Dr. Pelc started to accept Veterans who were diagnosed with sexual deviant behaviors. I recall when I first heard that these individuals would be coming to our unit and was flabbergasted to hear this because these Veterans represented the perpetrators of child abuse and exploitation that we all read about in newspapers, magazines or viewed on the television. Dr. Pelc had broken ground and established the first treatment program in the Veterans Administration system. This program started out very slowly and the first patient admitted was Fritz Danker. Fritz was from the Eastern end of the State and the report that came in stated that he had raped a thirteen year-old girl at knife-point and then darted across the state line to New Hampshire, wound up in White River Junction VA Medical Center in Vermont and White River transferred him to the Northampton VAMC.

When I reported for duty no matter the shift I was assigned to, I would always read the shift reports to find out what had transpired in a twenty-four hour period. I read the report about a new admission that was a transfer from Vermont along with the events that brought him to this VA in Northampton. As I was reading, a co-worker stated, "What do you think about our new admission?"

I finished reading the report and placed it on the desk and just sat there wondering what this pedophile would look like! I had read so many stories about these individuals because it was bursting out of the closet at this time. There were movie stars, politicians, clergy and some law enforcement people who were telling their stories of childhood sexual abuse. I also learned through these readings that 75-85% of the perpetrators are family members or a close friend of the family. I imagined just what this Fritz Danker would appear to be when I saw him in the morning. My imagination was declaring war on rapists and child molesters because I was visualizing sub-human creatures that were crawling out of cesspools or septic tanks covered with all kinds of crap and disguised as an ice cream man or a clown to totally confuse the child and getting their attention to fool them into trusting them. I soon learned that my descriptions fell short by hundreds of miles.

At 6 a.m. all the patients are awakened and have to report to the nurse's station for their medications. I was sitting at the secretary's desk recording blood pressures when I heard the nurse say, "Mr. Danker, here are your meds! "

I raised my head from my recording to see an average-height, Caucasian; well-groomed, neatly-dressed man sporting wire-rim glasses. He was very cooperative and polite and thanked the nurse for his meds. He then retreated to the dayroom where he watched some TV before going to the dining hall for breakfast.

Fritz tended to be a loner, even though he was very compliant with the rules and regulations of the VA. He never mixed or conversed with any of the general population of the ward and would sit at length on the porch reading and smoking cigarettes. It was on one of these occasions about a month after his admission when I was taking a smoke-break on the porch and Fritz came and sat down in the chair on the opposite side of the table I was sitting at. The ashtray was placed in the middle of the table and Fritz inquired if he could share the ashtray with me. I gave him an affirmative nod of my head to let him know that it was fine. He appeared relaxed and lit his cigarette and softly commented about the nice weather we were having that evening. We conversed in general conversation for about five minutes when Fritz looked at me and stated, "Do you know the reason I was admitted to this VA?"

I slowly turned my head towards him and responded with, "I know the reasons for every patient admitted to this ward!"

Being that we were the only two people on the porch at this time, I inquired if he really did all those offenses that were written about him in the admission report. He readily admitted to these offenses and then attempted to explain to me his reasoning for doing so. I was haphazardly hearing him because I couldn't believe that he admitted to doing such a deviant act against a child. My mind was spinning with thoughts that he not only raped and molested this child, but rather he had raped and molested her whole family. I was focused on the parents of that child and thought how they were blessed with a healthy, normal baby and were raising this child to best of their ability and then along comes Fritz and blows every ethical, religious, physical and emotional teachings right out of the mind of their daughter. These thoughts were in my head as I sat there and stared at a squished fly on the door screen. I vaguely could hear Fritz's voice as he continued to babble on about whatever it was he was saying. My mental isolation was trespassed when Fritz touched my arm and asked, "What is your opinion?"

I turned my head and responded, "What is my opinion about what?"

It was very apparent that he wanted to know what I thought about his actions. Before I would release my opinion, I inquired if he wanted a personal opinion or a professional opinion. He stated that he wanted my personal opinion. Without hesitation, I reached across the card table, grabbed his shirt just below his neck and pulled him halfway across the table and with gritted teeth gave him my personal opinion. I have never been a parent, other than a godparent, but after I concluded my opinion to him, I further stated to him that he would have been better off if he had asked for my professional opinion. My professional opinion was a lot different than my personal opinion. Fritz was the first with the diagnosis of "pedophilia" to be admitted to Ward 8, but it wasn't long before they started to be admitted on a weekly basis.

Chapter Five

Being assigned the beeper (pager) was an automatic assignment for one nurse and one CNA on each shift. The beepers were used to warn the team that there was a psychiatric or a medical intervention. Whoever is appointed to the team and is carrying the beeper has a duty to respond immediately when that beeper goes off. The assignment of the beeper is on a rotation basis so that the same workers are not given it every day. It averaged out at about twice a week that the same employee would carry it.

I recall one situation in that I was assigned the beeper on the midnight shift on Ward 8. My beeper went off at about 2 a.m. and it stated that it was a psychiatric intervention in the admissions area in Building 1. Everyone appeared to arrive at the same time. The midnight supervisor was in charge and I knew him very well because he used to be the 4 p.m.-12 Midnight nurse on Ward BX when I had worked there. His name was Brett Mitchell and he was one of the nicest and most considerate persons that I had ever met in the VA. Brett had the team gather around him and directed our attention to this small-framed Veteran who was highly intoxicated and sitting on the floor in the admission area. As I observed this small quiet man sitting on the floor, I wondered why an intervention was called! He didn't appear to be a problem, he wasn't acting out and he was neatly dressed in whites that made me think that he worked in a kitchen/cafeteria or was an orderly in a hospital or clinic. The Veteran was cowered down and started to mumble something that none of us could understand. A male team member started to approach this Veteran when he suddenly bolted to his feet and appeared to defend himself from this male team member as he was screaming, "Fucking Gooks! You're never going to take me alive, fucking Gooks!"

Every limb of his body was in motion. It was very obvious that this was a Vietnam War Veteran and his intoxication put him in a flashback in which he was back in the jungle in Vietnam. Needless to say, the entire team had to physically subdue this Veteran and keep him from harming himself or others by grabbing a limb in an attempt to calm him down. He started to bang his head against the wall, so I came from behind him and placed my right arm around and under his chin to still his head. He slowly rotated his head so that his chin was below my arm and proceeded to bite my forearm with such intensity that I went into momentary shock and was staring directly at the supervisor, who in turn was looking directly back at me. In a low voice Brett asked, "Is he biting you?"

I was in such pain that I couldn't even verbally answer Brett, so I just affirmed it by slowly moving my head up and down. The first problem was solved in that we had subdued this Veteran from harming himself or others. The second problem was to safely attempt to pry his teeth out of my right arm. The bite was so intense that it went through the sleeve of my winter jacket I was wearing and punctured the skin on my arm. He wasn't loosening up at all and if they were to pull him off he would have taken part of my arm with him. I told the supervisor that there is only one thing to do and I have to do it. With my left hand, I placed it near his face and proceeded to flick both his nostrils, thus surprising him and he immediately opened his mouth and released the bite hold. Upon release, Brett asked me to remove my jacket so that he could see if the skin was broken. As I did so, I viewed a full set of teeth prints on my forearm and some had also been bleeding. Brett instructed me to roll up my sleeve because he had to give me a tetanus shot. After the shot, he bandaged my arm and completed an incident report and I returned to the ward and completed my shift.

I have always felt that there is no Veteran in the VA that is there for a runny nose or hang nails. There are definite reasons for Veterans to be admitted and cared for whatever medical and psychiatric problems that exist in them. There were about two handfuls of Veterans that were termed as "snowbirds" because they would spend their summers in New England. Then, as soon as the weather started to get cold, they would spend their winters in VA's in Florida or the Southwest. The Veterans that would normally follow this pattern were Veterans who were not involved in war. War Veterans would avoid climates that would trigger possible flashbacks in them. Korean War Veterans who were stationed in the mountains, near the 38th parallel, avoid snowy climates because these are the conditions that they were exposed to in Korea during the winter. I have had Veterans tell me that everyone thinks that Korea was in a warm area near the equator. Korea was very cold during the winter and attempts to climb the knee-deep, snow-packed mountains were bone-chilling and many soldiers suffered frostbite. The Vietnam War Veteran avoids humid, tropical, rainy areas because these areas remind them of the jungles of Vietnam and the long monsoon season that this country experienced for several months of the year. I also recall Vietnam Veterans that would gravitate to the rainy tropical surroundings because they feel that mentally, they are still in Vietnam.

Being assigned to Ward 8 proved to be very educational to me because of the mixed bag of psychiatric diagnoses. When we started to get more and more patients with the diagnosis of pedophilia, we were also starting to get Veterans who were the victims of pedophiles. I recall that there was one period of time where the staff felt like they were walking on egg crates because half the ward were perpetrators and the other half were the victims of perpetrators and one did not know about the other. It was a Sunday afternoon and most of the Veterans were on pass and were expected to return to the unit by 7 p.m. A female patient that was usually on pass for the weekend was sitting in the dayroom reading the newspaper. In her past, she was a victim of sexual abuse and the Veteran she was dating and frequently went on weekend pass with, was a perpetrator. She thought that he was discharged last Thursday, but in actuality his court case came up and he was found guilty and was sentenced to jail. She thought that he was discharged to his home. I was sitting in the nurse's station doing some paperwork and every now and then I would lift my head to observe the dayroom and the five patients that were there. Everyone looked content and appeared to enjoying the lazy Sunday afternoon. Suddenly without warning, the female Veteran bolted from her seat, threw the paper on the floor and proceeded to quickly approach the nurse's station. The other Veterans in the dayroom followed her with their eyes and wondered what had upset her. When she reached the nurse's station, she pointed her finger and angrily stated, "You're all a bunch of dirty bastards!"

I looked over the rim of my glasses and inquired why she made that accusation to us. She continued her verbal outburst with, "Why didn't you tell me that asshole was a pervert? You let me walk right off this ward with him and you knew he was a PERVERT!"

I visually surveyed the dayroom and noticed that the remaining patients were all facing the nurse's station and very interested in the subject that this female patient was expressing in her rants. It was at this point that I realized that she must have read the whole court case in the paper. I gingerly stood up and approached this Veteran and invited her to discuss this matter in the confines of an office, because the dayroom was not the place to discuss these matters. She obligingly accompanied me into an empty office where she was able to unload her emotions in a private area. She also fully understood the government laws of confidentiality after I thoroughly explained them to her. She humbly apologized for the outburst and the name-calling of the staff in the dayroom. She left the office much calmer than she was previously and returned to the chair she was occupying, picked up the newspaper that was on the floor and resumed reading the remainder of the paper.

The Veterans Administration Medical Center in Northampton, MA was built on Bear Hill in the Leeds section of the city. I used to wonder why they called it bear hill because I had never seen any bears. My opinion changed drastically when I went for a walk with a patient around the outside roadway. Walking on this road, behind the recreation hall, was a female black bear and her two cubs. Needless to say, we scurried between two buildings and safely returned to the ward without incident. On another occasion, I was assigned to the 12 Midnight – 8 a.m. shift to cover for the vacation of a fellow employee and it turned out that it was also my turn to be assigned to another ward for the night. I was assigned to Ward 4Lower, which at that time, was the admission ward. I was assigned to special-observation duty of four patients. All four patients were asleep and being a very muggy summer night, I found that the air was heavy and very uncomfortable to breathe. There was no air conditioning and the only fans were circulating in the patients rooms. I opened a side door that led down a ramp to the backyard just to try and get some air circulation. I placed the chair in the open doorway and gazed up at the night sky that was full of stars. I was sitting there for about ninety minutes when I suddenly noticed a big dog in the yard. The dog looked like a Newfoundland. The dog was at the far end of the yard and I assumed he was trying to find a spot to do his business. He was moving around sluggishly and was grunting. There were no lights in the back so it made it difficult to see. The so-called dog was getting closer to the ramp area when suddenly he stood up on his hind legs and was heading for the ramp and me. I immediately kicked the chair out of the door and closed the door. This was no dog, but instead a huge male black bear that was looking for something to eat. I asked another employee if they would take my watch so that I could report this bear incident. My co-worker told me that my report would be the third one of the night. He stated that there was a bear in the tree by the power plant and there was also another bear spotted in a tree near the recreation hall. I was surprised to hear so many bears that were spotted on the VA grounds at that time of night. I made my report and returned to my post outside the special observation room where all the patients continued to remain asleep.

The evening shift on Ward 8, I found to be very enjoyable because the porch was completely screened in from floor to ceiling and everyone delighted in sitting out there to talk, smoke a cigarette or just to feel the balmy summer breezes that carried the scents of the woods that totally surrounded the compound. I was sitting in the chair just to the right of the main entrance door to the ward when I noticed a defined cut in the screen. The screen seemed to be placed back into position so that no one would discover that it was cut. I walked over to the screen to observe it more closely and I could see that someone cut the screen in the shape of a large right angle. I returned back to my chair and wondered who would do such a thing and then try to cover it up. Patients were allowed to walk the grounds until 10 p.m. and then they had to be back for patient-count at that same time. It was also at 10 p.m. that all the wards were locked. At this time, Ward 8 was admitting several problematic patients with personality disorders. Garth Taylor was one of these patients who wanted to be in the hospital, but didn't like the idea of the ward being locked at 10 p.m. He hung around with Vietnam Veterans, but I am not sure if he was a Vietnam Vet. Garth liked pushing the rules and regulations to meet his own needs and really didn't care what anyone thought about him or his actions. He was a charmer, or at least he thought he was a charmer. He would always say or do something with a big smile on his face and many times it worked for him, but with me he got nowhere. I had a feeling that Garth was the one who cut the screen on the porch, so I decided to set a trap for him. Two days previous, patient-count was taken at 10 p.m. and no one could find Garth. At 10:05 p.m. Garth entered the ward from the porch and stated that he was on the porch sitting behind the door. I never bothered to report the cut screen because I had a strong feeling that this was Garth's exit and entrance point. I told the nurse that I was going to try something that just might catch a culprit. I turned the porch lights off and sat in a chair by the table and didn't smoke a cigarette because the red flame would give me away. I sat there ever so quietly and listened to the sound of the crickets in the yard. Without any warning, Garth burst through the cut screen and immediately sat in the chair and acted as if he was there all the time. I slowly turned my head in his direction and stated, "Welcome back!"

He appeared speechless and attempted to give some flimsy excuse, but I wasn't buying anything. I also assured him that the screen would be repaired tomorrow and if it or any screen is cut again, it would be grounds for immediate discharge according to the rules and regulations of the Veterans Administration. The cutting of screens is destruction of Federal properties and results in immediate discharge and the possibility of monetary payment of the damages or replacements. I further stated that his actions will be going on report and that he should be prepared to meet the staff at meeting tomorrow concerning this incident. When I finished saying what I had to say, Garth just sat there with his mouth gaped open, not so much for what I had said, but rather for being caught red-handed for one of his rule-pushing escapades.

There were quarters for five females in the Ward 8 program. At this time, there were two young females, one middle-aged female and two older females. One of the older females was Adele Slotnick who had had several admissions to the Northampton VA over a period of twenty years. Adele was schizophrenic and would hear voices. Several times Adele was observed talking to herself or answering something that she heard from the voices. She was one of the most unique patients that I had ever met because she possessed a memory of several past movie stars and she would tag a female employee with one of these movie stars name. I was referred to as "Sophie Tucker" and Penny Nimms, a nurse was referred to as "Myrna Loy"! All the male employees were also given stars names, but never on a permanent basis as were the females. I overheard Adele talking to another patient and in the conversation mentioned two movies stars names referring to a male employee. She said, "He thinks he's Errol Flynn, but he looks like Groucho Marx!"

She was very comical for the most part, but she could also be very nasty. She was nasty with the female employees, especially when she stared without blinking. It was as if she was zeroing in on her target. I had taken the ward patients over to the mess hall for supper and I was the last one to enter the mess hall. I sat at a table near the door and directed the patients to sit at the group of tables that were against the wall when they returned with their full trays. Adele was sitting at the first table eating her supper and was staring directly at me. After she placed her tray and utensils by the dishwasher, she proceeded down the aisle to the door I was sitting near. I knew I was going to catch hell and sure enough she started at the top of that aisle and with a loud defined voice, she said, "I know you Sophie Tucker and I'll patronize your music, but you're nothing but a PIG!!"

She usually would add "whore, lesbian or lesbian-whore with it, but she omitted it this time. Perhaps the reason she omitted it was she had already arrived at the door and pushed it open and departed without further incident. After she left, I turned to observe the patients that I escorted to the dining hall and was surprised that all of them were looking back at me. Many of these patients were new to the VA and were not familiar with each other, let alone, Adele! I decided to ignore the situation because, after all, I am working in a psychiatric hospital and anything is bound to occur in that setting.

Every day was different and every day is unpredictable in a psychiatric hospital. Certain routines do not change, like medication distribution times, 6 a.m. wake-ups, maintenance of ADL skills and set meal times in the dining hall. The patients appeared to fall into the daily routine of hospital-life very easily. As I escorted the patients back to the ward upon completion of their supper, I was asked by a few patients if I was able to play spades with them. I informed them that I had to do the blood pressures and to record them before I will have the time to play. Fortunately, there were only six patients who needed those recordings, so by seven-thirty, four of us were sitting at the table involved in a very competitive card game of Spades.

When I was getting the blood pressures earlier, I noticed that Adele had approached the nurse's counter and was staring at Penny Nimms, the nurse who was writing notes in a chart on the other side of the counter. Adele just stood there with her arms resting on the top of the counter. Adele must have had a goiter problem because her eyes were very bulbous as she stood there staring at Penny. As I completed my blood pressures, I entered the office when I heard Adele say to Penny, "Myrna Loy sucks cocks in the gutter!"

Without hesitation, Penny slowly dropped her pen and looking at Adele stated, "NEVER once have I ever done that in a gutter!"

Upon hearing that remark from Penny, I grabbed the first chair I could find because I couldn't stop laughing. Adele had vacated the counter and Penny looked in my direction, lowered her head and began to laugh as well. We both felt that this was one of Adele's off-days and would probably have a better day tomorrow.

On the behavior modification ward they had a pay system that was based on chits. Chits were small pieces of paper that the patient earned during the day and the highest amount of chits earned daily was five. Each chit also represented a dollar, so the most any patient could get was $5/day, if they made all their chits. Some would get two dollars, some three dollars, but most of the patients would behave and earned their $5/day. Most of the monies were spent on cigarettes which were sold in the canteen for $1/pack and not one brand was generic. All cigarettes were brand-named such as Winston, Lucky Strike, Camel, Newport, Salem etc. Most all of the patients were smokers so it made sense that they would spend their daily money on cigarettes, but it was also tragic because many of them died of cancer of the lungs or throat in the years to come.

Integrating with the patients by playing cards, Ping-Pong, discussing the daily news issues or just sitting and having a general discussion was always an enjoyable task for both the staff and the patients. Many feelings were expressed during these times and regardless of their diagnosis, these Veterans displayed real concern about the various topics of discussion. Several of the schizophrenics were on Haldol injections which began upon their admission to the hospital. They were very paranoid and didn't trust anyone or anything and would strike out at anyone who entered their space. It usually took a team of three or four employees to hold the patient still so that the injection could be given correctly and safely. This team process would occur only at admission because the patient was at the height of his decompensation and didn't understand where he was, let alone receiving an injection. After receiving the injection, the patient was released by the staff and every time we would receive verbal hell and were called every name in the obscene book. There was no need to try and explain the benefits of the injection to the patient because they wouldn't understand anything that you said to them, nor was he/she in any mood to even listen to you. It took two to three weeks for the patient to feel the effects of the medications and would be pleasant, respectful and polite in their behaviors and mannerisms. Some would recall their admission day and remembered how they acted and would apologize to the staff for these terrible behaviors. Others had no memory at all of their admission. No staff member ever brought the admission date up to any of the patients because after all, no one was admitted to have their ears flushed. There was always a legitimate reason for every admission in the Veterans Administration Medical Center.

It was out in the Oval that I experienced my first patient that was referred to as a "runner". Kirby Arthur was a 100% service-connected Veteran who had several admissions to the VA, particularly the Northampton VA. He was from Connecticut and I assumed that he had been transferred to Massachusetts because he had exhausted all the VA's in Connecticut and he continued to be in need of treatment. Kirby was schizophrenic and he would frequently disregard his medications and not take them, thus he would get verbally loud and obnoxious. He was also frequently escorted to the VA admission office by some area police cruiser because he would announce that his residence was the VA hospital. After his admission, Kirby would be escorted to the ward and would be showered, placed in pajamas and given something to eat. He always seemed to smile or laugh and acted like he did nothing wrong. He would remain in pajamas for three days and tray service would be provided to him on the ward. When he was allowed to dress in his own clothes, he was also allowed to have ground privileges in which he could go to the recreation hall, canteen, library or the VA store. Kirby would never walk when he had privileges, rather he would run, like a bat out of hell from the escorted group on the return trip from the dining room to the ward. He was given the nickname of "Speedo" because he was like the wind and there was no catching him when he was in full running mode. He would run down the tunnel around Ward 9 and disappear into the woods that surrounded the VA hospital. He was gone! The only thing left to do was to put him on the report and to notify admissions. This was nothing new to the admissions office; they would see these reports about Kirby about three to four times a month during late spring, summer and early fall because the weather was nice. Kirby never ran during the winter, rather he was like a bear and would literally hibernate for winter by rarely leaving his room or sleeping in a chair in the dayroom.

Ginger Shevlin was a nursing assistant who worked the 4 p.m.-12 midnight shift on Ward 8. She was a character and had been employed with the VA for about twenty years at this time. She was short, shaped like a pear with short-cropped hair that was bleached blond and whenever she had to approach a patient she appeared to be very apprehensive and talked in a low voice. She walked cautiously and quietly as if everyone was asleep and she didn't want to wake them. I recall an incident when there was a female patient restricted to the ward for some offense that she had committed during the day. When patients are on ward restrictions, cigarettes are given on an hourly basis and they are not allowed to leave the ward unless they are escorted by a staff member. Ginger started to do rounds as I was sitting in the nurse's station writing notes. I was positioned at the desk that was on the other side of the counter and was able to view the entire dayroom. I noticed Ginger walking into the crafts room where she was talking with the restricted female patient who was in there. I returned to my writing when suddenly Ginger was standing in the doorway of the office which was on my right side and very quietly stated to me, "Linda, Missy is in the craft room smoking!"

I slowly raised my head, looked over the counter and directly through the craft room door where I saw this small stature, neatly-dressed, cocky, restricted female patient who was flauntingly smoking a cigarette and laughing nervously as she stared back at me. I turned my head to Ginger and asked, "Where did she get the cigarette? Go and take the cigarette away from her!" Without even budging from the doorway, Ginger remarked, "I already asked her for her cigarettes and she told me to go screw myself!"

I stood up and proceeded across the dayroom to the crafts room. When Missy saw me coming halfway across the dayroom, she immediately extinguished her cigarette in the ashtray and was sitting there with her pack of cigarettes in her extended arm getting ready to hand them to me. I retrieved her cigarettes and lighter and reminded her that she is on restriction and that she does not have the liberty of smoking freely, she will have a cigarette on the hour and not before. I noticed that the time was 6:30

p.m., so I told her that she would not get the 7 p.m. smoke, but rather she would get the next cigarette at 8 p.m. She sat there just smiling at me as I turned and returned to the office to finish my writing. As I sat there trying to gather my thoughts and remember where I had stopped my note writing, I noticed through my peripheral vision that my little friend Ginger was again standing in the doorway. She appeared to be nervous and apprehensive as she hesitantly told me that Missy was smoking a cigarette again in the craft room. I quickly raised my head and viewed Missy sitting in the same chair and boldly smoking away. I turned my attention to the pack of cigarettes and lighter that I placed on the desk when I returned after I had taken them from her. I was a little perplexed and wondered where did she get the cigarette? I returned back to the craft room to confront her about her possession of a cigarette! She sat there laughing and extended her hand towards me again, holding another pack of cigarettes. It was then that it dawned on me that she must have a carton in her room. I escorted her to her room and told her to hand over any packs of cigarettes that she had and that I would put them in the med (medication) room in the office. I saw three packs of cigarettes on her closet shelf which she politely relinquished to me, but her mouth dropped when I told her to open her bureau drawers, check her jacket pockets and inside her shoes and socks which yielded five more packs of cigarettes. I gathered the cigarettes from her room and placed them in the med room and before I left her I told her that her next cigarette had been moved to 9 p.m. as a result of this second infraction. I returned to the office and Missy returned to the craft room sitting very quietly and no longer laughing.

Incidents of patients who attempt to push the rules and regulations just to see how much they can get away with really doesn't occur that often. These are the cases that Ginger had difficulty confronting. She was very nice and absolutely avoided anything that was confrontational. She would always come running to me with these problems. When everything was quiet one evening and

61

Ginger was in the office with me and we were just talking in general, I stated to her, "Ginger, how did you ever manage to stay working here for over twenty years? You're so quiet and soft spoken…you should be in a convent somewhere!"

Ginger burst out laughing and said, "Just call me Mother Superior"!

Little did she know at that time, but that was her nickname from that point on. Staff never asked about Ginger, rather they would say," Is Mother Superior on duty tonight?"

There were several quiet times that I would spend sitting on the porch or walking around the grounds on my break just to be alone and to think. My thoughts would go back in time and I would wonder about the thousands of Veterans that have walked these grounds and have died on the medical wards or even in the woods surrounding the medical center. The surrounding woods harbor a menagerie of animals such as skunks, raccoons, deer, feral cats, bears and wild turkeys. I never saw it, but it was reported by the medical center police that there was a moose that was walking around behind Ward 9.

Chapter Six

Dr. Lionel Pelc was starting to build up his Sexual-Deviant Behavior Group and it seemed like these patients were coming in in droves and I was starting to feel that these patients made up the majority of patients on Ward 8. There was a spattering of the other diagnoses, but it appeared that the bulk were pedophiles. It was at this point where I had had enough and when Dr. Pelc arrived for work that morning I proceeded to go up one side of him and then down the other. I wasn't holding back anything and whatever was in my head was coming directly out my mouth. "LIONEL!! You have got to be the biggest pervert of all!" You think you're helping these misfits out! Well I have news for you! I read that the cure rate is less than 2%. Oh! Sure, you're getting funds and grants for this project that will assist in keeping these jerks out of jail for a period of six months to a year and allowing them to be very comfortable and protected in a VA setting. WELL! I want to know one thing and I know that you do not have the answer for me! WHO IS TAKING CARE OF THE SMALL CHILDREN THAT THESE PEDOPHILES HAVE ABUSED SEXUALLY, MENTALLY and EMOTIONALLY? Not you, not the Federal government!"

I couldn't believe that I was capable of verbally attacking a psychologist when everyone was aware that I held a great deal of tolerance for just about everything. Dr. Pelc allowed me to rant and rave at him and never once interrupted me or walked away, but rather listened intently while he sat there stirring his coffee. When I finished I sat in a chair in the office and could only shake my head to attempt to make sense of this so-called therapeutic situation for pedophiles. I apologized to Dr. Pelc for my vicious outburst and as he looked at me with a small smile on his face he said, "LINDA! You have probably worked this unit the longest of any other aide here! I appreciate your dedication to these Veterans and I also understand that you have had enough and have reached the end of your rope with this clientele. I would like you to inquire about an opening on the Post-Traumatic Stress Disorder unit as a mental health associate. If you want, I will recommend you. That unit is on Ward 7Upper and deals entirely with Vietnam Veterans. I know you will do well there. I have observed your interactions with the few Vietnam Veterans we have had here, so I know you will be a wonderful addition to that unit."

I sat back for a few minutes to absorb the offer that Dr. Pelc just offered me and agreed with it. That afternoon I walked over to Human Resources and filled out the application for a Mental Health Associate.

The waiting period for the position of mental health associate was about three weeks before any of the candidates would be in-formed whether they were accepted or not for that one position. In this interim, I continued to serve the Veterans on Ward 8 and I was also assigned on the midnight to eight tour to cover for a nursing assistant who was on annual leave for two weeks. I always arrived at work for 11:30 p.m. and there was usually about two or three patients still awake watching TV. On my second night of working this shift, I entered the ward to see the TV off and only one patient sitting in the dayroom. Lester Algers was the patient who was awake and was quietly sitting by the restroom door. He greeted me as I came in with a gentle "Hello Miss"! I returned the greeting and entered the nurse's station to hear the report. Lester was another schizophrenic who reminded me of "Man Mountain Dean". He was huge, probably standing 6' 7" and weighing close to 400lbs. I remember when I first saw Lester. I felt that he was going to kill me, but I soon realized that he was a gentle giant with a lot of respect for everyone. I only remember him becoming angry once and he walked away from the person or situation that got him irate. Upon hearing the report, I returned to the dayroom and exiting the office doorway Lester was beckoning me from his chair in the dayroom. His eyes were big and he looked to be a little stressed. When I neared him and inquired if he had any problems, he proceeded to tell me of an incident that he experienced about fifteen minutes ago.

"I was sitting here in this chair and I saw an old friend of mine sitting in the chair next to the TV. So I got up and walked over to shake his hand and when I was close enough, HE DISAPPEARED! He wasn't sitting there anymore! I think I saw a ghost!"

I reassured Lester that he probably thought he saw his friend because he was probably thinking about him at that time. Knowing that schizophrenics hear voices and sometimes see things that do not exist, my explanation seemed to calm Lester down to the point that he was willing to retire to bed. I made my way to the second floor, did the rounds and then settled in a chair in the alcove just below the intercom system that was used for emergency situations. The system is always on and the main box was on the counter in the nurse's station. I was checking off the patients who were sleeping making sure that all were accounted for when over the intercom I could hear Lester reciting the same story he had told me earlier to the nurse. Lester must have been standing very close to the main box because he sounded so clear as if he were sitting in the chair next to me in the alcove. I stood up, pressed the speaker button and in a long drawn out whispery voice said, " Les-s-s-s!"

He suddenly stopped his story and asked the nurse if he heard that sound. "I think that damn ghost is after me!"

I heard Bart the nurse tell Lester that he didn't hear anything. Lester proceeded to continue telling his story, when again I pressed the speaker button and said, "Les-s-s!"

There was complete silence for about thirty seconds when I heard, "Yes, Miss!!" over the intercom. I couldn't help but smile and told Les to retire to bed because 6 a.m. comes around very quickly and that's when he has to get up and get his medications and get ready for breakfast. He pleasantly bid me "goodnight" and retired to bed.

Many times I would wonder why families would abandon their family members that were in a VA hospital. It didn't occur very often, especially with the recent admissions, but the Veterans that have literally taken up residence on some of the wards for long periods of time have never mentioned any visits or phone calls from their families. It was sad and it pulled at my heart strings especially over the holidays. Many Veterans would go home for Christmas, Thanksgiving, Easter and New Year's Day and these holidays would also include the days before and after the holiday so that they had a 3-4 day pass. For the Veterans that were left behind and remained on the wards, the staff would make every effort to celebrate the holidays with these family-forgotten Veterans. On Thanksgiving, the hospital would serve a terrific meal in the cafeteria (Building 5). The meals were served on paper platters because there was so much that a regular plate was unable to hold. There was salad, potatoes, stuffing, cranberry sauce (2 kinds), butternut squash, green beans and turkey and gravy. There were olives, celery and carrot sticks for appetizers and apple or pumpkin pies for dessert. I enjoyed escorting the Veterans to the dining room for these meals because they would walk at a fast pace to get there as if they feared that everything would be gone if they didn't hurry. When everyone was done eating, they would walk sluggishly back to the ward and enjoy a cigarette on the way. There was also a lack of conversation because no one felt like talking and would just try to enjoy their smoke and allow the digestion process to take place.

At Christmas and Easter the main meal was ham and this also had all the fixings to go with it. The desserts were usually apple pies, but occasionally there would be strawberry short cake, blueberry pie or chocolate cake. Every ward would decorate for the different holidays with pumpkins, Easter egg decals, and baskets filled with candy, which were placed strategically throughout the ward. Christmas trees decorated with ornaments and paper chains that the patients made while everybody (patients and staff) merrily singing carols as everyone participated in the decorating.

In July 1984, I had been given the news that I was appointed to the mental health associate position on the Post-Traumatic Stress Unit on Ward 7Upper. I couldn't believe that I was the one selected because the other candidates that applied were employed longer than me. I recalled that Dr. Pelc stated that he was going to send a letter of recommendation and this was probably the result of my being selected for this position.

Ward 7 Upper was one of the smaller wards at the VA. The ward had the capability of holding 21 Veterans who were committed to a six-month-stay in the PTSD program in which the primary candidates were Vietnam Veterans. As I walked through the door on my first day as a mental health associate, I observed three Veterans talking to staff members around the nurse's station. When I approached the station all eyes were looking at me and mentally questioning, "Who is this female?" I learned quickly that Vietnam Veterans do not accept individuals right off the bat and I knew that I would be checked over by every Veteran on the unit. Marty Murray was standing at the nurse's station when I approached the desk. Marty was a Marine who hailed from Worcester, MA and was also president of the patient counsel. I knew the nurse he was talking with and we started trading joking remarks to each other. Marty sported long hair that was gathered into a ponytail and also possessed a lengthy beard. This must have been the icebreaker because I was told by the nurse that Marty stated to her that I could stay. I felt that this was only another change in my employment at the VA and whether it was for a promotion or to remain at the same pay level, I was still working for the Veterans. I found out three weeks later that my reputation had been positively noted on this unit prior to my arrival and that Dr. Pelc had written one hell of a referral letter. I was also told that the PTSD unit has a patient council that is involved and vote on applicants applying for positions on their unit along with the staff members. It was at this point that my immediate acceptance to this unit did not seem strange any longer because everybody knew me.

Working with Vietnam Veterans was difficult because they did not trust anybody and particularly they did not trust their government. Vietnam Veterans were called "babies" and "whiners" from Veterans of Korea and WWII. Vietnam Veterans were not accepted to VFW's, American Legions, DAV's etc. because Vietnam was an undeclared war and it was occupied by the French Foreign Legion. These comments would infuriate the Vietnam Veteran because they fought in the longest war in American history. The Vietnam War lasted fifteen years and it is pathetic to view an American history book and to read two to four pages that covered the entire war. Many World War II and Korean Veterans have been asked to speak at various schools for Memorial and Veterans Day, but a Vietnam Veteran was never asked until the mid-nineties when the war was twenty-years old. Vietnam Veterans feel that they are more victimized in their own country than they were in Vietnam. Many made statements to me such as, "I wish I never came home! I'm not accepted here! In Vietnam you were accepted and you had true friends and we belonged to a family of soldiers that fought shoulder to shoulder against an enemy that sported no defined uniform. You had no idea who the enemy was because they all dressed the same!"

As I sat there listening intently to every word that came out of their mouths, I was overcome with a feeling that I heard these statements before, uttered by my own brother. My heart went out to these Veterans and I was a step ahead of other employees in understanding PTSD because I was the only family member that my brother trusted and communicated with after his return home from serving eighteen months in Vietnam.

The time that I spent on 7Upper was very short because there were plans in place for the entire ward to move to ward 12Upper. This ward was much larger and the plan was to admit more Veterans to the program and increase the staff to accommodate the increase of Veteran population. The program was for Veterans to be admitted for six months to intense group and individual therapies. I was indirectly involved in the move to 12Upper because I was working the 4 p.m.-12 midnight shift. On this shift we were involved in the organization of this unit by placing things in file cabinets and to arrange furniture in the dayroom and conference room so that it did not appear as if things were just stuffed there, but neatly and comfortably placed. Veterans that were already in the program had the opportunity to select their own rooms. Anyone admitted after we were settled would be assigned a room.

Cathy Danvers had been working this unit from its inception. She was a mental health associate as well, but she took over the task of admissions coordinator by contacting all the Veterans on the list that were interested in the program. Veterans were not just admitted to this program, they had to be interviewed by MHA's (Mental Health Associates) who were assigned to them. Interviews lasted two to three hours depending on the amount of information the Veteran was willing to give. After the interview, the information was processed at the staff meeting followed by an acceptance or denial letter that would be sent to the Veteran the following week. Ms. Danvers office had no organization at all. I would wonder why she wasn't organized, especially when you are dealing with so many applications of soldiers interested in coming here. I remember seeing a big stack of DD214's (discharge papers) held together with a rubber band. She also had acceptance and denial letters held together with a rubber band, as well as phone numbers and addresses on little note pads. The office consisted of a desk, desk chair and about five straight back chairs against a wall. Needless to say, I didn't venture into Cathy's office too often even though we were very good friends.

Seth Dickerson, MSW (Masters in Social Work) was the Director of the PTSD program and Dr. Burger was the ward psychiatrist. There was a speckling of MHA's that I had worked with on other wards, but the majority of staff on 12 Upper were either newly-hired individuals or people that I had never worked with on other wards. This was a new experience and a new title for me and I was excited and pleased with this assignment. Cathy Danvers was very close to Seth Dickerson at work and she stated that when the time comes that Seth leaves, she will also leave because she didn't want to work with anyone else for a supervisor. In reality, Seth was never her supervisor because all the MHA's were under Psychiatry Service and Dr. Bartholomew Bevins, M.D. was the Chief of Psychiatry Service so he was our supervisor, not Seth. Dr. Bevins stayed in close contact with Seth and he would inquire about the status of each MHA so that he could write a proper evaluation about each at evaluation time which occurred twice a year.

When the ward was settled and the program was getting in gear, the admissions increased from 21 to 37. The program itself continued to last for six months and it was understandable that not many Veterans wanted to dedicate their lives to five days a week of grueling therapy so sometimes the admissions were slow. When word started getting out about the program, there was an increase of interest in phone calls by Veterans seeking out information about it. There is nothing stronger or more powerful than the "Veterans Grapevine"! Word passes from Veteran to Veteran faster than AT and T can send a call to Europe. I was amazed when I heard that calls were coming in from Florida, Michigan, Tennessee and even Puerto Rico from Veterans inquiring and interested in the PTSD program in Northampton, MA. There were many from the New York and New England areas as well, but the fact that Veterans communicate so quickly with each other, it created an explosion of admissions for evaluations and it made it difficult for the staff to keep up with the referrals. There were times that I felt like I worked on an assembly line, interviewing one Veteran after another. Cathy Danvers would leave a note in our mailboxes with the name or names of the Veterans we would be interviewing on those days.

It was on Ward 12 Upper that I met many other staff members who were either transferred from other units or were new employees to the VA. The staff consisted of one psychiatrist, three psychologists, two social workers, one social work associate, one head nurse, five registered nurses and about twelve mental health associates. Everybody knew their job and the jobs were performed to the best of our ability for the care and concern of the patients in our charge. All the patients that were admitted had severe PTSD and agoraphobia, which is the fear of crowded places. I recall seeing several Veterans who continued to hold their suitcase in their hand and stood quietly at the door. They were having second thoughts about being on an inpatient status in a VA hospital, but after conversing with a staff member to assure them that they were not prisoners and could leave any time they wanted, allowed them to relax and give it a try. I seemed to have a direct mental communication with these Veterans and I was able translate their body language and facial expressions which allowed me to approach them in a comfortable and non-threatening manner.

Ward 12 Upper was setup like a huge letter "I" or an upright and upside down "T". Each end of the long hallway was capped off by a conference room at one end and a four-bed patient room at the other end. The nurse's station, doctor's office and Cathy Danvers office were right in the middle and opposite the large dayroom where morning meetings were held for every Veteran and day staff members during the week. There was also a tiny kitchen area for the staff where they could make coffee, tea or soup, but not big enough to sit and enjoy your coffee. So staff had to go to the nurse's station or an office for their lunch or supper.

The late spring, summer and early fall was a great time for staff to go outside and sit at the picnic tables to comfortably eat their meals. On a few occasions, the staff would initiate a potluck meal in which everybody brought something different and even the patients would bring pizza, Kentucky Fried Chicken or Chinese food and everyone just dug right in, socialized and everyone was more trusting of each other. The PTSD program succeeded well with these social interactions because the patients felt like they were more at home than in a hospital setting and it also made the six months speed by very quickly for them.

As the months went on, I found myself in a niche that I was very comfortable in. I loved the PTSD ward and I was getting close with these Veterans just as I had on the other units I had worked. I learned how to play pool from a Vietnam Veteran and when I started getting better than him, he put his stick up and asked other Veterans to play me. He was proud that he taught me the game and told me very nicely that I was a fast learner and that I would have been one hell of a soldier in Vietnam if I had ever enlisted. Compliments from Vietnam Veterans are an extreme rarity and I realized, at that moment, that I had received the highest honor a soldier could give, short of an oak leaf cluster with a silver star. These Veterans were comfortable with me and I was equally comfortable with them.

I was working the PTSD unit for seven months when I received a phone call from Clark Douglass, the patient that Sergio was infatuated with on ward 8, who had the long red beard and long red hair. Clark was a Vietnam Veteran and also possessed a bad drug and alcohol habit. Clark was interested in coming into the PTSD program and further asked if he could come onto the unit to talk to me. I told Clark that I would love to see him and talk to him and that he was very welcome to come and talk to me. Clark lived in downtown Northampton at Shay's Hotel and I knew that he would have to take the bus to the VA. It was Friday and we had a policy of never admitting anyone on a Friday because there is limited or skeleton staff on weekends and there would be no medical or psychiatric staff to attend a complex admission. The latest day for admissions was Thursday. Clark arrived on the unit a half hour after his call to me and I noticed him walking slowly down the hallway in my direction. He was wearing jeans and his Army jacket was wrapped around him and his hands were holding one side of the jacket over the other as he approached me at the front desk. I watched him coming down the hall and thought that he looked terrible. His eyes were sunken in, his face was red and his hair was matted which made me think that he was living in the woods, but this was February and I hoped he wasn't living in the woods. I directed Clark to a side office and when he walked through the door he opened his jacket and stated, "Look at me! I've lost a lot of weight and I can't sleep anymore because of the violent visions of Vietnam that will not go away! I need to come into the hospital because I fear that I'm going to die if I don't!"

As I looked and listened to Clark, I knew that he had total trust in me because he never called anyone else including doctor, nurse, or psychologist, just a little lowly mental health associate…me. I gave Clark a cup of coffee and told him that I have to speak to Cathy Danvers since she would have the final word as the admissions coordinator. When I returned to Clark I stated, "I explained to Cathy your situation and also told her that you were in rough shape and needed to come into the unit as soon as possible. She agreed with me and told me that she could admit you on Monday because we don't do any admissions on Friday. Clark, next week I will be on vacation for a week, but Cathy has all the information for your admission on Monday. I gave Clark $5.00 in coupon books so that he could get something to eat in the canteen and instructed him to arrive early on Monday for his admission."

When I arrived back to work after my vacation, I immediately inquired about Clark. Cathy called me into her office and said, "Linda, Clark never made it in here for admission last Monday. We were informed by the owner of Shay's Hotel that Clark put a gun in his mouth and his brain was splattered all over the wall! I know this sounds terrible, but this is how it was explained to us! This happened the day after he was on the unit for the visit with you. He never made it to Monday because he committed suicide on Saturday! I'm sorry, Linda!"

I sat there motionless and numb for about three minutes as the image of Clark raced through my thoughts and turning to Cathy I said, "You know, some things have to change around here and the first thing is that no admissions on Friday rule! I really feel that if Clark was admitted when he came to see me, he would be alive today! I'm not pointing fingers or accusing anyone of his suicide, but it usually takes something like this to change the rules."

I excused myself to Cathy and concentrated on my details of the day.

I never realized that an entire year had passed already. There was talk buzzing that Seth was going to be leaving, but I never settled for just talk, rather I always went to "the horse's mouth" to get a straight answer. It was at this time that I met Sophia Lindstrom, a social worker that was appointed to the PTSD unit from the admission unit where her excellent reputation was very well-known throughout the hospital. I had heard of her name, but I did not know her until she was assigned to the PTSD unit over six months ago.

It was a Monday morning, the first day of work for the regular office staff who worked Monday through Friday and I was in the tiny coffee room getting a coffee when I heard behind me a stressed voice saying, "How can they do that to him? He's such a nice and caring man! Good grief!! He started this program and they're kicking him out!" With my coffee cup in my hand, I turned around and saw Sophia standing there, shaking her head and looking down at the floor. "Who are you talking about Sophia?"

She lifted her head and quietly stated, "Seth! Some staff on this unit are forcing him to step down because they do not feel that a social worker should be head of the program, but rather a psychologist!"

I was confused and asked, "When did all this talk/rumor happen?" Sophia just shook her head in disbelief at the poison arrows of injustice and cruelty aimed in Seth's direction. With my coffee still in hand I knocked on Seth's door and he quietly bid me to enter. Seth was sitting at his desk with his left hand on his forehead and his right hand was writing something on paper. Without any hesitation, I asked Seth if he was getting pushed out the door. He took his left hand away from his head and gingerly stood up and turning his back to me he stated, "Linda, do you see the knife in my back!"

I was horrified and like Sophia, I was in total disbelief. How can anybody stomp on a staff member who has put their heart and soul into developing programs that benefit combat soldiers by teaching them different and more beneficial ways of dealing with their mental and emotional traumas associated with their being in combat? This was Seth's program, conceived in his mind and heart, planned on paper, presented to the administrative staff and finally setup and developed on Ward 7 upper. Now that all the heavy work was done, one psychologist, whom I am presuming to be jealous, wants to sit in Seth's chair and claim his credit because he feels that an MSW is beneath a psychologist and should not be head of any program. I guess the saying" what goes around, comes around" is true, because not only did Seth leave, but this psychologist was also removed from the unit as well.

When Seth departed the program, Cathy Danvers held true to her word and also departed from the VA. Seth transferred to the VA in Maine and where Cathy went was unknown, although a few people stated that they had seen her in supermarkets or stores in downtown Northampton. After their departure, things seemed to come to a standstill on ward 12 Upper. There were no new admissions because there was no one tending the office that Cathy vacated. Everybody was looking at each other and shrugging their shoulders and wondering if this situation was fixable.

Although it seemed like an eternity, in reality it was only one week that had passed when a call came to the nurse's station from Dr. Grant Burger, the ward psychiatrist. He had been attending daily meetings with the Chief of Psychiatry to discuss ways to replace the staff members that had retired or transferred and to put the PTSD program back on track. I was standing at the counter when the secretary informed me to pick up the extension because Dr. Burger wished to speak to me. Upon answering the phone, Dr. Burger informed me that he wanted me to open Cathy's office and take over that assignment. I went into momentary shock because there was nothing in that office to resume. No organization, drawers were vacant except for two rolls of application forms stuck in the middle drawer of the desk. I inquired of Dr. Burger, "What exactly do you want me to do in that office?" "Linda, I want you to open that office and call candidates to come into the program and to set up interviews for those that sent in their applications. Of all the MHA's, you were the one that was chosen because of your capability and organizational skills."

When the call ended, I sat there for about five minutes just trying to figure out what I was going to do in that office. I slowly stood up and headed to the locked office that Cathy had vacated and unlocking the door, slowly pushing it open and standing in the doorway, I observed an extremely barren office that consisted of a desk and a single desk chair. I entered and sat in the chair and my eyes slowly surveyed the walls, floor, ceiling and total spaciousness of the room. I was wondering, "How does one open up an office when you have nothing to work with!" There was nothing there! Oh sure, a desk and chair…BIG DEAL!!

Several patients and staff members passed by the door and stopped for a second to stare at me and although they wondered why I was just sitting there, they never uttered one word or asked any questions. Phil Kendricks was another MHA and he also served in Vietnam as a bush medic, meaning that he was out in the field of combat, not in a hospital setting. I was very familiar with Phil because he had worked at the State hospital with me and I felt that he would be my right arm in the organization of this office. Phil reminded me of the "Scrounger" from the movie "The Great Escape". He was my supply man and with his assistance he equipped me with folders, pencils, paper, file tabs, note pads, rulers, stapler and staples, paper clips etc. I inquired about the possibility of having two five-drawer file cabinets and the following day the cabinets were in the office. I also acquired a desk lamp and a bulletin board for the wall. I moved the desk to the middle of the office and against the left wall so that I could put some plants near the window area so that they would be exposed to the air and sunshine. That barren office was coming together and appeared to be developing a personality of its own. It became so comfortable that the staff would come there for coffee and luncheon breaks and to relax in general conversations. The staff was very considerate and would only come in my office at times that I was on break so that there was no interference in my work day.

Separating applications that were bunched together and matching them with the DD214's was a job in itself! I started to make individual folders for each candidate that applied to the program, separating the denials from the accepted and then placed them in the file cabinets alphabetical so that when the individual was admitted to the unit, the staff member only had to grab a folder instead of thumbing through a pile of application forms looking for information about them. All information would be contained in each candidate's individual folder.

Things on the ward started to settle down very nicely as furniture and cabinets and office supplies came together by having offices properly set up and organized. The same was true for the bedrooms, break rooms and conference rooms. Ward 12Upper was a functioning unit with admissions, discharges and a full five-day program (Mon-Fri) for Veterans with a diagnosis of Post-Traumatic Stress Disorder. My office appeared to be a haven for patients and staff alike, because I had an open-door policy and anyone was welcome to enter for whatever reason. Most of the visits were just to say "hello" and to tell me to have a great day, the other entries were the result of a staff member having problems with another staff member or even worse, a patient having a problem with a staff member. In the beginning, I was more a listener than anything else because I allowed individuals to vent their problems. It was a rare occasion for someone to inquire about my opinion concerning assignments, personalities or attitudes.

As time went on, all the high professionals on Ward 12Upper were getting more and more inundated with work. Several new groups were established as a result of the increase in patient population on the unit. My office was running like clockwork and the dust from all the moving was settling. Things were running smoothly and everyone, patients and staff alike, knew their daily assignments. I have always been suspicious when things are running good because there has always been a wrench that gets thrown into the gear shaft of progress. There was talk going around that many of the patients were dissatisfied with the ward psychologist and they were refusing to attend his group. From what I could understand of the patients complaint was that this psychologist did not believe that there was such a thing as PTSD and apparently was stressing his opinion to the Veterans that were on the PTSD unit and suffering with it. Before anyone could count to ten, the psychologist was removed, the ward was shut down for two weeks and there was a congressional investigation going on.

During the two-week shutdown, all the staff were meeting to establish new rules and regulations for the PTSD unit. We were all informed that the unit would be moving from Ward 12Upper to Ward 8. It was also at this same time that Dr. Burger announced that he had accepted a position in a neighboring community and would no longer be working for the VA. I sat in total disbelief at the confusion and chaos that was going on! At least that's what it appeared to be to me! Old rules and regulations were compromised, so we had to have new ones. Staff resigns so we have to get replacements and along with this, we have to move the entire unit to another ward. It was during this chaos that I first realized that the VA is constantly in transition. If it doesn't work, you fix it. If it works…you still fix it!

Packing my office up and moving it to another ward on the other side of the oval was not a chore, the chore was unpacking and settling things in another office and wondering if there would be another office to accommodate the equipment that I had on Ward 12Upper. Ward 8 was quite comfortable because I was given a corner office that had three windows and was spacious enough to fit all my equipment and furniture very nicely. The laundry truck was the primary mover of furniture and equipment from one ward to the other. Sometimes, the move was for a two-day span and other times the move was well over a week. The movement of the PTSD unit was about three days before everyone was settled because the Veterans assisted in moving their own belongings to the new ward and their new rooms.

The new staff were setting up their offices and at times our introductions seemed like we were greeting each other at Grand Central Station while we were going in and out of a doorway trying to acclimate ourselves to the new unit. Dr. Manuel Benedicto was the new psychiatrist assigned to the PTSD unit. He had been working in this VA for several years and I had observed him many times walking on the VA grounds. He always walked at a fast pace and I remember thinking that he probably was late for a meeting, possibly had to interview someone or maybe he just had to go to the bathroom and that was the reason his pace was so fast. In the weeks that followed, I learned that that fast-paced walk of Manny's was just part of his personality. He requested that the staff call him Manny because he felt more comfortable and it also made him easily accessible and approachable to staff. After all, Manny was the head one of the unit and all the responsibility of the unit, good or bad, was on his shoulders. I also learned that Manny never wanted to come to the PTSD unit and work with Vietnam

Veterans because he didn't want the Veterans to be uncomfortable with his presence. Manny was from the Philippines with a small stature and had strong Oriental characteristics and he felt that these features would be threatening to Vietnam Veterans and place them back in a Vietnam combat setting. I introduced Manny to a Vietnam Veteran that was just admitted to the ward and as this Veteran froze in the doorway of his office, Manny stood up, extended his hand and stated," I no gook! I from the Philippines and if you don't mind, I would like to interview you."

The Veteran would slowly follow him into the office and would request that the door remain open. This request was not only honored by Dr. Benedicto, but by every staff member who had an office. Vietnam Veterans abhor closed-in places and will avoid them at all cost. They need an exit that they can quickly run through when they cannot talk any longer. Another diagnosis that always accompanied PTSD was agoraphobia. Agoraphobia is the fear of crowded places (buses, subways, theaters, concerts, restaurants etc.).

Everything appeared to be falling in place on the unit, groups quickly started and the admissions appeared to be never-ending as the rest of the staff became comfortable in their new surroundings. Sophie Lindstrom, the social worker, was like the ever-ready battery because she was constantly on the go, doing her job and I surprised her one day when I called her "Scrappy". She darn well earned that name because she put her heart and soul into helping every Veteran. Scrappy Lindstrom and I became very good friends and she was a wonderful individual to converse with. She hailed from Worcester, Massachusetts and possessed a regional dialect that was not totally Bostonian, but extremely close to it. Scrappy was the first of the administrative staff to compliment me on my organizational skills in setting up the admission coordinator's office so that all interviews were streamlined because all the information was in each personal folder and they didn't have to run all over the place seeking information. She also told me that my system decreased the amount of time that the staff questioned the patients during their initial interviews. In these folders, I had a face sheet with every staff member's name that was scheduled to interview the patients. When they completed their interviews, they signed and dated next to their name on the face sheet and this method prevented patients from being overlooked or being seen multiple times. The face sheet was a record for everyone, staff and patients alike, that reminded us that every Veteran is entitled to care and treatment in the Veterans Administration. After all, no one working in the VA would have a job if it wasn't for the Veterans that walk through their doors. Over the years, I have shaken thousands of Veterans hands and have thanked them for allowing me to work for them.

CHAPTER SEVEN

Prior to moving to Ward 8, Dr. Grant Burger asked me to do the scheduling of all the MHA's on all the shifts because he was too busy to do it and frankly he had no idea where to start. I admit I was a little clumsy with the scheduling when I first started, but meeting with each one of the MHA's and hearing what their requests were and applying any specific needs, such as vacations, days off, National Guard weekends and specific holidays, had to also be considered. After I patiently surveyed the MHA's on each shift, I proceeded to develop my own schedule that made sense to everyone involved. All the MHA's were pleased with the scheduling of their time and no one worked over five days straight without having a day or two off. The time sheets and scheduling were carried over to Ward 8 where I continued to do them for about six months. We were then assigned a new psychologist and he decided to take over doing the scheduling of the MHA's. It was understandable, because after all, he was our supervisor and he had the right to do the scheduling. It didn't take us long to realize that this was a "psychologist from Strangeville"! His ways of doing things were right off the wall! He had no conception of doing a time schedule and didn't consult any of the MHA's that he was in charge of supervising. As time went on, even the patients were complaining about his style of therapy and didn't want to attend his groups. I felt bad for my fellow MHA's and on several occasions they would approach me and beg me to take back the scheduling of their time. Regretfully, I told them that there was nothing I could do about it!

Dr. "Strangeville", whose given name was Garfield, wasn't easy to converse with because it was his way or no way and that was his attitude. He wouldn't even listen to the patients when they asked questions or inquired about his technique. So, as time went on, I not only had co-workers approaching me, but also patients who wondered how this man ticked and I told them that my hands were tied and that he was also my supervisor as well as the other MHA's. Dr. Strangeville had set up the time schedule for the MHA's on a rotation basis. They worked two days on the day shift, two days on the afternoon shift and two days on the midnight shift. The day shift MHA's followed this schedule and worked six days in succession. On their first day on the midnight shift they ended up working for sixteen hours straight because if they worked the 4 p.m.-12Midnight shift on Wednesday and were scheduled for the midnight shift on Thursday, they had to stay for another eight hours because Thursday started at midnight. It really was sad to see exhausted MHA's walking in circles or putting their heads back to relieve the tension because it felt too big for even their necks to support. I had one MHA who was so desperate that he got on his knees and begged me to please get the time back and make his life normal again. No matter where I looked, there were pleading eyes staring back at me and sadly there was nothing I could do about it.

It was about two weeks later when Dr. Strangeville requested that I meet him in his office. I knocked on his door and he bid me enter, which I did and observed him standing at his desk. Without even looking in my direction, he picked up a thick folder and handed it to me and stated, "This is the time for the MHA's and I am giving it back to you because I have accepted a position at the VAMC in Togus, ME and I will be leaving next week!"

I hesitantly asked him, "How long have these arrangements been in the works?"

For as long as I knew him, which was about five or six months, he was never soft-spoken or displayed a smile to anyone and I found myself looking at a man who was truly embarrassed or emotionally hurt or broken. He was awkward in his stance and was mumbling words that he previously had expressed with such directness and strength. I took the folder from his hands and sincerely wished him the best in his new position and his transfer to Maine. As I exited the office and walked down the short corridor to the dayroom my intentions were to return to my office and attempt to fix the scheduling mistakes as soon as possible. As I rounded the corner and entered the dayroom carrying the time folder in my right hand, the three or four MHA's that were in the dayroom suddenly stood up and erupted into cheers. I quickly turned my gaze to the front door because I was expecting to see some high official walking through it and that was what caused the cheering. When nobody was seen at the door, I turned around to the cheering MHA's; they encircled me and continued their cheers, it was then that I realized they had spotted the time folder in my hand and were ecstatic. I was hearing statements like, "YAY, she's got the time schedule back!"

Another MHA was looking up at the ceiling saying, "Thank You God! We will be able to live again!"

The eyes that were pleading with me two weeks ago were now sparkling with happiness. I told each of them not to go too far because I would need to speak with each one of them so they could tell me what days they worked last week, what days for the present week so I could possibly change the schedule for next week so as to make it more feasible for everyone to live by. When I finished rearranging the time schedule and after speaking with the MHA's, all the tension and stress that you could previously cut with a knife had dissipated and vanished because they were comfortable and they knew that things were back to normal.

Jake Peterson was a Marine who served two tours in Vietnam. One of these tours was the 1969 TET Offensive. I referred to him as the "elusive Vet from Cape Cod" because I had received several calls from him and also had scheduled him six times to come in for a two-day evaluation and he hadn't shown for one of them. My schedule book was getting to be very messy with all the white outs and reschedules that I made on Jake. I had even received calls from his boss begging me to please do something to help Jake because he was drinking on a daily basis and had missed quite a few days of work. His boss had stated that he was extremely fearful that Jake would die from his drinking and was pleading for an intervention from the VA. I explained to the boss that I thoroughly understood his concerns, but the VA doesn't force anyone to be admitted because all admissions were on a voluntary basis. I further explained that the only thing I could do is schedule Jake for another two-day evaluation because he has to have this evaluation to prove that he has PTSD before he can be admitted to the program. Many weeks had passed and everyday there were two to four admissions to the program. I was walking into the nurse's station with an arm full of applications for the mail, when I noticed a neat, clean-shaven gentleman in khaki pants and a sport shirt standing at the counter. I placed the envelopes in the outgoing mail and turned and noticed that there wasn't anyone at the counter. I approached the counter and looking at this neatly-dressed gentleman I stated, "Can I help you?"

He looked at me with a crooked smile on his face and replied, "Jake Peterson, in person!"

I was stymied for a minute and then looked directly into his eyes and said, "You're the little shit that I have been chasing all over this State! I can't believe you're here!"

"You must be Linda", he stated as he held his hand out to greet me. I explained to Jake that I was going to get an MHA to show him to his room and allow him to get a little settled before he gets hit with a barrage of questions.

Working with Vietnam Veterans was the most challenging position that I held at the VA. The only element that they all held in common was the fact that they were involved in combat in Vietnam. It didn't matter which branch of the service that they served or the rank that they held; everyone had their own story to tell based on their own experiences in war. As each Veteran was admitted, I learned very quickly the difference between a true heavy combat Veteran and a "wannabee". The heavy combat Veteran was extremely quiet, isolative and usually dressed in plain everyday clothes. He also appeared to be suspicious, but cooperative and rarely ever smiled. The "wannabee" would enter the ward extremely boisterous, demanding and usually sported camouflage clothing as if he was advertising in a sporting goods store. These Veterans were also in Vietnam, but were never directly involved in combat. Instead they were file clerks, cooks or supply clerks. I have even heard the stories from men who were in the service, but never assigned to a war area that would try to claim PTSD because they heard a drunken Vietnam Vet tell of his experience in war and would attempt to claim that soldier's experience as their own. That is pathetic when a non-combat Veteran stoops that low to claim a war Veteran's experience, but it is done!

Heavy combat Veterans had difficulty sleeping and sometimes would fall asleep in a chair in the dayroom where there was a lot of noise going on such as the TV displaying a ballgame with the volume on high because there were three to four others playing pool and were talking loudly about their game or just in general conversation. At night these soldiers were on alert because their eyes were constantly piercing the darkness looking for any movement and their ears were listening to any little rustle or sound that they felt was not normal. Nighttime is difficult and stressful for every Vietnam combat Veteran because all fights and attacks occurred during the night hours. The Viet Cong had no uniform to speak of and they dressed like a common villager which made it impossible for the American soldier to distinguish a civilian from the enemy. During the day the Viet Cong would mingle among the villagers and townspeople and act like the average civilian going about his business. At night they donned a full metal jacket, equipped themselves with AK47's and their mission was to kill as many American soldiers before the sun rose at dawn. I had heard these and similar stories from every Vietnam Veteran who was admitted to the PTSD unit at the Northampton VAMC.

Veterans were coming in from all over the country to our program which changed the acceptance of just receiving Veterans from VISN 1, which was all of New England and Puerto Rico. Martino Miguel was a very good-looking Hispanic from Hartford, CT, who after a week of his admission approached me and asked if he could talk to me in my office about a stressor that he had been carrying around since he was in Vietnam. As Martino was sitting in the chair next to my desk, I recalled the first time that I met him which was on Ward 12 Upper just before we moved over to ward 8. Martino began with a general conversation as he gently led into his description of the stressor. He sat very erect in the chair and I could tell that he was having difficulty talking about it. I gave him all the time he needed and patiently waited for him to gather his thoughts. He sat back in the chair his right arm resting on my desk and turning his attention to me, he began his story.

"You know! Men get very close in war and I had a very good friend who was killed on a search and destroy mission. He was an Afro-American and a great guy! We were always sent out together in a squad and I always had the radio and walked point. That was the assignment that was always given to me. I didn't mind it and I knew that if we were attacked that the radioman is the first one that they take out because the enemy doesn't want any communication going back to base camp. Our squad went on patrol every day and there were several times that we were sniped at by the VC (Viet Cong). For whatever reason that overcame him, my buddy Bruno requested to carry the radio and walk-point. He stated that he needed a little change in the squad formation so we switched positions for the day. The jungle was very quiet; no one could hear a sound of a monkey, lizard or the rustling of leaves. We were walking in diamond formation and while I was positioned in the rear of the squad, my buddy Bruno was walking right-point and carrying the radio which was my position that he requested to have for the day. We started to feel an eeriness come over us when suddenly Bruno accidently stepped on a land mine (claymore) and his body was blown into a hundred pieces. I crouched down and aimed my rifle as parts of Bruno's body were raining down around us. When things were settled and we realized that the enemy was gone, we started to collect the body pieces so that we could bring him back to base camp. We gathered everything but his right arm. I couldn't find his right arm and to this day I still have flashback dreams of trying to locate his arm. I lost a very good close friend that day and I feel guilty for major things, such as he requested my position and stepped on that damn mine and I sent him home with a missing right arm. Bruno was a whole man when we went into the jungle, but came out a partial man".

I offered Martino a cup of coffee and as he sat there drinking it, he expressed his gratitude for my allowing him to speak of this stressor. Before Martino left my office, he stated to me while staring at the wall, "You know, I may be sitting in this chair, but my mind is constantly in that jungle looking for my buddy's right arm!" With this said Martino slowly rose and exited my office.

Mondays were always the busiest day of the week because many admissions occurred, both two-day evaluations and six-week admissions and it was also the day that I mailed many applications to Veterans who were interested in the program. The entire staff was hustling and bustling all over the place. Discharges usually occurred on Thursday and Friday, but the discharge process started on Mondays; meaning that all t's had to be crossed and all i's had to be dotted before the Veteran could be discharged.

The PTSD program was constantly changing and new rules and regulations were implemented to meet the needs of the patient population. One huge change pertained to the drug and alcohol and substance abuse policy. When the program began, the rule was three strikes and you're out meaning that the Veteran could use substances twice and on the third time they were discharged from the program. We realized that this rule wasn't working because eight out of ten admissions had alcohol or substance abuse problems and they would push this rule to the hilt. We also realized that this old rule was constantly interfering in their treatment because if they returned to the unit under the influence of alcohol or drugs, we had to transfer them to the detox ward for three days. Thus, they've missed three days of therapy on the PTSD unit. Upon realizing that this rule did not work, the team agreed to a zero tolerance policy and tests for alcohol and drugs were given at admission. If the alcohol or drug urine tests were positive, the Veteran was informed that he could not be admitted. When this new rule was instated, there were several Veterans that were denied admission because their tests were positive. The rule change proved to be very productive because it separated the Veterans who were motivated to treatment and striving to make some positive changes in their lives from those who basically just went through the motion of filling out an application and continuing with their substance abuse. I would like to believe that it was this rule change that brought Jake Peterson to us, but I know that he was just not ready all the other times that I scheduled him for admission. He was ready now and I thanked God for it.

Somehow Jake was assigned to me and I believe it was Dr. Benedetto that arranged this assignment. I had heard that Jake was not talking in group and he mingled with very few Veterans on the unit. There was never a day that went by that Jake didn't stop at my door to say "hello" and inquire if he could come in to talk. I think Dr. Benedetto realized that Jake was comfortable with me and if the team needed him to open up and talk about his combat stressors, then I was their best bet in getting Jake to talk. Jake was extremely intelligent and very talented. He built his own boat and was employed with a boat builder on Cape Cod. He also showed me pictures of the beautiful sail boat that he built right from scratch, during some of our general conversations. After three weeks had passed, I decided to ask Jake why he is comfortable with me and not in group. Jake turned his clean-shaven face with a semi-smile towards me and stated, "It was your voice that I heard on the phone or my answering machine giving the many appointments to come into this program. You were the one that my boss called and spoke to for assistance for me. You were also the one that gave me that wonderful "from the heart" greeting when I was admitted a month ago. Linda, you never gave up on me and you never turned your back or gave up hope on me.....Why should I not return that same respect to you!"

Pete Santini was another Marine who came to the Northampton VAMC, PTSD unit from New Jersey. Like many others, he was a gifted artist and sculptor. He was very visible on the ward because he was always drawing something or someone, where he comfortably sat at a table on the porch or at the picnic table that was in the front yard. He constantly carried his sketch pad with him and he used no models; everything that Pete drew was totally from his memory. With his sketch pad under his arm and a roguish smile on his face, Pete knocked at my door and requested if he could have a tootsie pop. I was always well supplied with candy and tootsie pops for the children of the Veterans, but I soon realized that the top sought candy for Vietnam Veterans was the tootsie pop. So I always had five to six bags in my desk drawer. When I found out that the employees were going in my office and helping themselves, I put my candy stash under lock and key in my file cabinet. Pete entered my office and sat in the chair next to my desk as I was grabbing a handful of tootsie pops from my drawer to give to him. He wanted to show me the drawing he was working on and further stated that he had drawn it from memory of a portrait of a woman from the "Gay Nineties". Pete was fixated on that era and explained that women were absolutely elegant at that time with their long dresses with the puffy sleeves, floppy straw hat and a parasol that sometimes matched the pattern of the dress. The hair was always long, but it was put into a French twist or braided and placed on top of the head. Pete flipped the cover of his drawing pad over and turning it towards me I was amazed to view a beautiful woman with a high lace collar, hair in a twist with small ringlets hanging just above the back of her collar on the dress. I was speechless for a minute because this picture was drawn with a charcoal pencil and viewing the intricate and delicate work he did in the lace of the dress was utterly fantastic. I sat back in my chair and as my eyes slowly turned to meet his and with true sincerity I said, "You are truly a gifted artist and I also know that sugar is food for the brain, so feel free to ask me for any candy you desire because I want nothing to happen to that brain of yours!"

Pete smiled and took his tootsie pops and from that time on became a frequent visitor to my office.

Time passes very quickly when you have a full day of working incessantly and sometimes I worked right through my lunch and break times. My job was not grueling, but it was tedious and I enjoyed it being that way because the weeks seemed to fly by. In December 1986, I was sitting at my desk and just gazing out my window watching the gently falling snow slowly covering the ground when I heard a knock at my door and turned to see Pete standing there requesting if he could enter to ask me a question. I nodded my head and he sat in the chair by my desk. He appeared to be more serious than usual and I was wondering what was so important about the question he was going to ask me. After he positioned himself comfortably he said, "Linda, I would really like to know what your opinion is concerning what I am going to tell you! I went to the University of Massachusetts (UMass) and inquired about their art program because I would love to pursue my degree and possibly my Master's as well. I would like to know how you feel about my going to college!"

From the expression on his face, I knew that Pete had his heart set on doing this so that he could accomplish a well-desired goal. I looked in Pete's eyes and inquired how long had he been thinking about going back to college. Why UMass when he was from New Jersey!

"Do you have any intentions of returning to New Jersey Pete?" You also have a diagnosis of agoraphobia in which you cannot tolerate crowded places. Are you aware that UMass is also referred to as "Zoo Mass" because it is so huge and crowded with students! The campus is immense and people were known to get lost up there even with a map."

Pete gently smiled at me and stated, "Linda, I have already talked with the head of the art department there and I told him the project that I wanted to do to earn my degree. He was flabbergasted and his mouth dropped open when I explained my intent".

Pete explained to me that he wouldn't be attending any classes, but would be completely alone at the art department foundry and would be making a statue out of bronze. His whole mark was based on this statue and he further stated that this statue was going to be sent to Bristol County, Pennsylvania which was the hometown of a lieutenant that he served with in Vietnam. I gave Pete my blessing and highly complimented him on his smooth accomplishment in being verbally accepted to the University. He never filed an application for registration, but rather he had an interest in viewing the art department at the University. So, when he was on a pass and decided to go to Amherst to check out the college, the opportunity presented itself and the art department was open so he entered and communicated with several art instructors. This was a Sunday and Pete was thrilled that there was an art show that day that was open for the public. Pete happened to be in the right place at the right time and sold himself to the art department at the University.

Months had gone by and Pete was strongly invested in his art project. He would leave the unit at 8 a.m. and would frequently return at 9 p.m. As he walked through the unit door late in the evening, he appeared to be tired, but was also extremely satisfied. Pete showed me some pictures that he had taken of the project which showed parts of the body. He said that bronze is very heavy and he has to make it in parts and then he would solder the sections together. It took almost two years for him to finish this project and the statue weight was over two tons. When I viewed the pictures of the completed project, I was dumbfounded to see such detail in bronze. The statue was a depiction of two Marines, one was a sergeant and the other was a lieutenant. The sergeant was holding the dead body of the lieutenant who was killed in action. I looked very closely at these pictures and I said to Pete that this sergeant looks very much like you! In a low voice Pete stated, "It is!! That is me! That happened in Vietnam and that image has been with me every waking moment since I returned from Vietnam. We were on a search and destroy mission and we were ambushed and my lieutenant was shot. I rushed to him and cradled him in my arms and after calling for his mother, he died a moment later. I became so numb that I didn't care if I lived or died. Making that statue was very therapeutic for me because it has softened, if only a little, the impact of those horrific memories of war that I know will follow me to my grave!"

Jake Peterson, the elusive Marine that I chased all over the State of Massachusetts, was starting to loosen up and began communicating in groups. He continued to remain cautious in what he said in group because he had expressed to me that he didn't trust everyone in the group. Jake and I continued to have our talks and many times we would walk in the outside oval where I noticed Jake eyeballing the woods as if he was on patrol. Jake was raised in a middle-class religious family near New London, Connecticut. He was the oldest of four children, two boys and two girls and always lived near the ocean. I would wonder why Jake didn't enlist in the Navy instead of the Marines because of his maritime experience. He shrugged his shoulders and muttered that he just wanted something different. When Jake arrived in Vietnam in 1968, he was one of two Marines that were assigned to train the soldiers of the Republic of Vietnam Army (RVA) to fight the Viet Cong.

Although he went out to surrounding areas, his home base was in Saigon. Jake fell in love with the daughter of the Vietnamese ambassador and he married her within six months of their meeting in a Buddhist temple in Saigon. His instruction and training of the troops took him away from his wife for weeks at a time. As Jake was telling me this story, he opened his wallet and showed me a frayed photograph of a very pregnant , pretty Oriental girl named Lin. This was a picture of his wife and his soon-to-be-born baby. Jake lost his wife and his unborn child in the TET Offensive of 1969. This Offensive almost wiped out a good portion of the city of Saigon and tragically, the area where his wife lived was totally blown away. Jake fought in the TET Offensive and didn't even know that his wife and unborn baby were killed for over a week. When he finally had a chance to return to his home and try to find his wife, he found himself standing in the middle of the street and couldn't recognize his home because everything was leveled. The casualties were great for the Americans and the RVA's, but the casualties for the civilians were horrendous.

Upon returning to the United States after serving thirteen months in Vietnam and still numb from the loss of his wife and baby, Jake completed his final year in the Marine Corps at Camp Lejeune assigned to a desk job. When he was discharged, Jake returned to Connecticut and his parent's home, but this stay was short-lived. Jake decided to head back down South and settled in New Port Richey, Florida. He got a job employed in a sailboat-building company and liked this job, but he was missing several days of work resulting from his chronic alcoholism. Jake was drinking so heavy that he was spending most of his paycheck on alcohol. Jake also had a live-in girlfriend whom he was arguing and fighting with every time he was home. The arguments centered around his chronic abuse of alcohol which he was doing on a daily basis. One particular day, Jake had a screaming argument with his girlfriend which resulted in her leaving the house and going left down the street and he separated by going right up the street. He went about two to three blocks and entered a bar, sat on the stool and continued to imbibe. He had remained in the bar for about six hours when he had heard his name called from the doorway. Jake turned on his stool to see two uniformed policemen inquiring about someone named Jake Peterson. With slurred speech and very tipsy, Jake informed the police of his identity and added that he had not even been thrown out yet, let alone be escorted home by the militia. The two cops approached Jake and told him that they were not there to arrest him, but rather that they had gone to his residence and it was the neighbor that informed them on where to possibly find him. Jake was puzzled from this statement and asked, "Why are you here for me?"

Looking at Jake and speaking in a low voice, one officer stated, "We need you to come to the morgue to identify a body!"

This single statement appeared to have sobered Jake up and wondered why he had to go! The officer informed him that they found an abandoned white van pulled over on the shoulder of the road in the outskirts of town and when they checked it out they found the decapitated body of a female inside it. We found this card with your name on it on her person and we need you to identify who she is. Jake went with the officers to the morgue and identified the body as that of his girlfriend. Jake was still numb from the loss of his wife and baby, but this new incident put him somewhere close to the epicenter of numbness, to the point of being non-retrievable. I fully understood why Jake drank to oblivion, why he never got married again and why he never had another relationship. It was because he didn't trust anything or anyone and the stress, fear and pain he carried was overwhelming and intolerable.

After losing his girlfriend and job in Florida, Jake returned to the New England area and settled at Cape Cod. He procured a similar job in boat-building as he had in Florida and started to seek some treatment from the VA Outpatient Treatment Center of the Cape and Islands in Hyannis. This VA Outpatient Center was affectionately referred to as "The Hooch" by several Vietnam Veterans who had settled at the Cape. I became familiar with many of the counselors from the Center and received many calls from referring Veterans to the program at the Northampton VAMC. The first time that Jake attended the VA Outpatient Clinic in Hyannis was with another Vietnam Veteran he befriended on the job. Surprisingly, his first line of treatment was not for his PTSD, but rather it was for his chronic alcoholism, which never diminished from his move from Florida. Jake went to the clinic to appease his friend; he was never really interested in treatment or in quitting his drinking. As a result of this attitude, he would only attend the Center perhaps once and occasionally twice a month. Originally, Jake had called his parents prior to arriving at the Cape and asked them if he could stay with them a few weeks until he was settled. They denied him for the sole reason that they had no tolerance for his alcoholism, so he continued his trek and settled at the Cape. Jake was doing very well at the Cape and had resided at several places from Mashpee to Orleans and thoroughly enjoyed his job and the Ocean. Jake was a homebody and an isolationist who enjoyed being by himself and gave up drinking in bars to drinking at home. His mother had passed away and he was calling his father once every two weeks because his father was in poor health. He never mentioned his sisters because I think that they gave up on him when he was assigned to Vietnam. He heard from his father that his younger brother had joined the Peace Corps and was working in Belize. Whenever Jake called his father he made sure that he was sober so that he could speak intelligently to him. One day while working in the boat building company, Jake was approached by his boss who told him that there was a call from his father in the office. Jake answered the phone and his father informed him that his brother had been killed by terrorists and asked if he (Jake) would go to Belize to escort his brother's body back to Connecticut because with the father's poor health, he was not able to do it. Before he could give his father an answer, Jake was silent for a minute and tried to slow down the stream of thoughts that were racing through his mind. In his mind he said, "-Good God! Will this ever end! WHY!! Will this black cloud of pain and loss that is hovering over me ever leave!"

He felt that he was in a cesspool of pain and death and wondered why it wasn't hitting him. He began to hyperventilate, but not loud enough for his father to hear over the phone. Then in a low, almost inaudible voice, Jake assured his father that he would bring his brother home.

Things were getting back to normal on the ward; this expression was emitted from many employees' mouths over the years. There was never anything "normal" in a psychiatric hospital. Maybe a day was routine or a week was routine, but there was never anything normal. I have never seen a normal person admitted to a psychiatric hospital or a predominately psychiatric hospital. I expressed to the others that we should use the term "routine" instead of "normal" because even the Veterans have picked up on the lingo and are questioning, "If I'm normal, what am I doing in the hospital for psychiatric treatment?"

So needless to say, the daily routine was getting back into the swing of things and the patients and staff invested their time into the treatment program.

The Christmas season was rolling around again and plans were being made for preparation of the big Christmas feast on the ward. This feast was always scheduled on the day that all the patients would be going on pass for Christmas. There was a lot of celebration because the families of the patients were also invited and the invitation extended to parents, wives, children, siblings, significant others and in some very rare cases, grandparents. When these feasts originally began, there were three twenty-two pound turkeys that were sufficient to feed the staff as well as the patient population. But, as time rolled on and the population and attending families increased, the number of turkeys increased from three to seven to ten. It was great and everyone was working together to get all preparations under way. The ward janitor decorated the ceiling with garland and plastic ornaments alternating them among the tiles. Santa Claus posters with Merry Christmas greetings were taped to the doors and walls and there was a seven foot artificial tree that was nicely decorated in the dayroom. Horticulture supplied several poinsettia plants that adorned the tables and the nurse's station. Every staff member brought in a casserole dish of a vegetable, salad or dessert that everyone could at least get a taste to enjoy it. Needless to say, the planning of these festivities began months in advance to make sure that everything would go smoothly for the day of celebration. With stomachs full and bags packed, the Veterans and their families would slowly depart to carry on their celebrations of the Christmas holiday, as the staff was left with the feeling of satisfaction that another ward Christmas celebration was successful.

In May 1987, I was on one of the many phone calls talking to the social worker at the Manchester, New Hampshire VAMC. We had received many referrals from them and I was presently listening as she described another potential candidate for our program. My office door was always open and I usually would visually scan the dayroom to see if there was anyone waiting to see me, even if I was on the phone. I noticed that Lucky Reese was the only patient in the dayroom and he was sitting on the love seat that was right outside Dr. Benedetto's office. I turned my attention back to the phone call that I had and listened to the vital statistics that the social worker was describing to me. I learned to multi-task very quickly when I was assigned the admission coordinators position on the PTSD unit. Everything appeared to be calm and quiet until the sound of silence was broken when Lucky jumped out of his seat and was screaming, "JESUS! He's killing him!!"

I heard a commotion coming from Dr. Benedetto's office and quickly threw the phone receiver that I was holding and bee-lined it out to the dayroom. Other staff members responded just as quickly as I did and trying to enter the doctor's office was futile because it was locked from the inside and the doctor had the only key to his door. Panic was starting to rise from the staff because no one had a master key or a similar key that fit the keyhole of the doctor's office. Some were starting to use their shoulder to hopefully push open the door, while others attempted to go outside and try to open the one window to his office that faced the back walkway to the building. It was terrible! You could hear the sound of someone choking and a desk being kicked. My adrenalin was declaring war on my muscles and my only thought was to break down the door. I stood about twenty feet away and using all my energy, I took a running jump and successfully kicked his door in. The entire door knob and lock ripped out of the door and slid across the floor like ice skates on a frozen pond. The staff merged in to restrain the individual that was choking Dr. Benedetto from behind. The doctor had blood coming from his nose and mouth and his shirt was torn from his right shoulder and was hanging down to his knees. The doctor appeared to be confused because he was walking in circles around his office and it was obvious that he almost "bought the farm". When the police arrived, the staff explained what had just taken place and when they asked for the identity of the individual that choked the doctor, no one had a clue of who this man was. I approached the nurse's station and asked the secretary if she had any information about the identity of the intruder. She explained that he came up to the counter and inquired to which office was Dr. Benedetto's, so she pointed it out to him and he nonchalantly went his merry way towards the Doctor's office. I remember noticing an individual entering Manny's office, but I assumed that he was going for an evaluation from the doctor as a possible potential candidate for the PTSD program. I learned later that this intruder was well-known to Dr. Benedetto and that he was one of his patients fifteen years ago. Manny explained that he told this patient in a one-to-one meeting that he felt very strongly that this patient was a repressed homosexual and if he continued to deny these feelings, he would be in and out of psychiatric hospitals the rest of his life. The patient had exited his office and continued to deny these thoughts and feelings. Manny further explained that this was an act of revenge because the patient didn't like what he said fifteen years ago and harboring these thoughts to this present day, he had full intentions of quieting Dr. Benedetto, permanently! I remained puzzled with one part of this situation, "How did someone from the outside just walk onto a ward without the ward receiving a call from admissions and announcing a visitor?"

I called admissions and inquired how this visitor got past them and they informed me that he was a patient on the admission ward which proved what Dr. Benedetto stated fifteen years ago; that he would be in and out of psychiatric hospitals the rest of his life. There was one change of placement that occurred without hesitation; this patient was sent to the Cedar Junction Psychiatric Unit at Walpole for a 60-day evaluation for the criminally insane for his attack on Dr. Manuel Benedetto.

More and more Veterans were being admitted for anger issues that they were carrying over from the outside and bringing them into the program. There was a lot of non-compliance, barking at the staff, resistance in group attendance and bucking the rules and regulations. This anger was like a cancer that had metastasized to the staff. Everybody was snapping off negative verbal remarks and no one had any patience with each other so that when a response was not given instantly , it seemed like the anger escalated to a realm where a simple "Sorry to keep you waiting!" was meaningless. Apologies were not accepted and demands were expected to be instantaneous. Even I was not excluded from this cloud of negativity that hung over everyone on Ward 8. Staff started to call in on a more frequent basis stating that there was a family emergency or just to take a mental health day. I started limiting people from coming into my office and just talking because the demand for paperwork completion outweighed the face-to-face interpersonal connection with the patients. It was at this high point of attitudinal negativity that Dr. Manny entered my office and sat in the chair at the side of my desk. I continued to write and tried not to notice him sitting there, but I noticed through my peripheral vision that he was staring at me. Without disturbing my writing he softly stated, "Linda, there is a great deal of anger on this ward and I want you to do an anger management class!"

I couldn't believe what my ears just heard uttered from his mouth, so I slowly turned my head in his direction and said, "Are you out of your flipping mind, I have one of the worst tempers on this unit!"

As we both held a direct unblinking eye contact he remarked, "Exactly, so who would know better to teach anger management than you?"

With this being said Dr. Manny got up from the chair and went to his own office. I sat there thinking about his statement and I couldn't even argue with him because he was absolutely right. It was always statements like this that would tick me off because he got to know me very well, sometimes too well, over the years that we worked together. He was just as aware that I knew him well also!

After sitting and just contemplating about doing an anger management group, I felt that I had better put my thoughts down on paper so as not to have them confused in my head. I had to first think of the clientele I would be teaching and knew I had to match my program to meet their needs. I thought of the Veterans, more particularly, combat Veterans and realized that the traditional classroom presentation would not be understood by the Veterans because about 85% of them continue to live in their anger world. A few days later I had my complete program written down and I presented it to the staff for approval or disapproval. My program was simple and consisted of six sessions. The program was as follows:

1. Assertiveness- (1) What does it mean to be assertive?

2. Anger Cognitive- (2) What do we understand about our anger?

3. Anger Affective- (3) How does our anger affect us, physically, emotionally and mentally?

4. Anger Management- (4) Culmination of the first three in order to achieve this.

I held the classes on Tuesdays and Thursdays in the classroom on ward 8. My first group consisted of eight Veterans because I was told that any more than that for an anger management class would result in losing a few patients interest and attention. I was surprised that my classes were a tremendous success and over time I even had staff in these classes who were interested in alternative modes in dealing with their anger. I never assigned any homework because my expectation was that everybody would verbally participate in class and would leave the class thinking about the material that was presented on that day. Even after I explained exactly how this course was going to run, I could see the curiosity on their faces as they wondered how I was going to teach them how to control their tempers and properly manage their anger.

CHAPTER EIGHT

There were eight Veterans assigned to my first presentation of anger management. These Veterans were assigned by their team leaders. Some showed an avid interest in this class, while some others entered the room and slouched in a chair folding their arms and closing their eyes displaying complete disinterest in the class. I was standing in front by the chalkboard with my arms folded and without uttering a word, slowly observed each candidate that was sitting in the room. There was direct eye contact with each one of them and not one of them asked me why I was silent. The ones that slouched down in their chairs started to sit up and put their feet under their own chairs instead of sprawling out after they received a poke from the Veteran sitting next to them. I didn't have to say a word because my direct eye contact was saying it all. When I knew I had everyone's attention, I proceeded to introduce myself and to explain the course that this class was going to take. I had already written the four sections of the course on the board and I noticed that some of them were eyeballing the sections. Picking up the eraser, I turned to the board and erased 2, 3, and 4 and left Assertiveness on the board and turning back to the patients and pointing to the word (assertiveness) I told the class that we are concentrating on assertiveness in the first session. I then asked the class, "What does it mean to be assertive?"

I received several responses from shrugging shoulders which informed me that these Veterans had no idea what it meant to saying that assertiveness was aggression. I explained that according to Webster's Dictionary assertiveness is a "positive statement or declaration, unduly confident or insistent". It is never aggression. I would always simplify the definition by telling them that assertiveness is very close to a compromise. With this being said, I decided to take them back in time to when they were children and told them that children are the best at being assertive because they are confident with themselves and I gave examples such as trading baseball cards or comic books or even playing the game of marbles or picking sides for a sandlot ballgame. The best were always picked first because they were confident in the position they were comfortable playing. In marbles you always played your favorite marbles last because you didn't want to lose them and if you were on a losing streak, you always quit before you used your favorite ones. I realized from this first class that taking the Veterans for a walk down memory lane was highly beneficial to them because it allowed them to escape the "soldier mode" that they have lived in since they enlisted into the military. As I continued with the succeeding classes, I noticed that these patients were in the class before I arrived and were raring to go. I also informed them that if they are going to get angry then you do it in this class, after all this is an anger management class…is it not?

As the weeks and months passed by and I continued to teach anger management, I noticed several changes that were very beneficial to the ward atmosphere. The changes that were most identified were that the number of individuals attending had increased and sometimes doubled. Fifty to seventy percent of the patients that completed the cycle requested to attend another cycle or two because they felt that there was an abundance of information presented in these groups and they thought that if they missed anything, they could pick it up in the second cycle. The interest and motivational levels also increased and not only with the Veterans, but with the staff as well. Everybody's attitude had improved tremendously and no one was barking or taking the head off of someone, but rather they were listening and communicating in a positive and courteous matter. Respect for each other had been re-established. I was proud of the fact that I established this program and that it rocketed to popularity with the Veterans. But, I am more proud of the fact that teaching this program has greatly quelled my own anger so that I no longer reacted to situations, but rather will listen with true interest and concern. Anger wasn't the only change that took place on Ward 8; there was a departmental change that also took place at this time. The Post-Traumatic Stress Unit was now under the psychology department and no longer under psychiatry. My supervisor was now the ward psychologist, not the ward doctor as it had been previously. Our new supervisor was Dr. Levi Keitel who was transferred to our unit from the substance abuse unit and to fill in the position that Dr. Strangeville had vacated. Levi was a true asset to the unit because he was down-to-earth and he was blessed with a listening ear which enabled him to hear each person and not jump to conclusions after hearing one person's complaint and making a decision about that. But, rather he'd have the two or three individuals in his office discussing their points of view. Upon completion of the points of view, Levi would make his decision about the situation which resulted in the decision he made being satisfactory to all.

I seemed to be acquiring more and more responsibilities in my job, but I wasn't paying it any mind. I enjoyed being busy because it made the time speed by quickly and there were days that appeared that there was not enough hours in the day to complete routine tasks. Dr. Levi had been working on the unit for about nine months when he approached me and inquired about everything that I do on a daily basis. He was my supervisor so I asked him if he wanted to know what I do on a daily basis or did he want a list of everything that I was responsible to do. He wanted to know everything that I did, classes I taught, scheduling of MHA's time, scheduling patients for 2-day, 2-week or 6-week admissions, preparing and sending applications, sending for military records, etc. I think I had mentioned about 52 different responsibilities that I did, when he suddenly stood up and stated, "Linda, I'm going to have you set up for a desk audit! I want you to be promoted to a higher grade because I strongly feel that you deserve it."

As he exited my office, I watched him leave when my mouth dropped open in total disbelief of what I just heard. This was the first time that a supervisor ever told me that he was putting me in for a promotion. Most of the time, on previous occasions, the promotion was never expected so that when it came about, it was a total surprise to the recipient. My desk audit was scheduled for the following week and passing with flying colors resulted in a promotion to the next grade and the 8th step. I also acquired an additional job title which was "Lead Mental Health Associate". This new title was used in conjunction with the admissions coordinator title.

Holidays were flying by and it seemed as if before one ended the celebration of the next one was already in full gear. My office had three windows in it and being a nice bright office it was attracting both patients and staff to sit comfortably and just chat at their break times. My office sported seventeen plants, a corkboard with family pictures displayed like a collage and posters of several of the Boston Red Sox players taped to the sides of my file cabinets. It was very comfortable and I was proud of the fact that many staff and Veterans complimented my decorative and arrangement skills and no one ever passed by without giving a friendly greeting followed by a smile when I graciously returned the greeting back to them.

On ward 8 I learned the many faces of Post-Traumatic Stress Disorder and the full depth of the definition of the diagnosis. PTSD is an umbrella that encompasses every type of trauma that has a psychiatric effect on individuals. The individuals that were being treated on this unit were primarily combat-related trauma, but the difference was that each Veteran had a different combat experience that caused his trauma. Some soldiers were "tunnel rats"! They would go down into the ground tunnels looking for the enemy, but these were highly hazardous because many openings had pythons or boa constrictors or even worse, there were highly poisonous snakes such as bush vipers and cobras that when bitten, death occurred within seconds. Others were assigned to search and destroy missions with a small amount of soldiers (about 5-6) that would step on claymores or trip a pongee wire that would instantly impale someone. Still others were door gunners on helicopters and their job was to clear the perimeter so the copter could land and pick up the injured. Many times the door gunner was killed and the copter was shot down and rescue attempts failed to retrieve survivors or wounded so as to bring them back to a safe area where they could be treated for their wounds. Physical injuries were readily cared for, but the psychological and emotional problems were escalating, but never reared their evil heads until they were back in the United States.

Several Vietnam Veterans never left Vietnam, at least on a mental and emotional basis. They physically returned to their homes, families, and even some jobs, but their minds, thoughts and feelings were continuing to fight a war that was on the other side of the world. There was no de-programming of Vietnam Veterans because they were pulled from a war zone and placed on an airplane, told that they were going home and then landed back in the United States in a little less than twenty-four hours. To add insult to injury, when they were disembarking from the plane they were pelted with rotten tomatoes and fruit. I would have many deep conversations with many Veterans and would ask them to recall their memory of the day that they arrived back in the States. They would hesitate in thought and become very somber and some would describe the day in one word, such as, "Okay", "Strange!" and even stated that it was a "sad day".

Boomer was a very pleasant, tall and slender Black American who sported a metal brace on his right leg. He always smiled and was casual in discussing the weather or general conversation of the day. To talk about himself or his family was a little more difficult because he never would go into any depth, although he would continue to smile and it was obvious that he was blocking conversations that were personable. I interviewed Boomer on the second day that he was on the unit. He told me that he was shot in the leg in Vietnam and the injury damaged a nerve in his leg which resulted in his having to wear a brace for the rest of his life. When Boomer returned from Vietnam, he stated that he was in his dress uniform and was wearing all the medals and ribbons, including a Purple Heart medal. His plane landed in Oakland, California and as he disembarked and was walking on the tarmac, he was pelted with rotten fruit and tomatoes by observers behind the fence and was called a "baby killer" and "hooch burner" and other slanderous names. He was in total disbelief when he heard some of the observers comment about his injury. He didn't believe that he was actually back in the United States because of these comments. He told me that he heard people yelling, "I'm glad you got shot, they should have killed you!" "Go back to Vietnam! You're not welcome in this country!"

The uniform that he wore with pride and respect was covered with garbage and his medals and ribbons on the left side of his chest that he so bravely earned were completely spattered with moldy tomatoes. When Boomer finished describing the day that he returned home from Vietnam, he was no longer smiling and was staring at the floor in my office. I offered him a bottle of water which he declined and then inquired if we were through because he wanted to take a walk off the ward to smoke a cigarette. After Boomer left my office, I quietly thought that Boomer was only one of many Vietnam Veterans that had a severe negative homecoming experience. It's no wonder that these Veterans drugged and drank as a result of the reception they received at airports, taxis, restaurants, and even their own families and friends that treated them like criminals instead of returning combat soldiers.

I started to realize that it was not healthy to work any particular program for any great period of time because I was told that

I had symptoms of PTSD. I always practiced not taking my job home, but that is easier said than done. I was fearful of taking any vacations because every time I returned to work I was informed that a Veteran had died while I was gone. It wasn't a typical death, it was suicide. Most were drug overdoses, but there were also several that put a gun in their mouths and blew the back of their heads all over the wall of a motel room. Some others drove their motorcycles or vehicles over a cliff or into a tree, killing them instantly. It appeared that these deaths seemed to occur every time I was on vacation or out sick for a week and there were several staff members who attempted to explain that these deaths were coincidental and that my being away had nothing to do with it. Usually these explanations were easily acceptable for me, but these deaths were too coincidental because I was the last staff member who conversed with many of these Veterans before they passed. I was perplexed and a little depressed when I learned of these deaths because there was no hint or suggestion that they were going to hurt themselves. I guess these Veterans had no idea that death was knocking on their doors because many of the deaths were the result of accidental overdose of cocaine or heroin. Prior to their entering the PTSD program, several Veterans were deeply involved in drug and alcohol use. They used alcohol and drugs to dull the memories of combat and even though several were married, the drugs and alcohol assisted to decrease the startle reaction when a car would backfire or jets were flying low over their homes. Substances did nothing to alleviate the nightmares and flashbacks they were experiencing on a daily basis.

Men get very close in war and some enlisted with the "buddy system" in which two or three friends that grew up together all enlisted into the same branch of service at the same time. Many were also deployed to Vietnam, but they were separated from each other as a result of their assignment. As a result of the separations, these soldiers returned to the United States at different times and in many cases, with soldiers that they didn't even know. It was only after their return that they found out who walked off the plane and who flew back in the baggage area and were escorted by six soldiers to the awaiting hearse that was parked on the tarmac near the plane. Vietnam Veterans held their feelings inside and they never wanted to talk about the war. They had no debriefing as did the Korean and WWII returning soldiers because the Vietnam Veterans were standing on their front door steps within twenty-four hours of leaving Vietnam. There is no comparison of Vietnam Veterans with Korean or WWII Veterans because Veterans of WWII and Korea came home on boats and went over on boats/ships. They were able to debrief with one another on the ships, so by the time they got home they were fairly adjusted and looking forward to being home because it took two weeks minimum to cross the ocean by ship. Treating Veterans from Korean War or WWII was a piece of cake to me because they were ready to talk about their experiences and in many cases they talked of comical situations from the war. I couldn't understand how any war could be comical, but these men stated that the situations that made them laugh were few and far between, but they most definitely existed.

Downtime on a Post-Traumatic Stress Unit is also a rarity, but periodically I managed to sit back in my office and reminisce about some of the old soldiers that I cared for at the State Soldiers Home and try to compare them with the Vietnam Veteran that I am presently treating. No matter how hard I tried there wasn't an ounce of comparison that I could equate to these wars. The only similarity I could fathom was that it didn't matter what branch of the service that they served in and it didn't matter what war they fought in and it didn't matter what rank they were because no matter how you slice the pie…a Veteran is a Veteran is a Veteran! And they have damn well earned the respect, honor and gratitude of every American man, woman and child for placing their lives on the line and protecting the freedoms that we continue to have today.

I was a co-leader in a process group with Scrappy Lindstrom, the social worker in this program. She was a phenomenal group leader and I credit her for my knowledge in teaching me social work techniques. Scrappy was also multi-lingual in many Slavic languages. She could speak Russian, Romanian, Lithuanian, Polish and I think Yugoslavian. I personally have never heard her speak anything but English at work, but it wouldn't have surprised me if she ever uttered Vietnamese to one of the Veterans just to see how they would respond. Our group had about ten Veterans in it and these Veterans were usually the most difficult ones to deal with in the program. They were difficult because they were never allowed to express any feelings about themselves. They were constantly being represented with gross negativity especially by the media. They expressed concerns about being clustered with some Veterans that went off the deep-end by reading in a paper or seeing it on TV that a "Vietnam Veteran" shot up a college campus in Texas or a Vietnam Veteran shot up a McDonald's in California and killed six or seven innocent people. They are not denying that these incidents occurred and that they were horrific and a terrible situation. They are angered that the specific reference of "Vietnam Veteran" was listed and feel that they are continuing to be punished by their own country. When the Korean War and WWII ended and the soldiers returned, they did not fit right back into the groove of living a normal life. There were problems and there were things that wives and relatives didn't understand about them. This is also true for the Vietnam Veteran as well, but the main difference is that if the Korean Veteran and WWII Veteran made the media for something negative that they did, they were never labeled specifically as a "Korean Veteran or a WWII Veteran"! They were just labeled Veteran! I was listening intently at this conversation that was going around this group room and I understood another aspect of the Vietnam Vet. Every Veteran in this group agreed with each other and some further stated that this specific labeling narrows their paths of opportunity because if they want to apply at college and they mention that they are

Vietnam Veterans, thoughts will automatically go to Texas and the gunman that went on a shooting spree. If they take their kids or even go by themselves to McDonald's, people will see the sticker in their vehicle window saying, " I'm a proud Vietnam Veteran" and they start to get nervous and think that we're going to start shooting up the place. Vietnam Veterans feel that it is not fair and they don't understand how they are being ostracized from other Veterans because they are equally proud of being a Veteran and serving in the greatest military in the world. All wars are dirty, bloody and reap tremendous losses but they are also very different from each other and one should never be compared with another. As I stated before, the only comparison is that a Veteran is a Veteran...is a Veteran!

My time on the PTSD unit was coming to a close and I would be shortly transferring to Social Service in the capacity of a Social Work Associate. Scrappy Lindstrom had transferred to the VA in Providence, Rhode Island and Phil Kendricks had decided to take a position at the Post Office for three months, but he didn't realize that this Post Office position was just a temporary position that took him through the Christmas holidays. He returned to this VA after his three month hiatus with no loss of sick time or vacation time that he had accrued. With these staff members gone, I had to change some of the scheduling and I even took some midnight to eight shifts to cover for staff that had family and children during the Christmas season. I hadn't worked this shift for several years and it didn't take me long to adjust my body clock back to staying awake at night. There was one night that was so bitterly cold and the north wind was blowing so hard that it made snow drifts on the roads and highways. It wasn't so bad on the roads, but as I steered my car up the road to the VA it felt like everything was stronger. Even the temperature was lower and now felt like it was ten below zero as the wind gusts broke small branches from the surrounding trees. I parked my car in the parking lot that was next to Ward 8 and entered the tunnel that led to the ward. It was

11:45pm and as the wind literally blew me through the tunnel and up to the door to the ward, I managed to turn the ice cold knob of the door and stepped inside and just stood on the rug attempting to thaw out. I noticed that there were about four Veterans sitting in the dayroom and the only things that I was able to move were my eyes. Jared was one of the Veterans sitting in the dayroom and upon eyeballing me asked me if it was cold outside. I slowly turned my gaze in his direction and stated, "It is colder than a penguin's balls sitting on an iceberg!"

He looked at me and stated, "Boy! That's cold!"

I responded with, "Now you know why they walk the way they do!"

I retreated to my office and made a pot of coffee and proceeded to do paperwork left over from the day shift, but I was also available to staff and Veterans if they needed me and I could always guarantee that there would be a Veteran that just wanted to talk because he was unable to sleep as a result of the flashbacks that he dreamed of on a nightly basis. If I was to ever count the number of times that I was stopped by a Veteran by being called on a phone, getting out of my car or getting into it, stopped on my way to lunch or an appointment/meeting or just relaxing on a rare down-time in my office, I was approached for the sole purpose of just asking a question that they think I have the better answer than anyone else.

It seemed like it was a blink of my eye when I was suddenly sitting in my vacant office waiting for the movers to transfer everything to building 20. The Veterans gave me a little going-away party in which they presented me with a cake, a card and an engraved Zippo lighter that had my name and date of birth on it. It was a beautiful silver lighter and being a smoker at that time, I sincerely appreciated it. One of the Veterans approached me during this gathering and stated, "Linda, do you know the symbolism of the Zippo lighter? Giving someone a Zippo lighter is the highest honor that a Vietnam Veteran could bestow on anyone! You see, Zippo lighters burned many huts in Vietnam. Soldiers were sent on "Search and Destroy" missions and after we cleared the civilians out, we were told to burn the village to the ground. If we suspected there were Vietcong being harbored in a village, we destroyed the village, otherwise if the village was safe we continued down the road without any disruption of the people or the village. So you see! Vietnam Veterans hold you in high-esteem and trust you unconditionally by presenting you with a Zippo lighter. It is also our way of showing our love and respect to you!"

Needless to say, I had a tremendous lump in my throat and was at a complete loss of words and was wondering if I was making a mistake in transferring to another service. My mind knew I had to leave, but my heart was begging my mind to stay. I really felt terrible because it was as if I was abandoning them. I assured them that I was only going to the other side of the VA and that they were welcome to see me any time they wished, as long as I was there and not on the road. My farewell/gratitude speech was short and concise because that lump in my throat seemed to have grown bigger and I didn't want my voice to crack or my eyes to well up in front of them. I took a deep breath and turned to see the movers starting to move my office to building 20.

Chapter Nine

Building 20 was situated on the hill of the entrance road to the VA from Route 9. It literally sits halfway up the hill and across the street from the employee homes which were primarily occupied by doctors and the director. Building 20 once housed the quarters for the employees who lived far away and in the basement was the daycare for the babies and toddlers of employees who worked the day shift and were unable to care for their children because they had to work during the daytime. On the first floor to the left housed the psychology department and the social service department. My new office was the first door to the right off the lobby and I shared this office with another social work associate. Brenda Curran was the other social work associate and we clicked right from the get-go. We were constantly joking at the end of the day and she would crack me up when she would dictate her daily notes and visits on her phone to the transcriber in the main building. I thought that it was rather comical when she would seriously state that "and he enjoyed his coffee and doughnuts" because it sounded like she had visited a client in "Dunkin Donuts" instead of his home. Brenda would hear me start to giggle at my desk and she would have to turn the dictation off and turn to me and ask, "What is so funny?"

Without hesitation, I attempted to describe how funny that statement was to hear, especially when I walked into the office and upon only hearing that statement, it made me think that that was the highlight of her outpatient visits for the day. Brenda started to laugh as well because she knew that I was aware of her dedication and respect of these Veterans and that this was an isolated incident and bad timing on my part when I walked into the office towards the end of her dictations.

This position introduced me to caring for outpatients at their homes or clinics. For seventeen years I had worked totally on an inpatient basis and now I had to get trip tickets to procure a government vehicle to travel all over Western Massachusetts to various rest homes, halfway homes, nursing homes and residential care homes. I found it exciting and different and I now realized what Luke Jefferson meant when he had asked me, "Linda, I hope you're flexible!" during my interview for this position.

Luke Jefferson, MSW is the chief of the Social Service department and my new supervisor. His secretary is Rose MacGregor and Rose started her employment on the same day that I had and she was the second person to enter the front lobby on that first day. Rose was a very good friend and she was only eighteen days older than me. Rose was Luke's right arm; anything that he wanted or needed from job descriptions to letters written for promotions or personal "thank you" notes, Rose was right there. It was also Rose who pointed me out to Luke as I walked across the parking lot at building 20 as I was returning to Ward 8 from Psychology service. She told me much later that that was the day she mentioned to Luke, "There goes your next Social Work Associate!"

I was totally unaware that that position existed or was even posted. I had a funny feeling that Rose wanted me working in the same department that she was working because we became very good friends when we both worked in nursing service and we saw each other every day. Now, the only times we were seeing each other was when I had to submit the work schedule of the MHA's to psychology service which is located at the opposite end of building 20 from the social service department, but now I am here in social service and I will adjust my schedule to meet the demands and care of the Veterans involved in social service.

Luke soon realized how flexible I was because many times as he was arriving at work, I was on my way out to go to residential care homes, VA clinics or to take an inpatient Veteran to get shoes or clothes at the mall and periodically, I would bring Veterans to a non-VA doctor that was referred by a VA doctor because the specialty treatment that they needed was not available in the VA. It became so routine to see Luke walking in as I was walking out of building 20. He would always inquire,"Where are you heading today, Linda?"

I would always smile at him and start singing Willie Nelson's song "On the Road Again"! Luke always whistled and as I crossed the parking lot to get in my car, I could still hear his whistle as it slowly faded like a train whistle that was going through a tunnel in the far distance.

I liked doing outpatient work because it appeared to be more hands-on than working inpatient. Outpatient assignments were more involved because you had to visit patients in their domiciles and if there were any problems, it was up to me to make sure that they were treated properly and efficiently. I would always meet with the house manager first because they always gave me a full report on the health of each Veteran that was living in the house. Many residential care homes housed several Veterans who were diagnosed with schizophrenia and in my experience, schizophrenics could be deathly ill and in a lot of pain and they will never complain. That is why it is imperative for any case worker to meet with every Veteran who is boarding in a residential care, private home, halfway house or single room occupancy. Several times I called back to the hospital to talk with the admitting doctor to relay the symptoms of a Veteran and was told to bring the Veteran in for admission because his condition was serious and if ignored could possibly be life-threatening. If a Veteran was intoxicated or high on drugs, then I had to notify the police and have them bring the Veteran to the VA.

It was a beautiful, bright and sunny morning in March when I was first assigned to take a government car to visit residential care homes in the Berkshires. I traveled along Route 9 on my way to Pittsfield and my eyes were squinting as a result of the sun's impact on the white snowfall that occurred two days ago. There were puddles on the road and streams of water that was running down the inclines. Snow was melting off the overhanging branches and every now and then a good size clump of snow would hit the hood or the window of the car, which would take me by surprise for about a second because of the sound it made from the contact. I would have loved to open a window and just enjoy the fresh air, but the oncoming traffic was producing high water sprays from their wheels hitting the puddles, splashing water on my car as if I was going through a car wash. I pulled into a muddy driveway which was my first stop to see two Veterans in a private home in Becket, MA. I introduced myself to the homeowners and then to the Veterans and told them that I would be dropping by once a month to see them and to evaluate how they were doing. These two Veterans appeared to be content, well-fed and were wearing clean clothes and personal hygiene also appeared to be good. One had a scraggly beard that definitely needed trimming and he also possessed dark brown nicotine-stained fingers from his profound smoking habit. The other Veteran had clean clothes that were disheveled and his hair needed to be combed because it looked like he never combed it; just walked out of the shower and let it dry in the position that the drying towel left it. Both these Veterans were very pleasant and sociable and I thought as I was departing this house and on my way to my next destination, that it would be nice if everyone I was visiting would be just as pleasant, but I knew that was wishful thinking on my part.

I was heading up Route 20 to Lee, MA to visit three homes that were in the Lee/Pittsfield area and like before, I was enjoying just being in the fresh air and feeling that I wasn't working because I was never on the road or assigned outpatient care. I arrived at the

Greater Hope House in Lee which housed about twenty to twenty-five Veterans at a little before 11 a.m. Most of the rooms were two bedrooms and there were only four that were single rooms. Usually, the single rooms had a waiting list and as soon as the room was vacated, the next Veteran on the top of the list had the option to decline or to accept it. It was a rarity for anyone on the list to decline a private room, but on the occasion that it did occur was the result of a Veteran pleased with the two-man room he was in and/or getting along very well with his roommate and did not wish to displace himself to a single room.

I was greeted at the door by one of the Veterans who shook my hand and bid me to enter. One of the staff had exited the kitchen and was wiping her hands on an apron as she walked across the large TV room to greet me and introduce herself to me. I reciprocated the greeting and introduction and was wondering if I was interrupting the Veterans lunch. She remarked that she was only in the preparation stage and that they were not scheduled to dine for forty-five minutes. One of the Veterans approached me and inquired if there was anything he could assist me with while I was there. I stated that it would be nice to have a group meeting for about fifteen minutes to hear any complaints, needs, medications or medical or psych appointments that these Veterans required. Everyone appeared to be well-groomed, clean-clothed and personal hygiene was excellent. Most of the Veterans spoke well and voiced their contentment of this house and their compliance with the rules and regulations of the VA and this domicile. After I dismissed the group, I informed the Veterans that I will be back again next month and if anyone has a problem they could call me at the VA or have one of the staff notify me and I will return immediately. I gave the staff my card and told them not to hesitate in calling me and that I am presently the VA worker assigned to the house. I knew that I had made a good impression on them because they all gathered around me to shake my hand and walked me to the door.

As I exited the parking lot of the Hope House, I turned right and went down a small hill to Route 7 which led me into the center of the city of Pittsfield. My next stop was the Williams House which housed four Veterans. These Veterans were very different from the Veterans of the other two houses because these Veterans had been living in this house for many years. Williams House was a private home and was run by the homeowner and she decided which Veterans that she wanted to board at her house. It was a big Victorian house that was situated smack-dab in the middle of the city so that everything was available to these Veterans within walking distance. When I arrived there were only two of the four Veterans that I met with because the other two were out at appointments or working a part-time job. I introduced myself to the homeowner and spoke with her before I talked to the two Veterans. I complimented her on her house and its upkeep and stated that for its size it was in excellent condition. She appeared to be very nice, but I somehow felt that I was disturbing her because she gave me one word answers to all my questions. She never carried on a sociable conversation, but rather stood with her arms folded across her chest like a knight in full armor defending his domain. I may be very wrong judging her in this manner, but this was the impression she was giving me. She introduced the two Veterans to me and I met with them for about fifteen minutes and like the homeowner, they also gave one-word answers to the questions I asked. I guess when people live together for long periods of time; they start to develop similar ways of doing and saying things. I affirmed that I would be returning on a monthly basis and that if they had any problems to please notify me. I left my card with the homeowner and each of the Veterans, bid them have a nice day and then returned to the VA to record the notes for all the Veterans I visited.

The travel back to the VA was much more pleasant because it was all downhill and the wash-off of melted snow from the mountains was now just a trickle compared to the streams that I encountered that morning. I also noticed that the trees were standing more erect and not bent over with laden snow on their boughs.

I pulled into a mini-mall area in Williamsburg to calculate the mileage on my trip ticket of all the stops that I had made that day. A completed trip ticket is handed in to the garage when the car is returned because it is the regulation of the VA when a government vehicle is used. The place, time, destination, and mileage of the trip must be recorded and is the responsibility of everyone who requests a government vehicle. Upon completing the trip ticket, I pulled the vehicle back onto Route 9 and continued my return to the VA hospital. I returned the vehicle and submitted both the ticket and car keys to the garage and then I trekked up that awful hill to Building 20 which was situated at the top of that road. Finally, making it to the top, I entered the middle door to Building 20, climbed four more stairs to the lobby and entering my office feeling that I just could not wait to sit in the chair, just to catch my breath and allow my heart rate to slow down. Brenda was sitting at her desk when I entered the office and she could tell by my symptoms that I had walked up the hill. She was very busy doing her notes and without even looking at me suggested that next time I should drive my car down to the garage and park it in their lot so that when I return I just have to get in my car and drive it up the hill instead of walking up it. Slowly turning my head in her direction, I stated, "Definitely, I will do that next time!"

Thursdays were staff meeting day for social work service. Luke would hold these meetings in the creative thinking room in Building 1. Employees came from the Springfield Community Care Center and the Northampton Community Care Center, as well as anyone who was available in the VA Hospital. These meetings were to give Luke an update on progress in the wards, as well as the satellite centers in Springfield and Northampton. Sometimes if the creative thinking room was booked, the meetings were carried out in the lobby of Building 20. This is where I first officially met Mike Jamison, MSW who was the director of the Northampton Community Care Center (NCCC). Mike was a pleasant, sociable man and he gave me the impression that nothing ever bothered him. Mike was always smiling and when he spoke, I caught a slight Boston accent in his speech. He was married and a fairly new father to a little boy. He lived in Springfield and commuted to Northampton every day. I thought that traveling from Holyoke was long enough, I could not imagine having to go from Springfield, but this distance didn't bother Mike at all.

I was working in Social services about three months when Mike Jamison approached me and inquired if I would like to work at the Northampton CCC. He explained that he was short a staff member for over a month and was impressed with my quick adjustment from mental health service department to the social service department. He further stated that he had already approached Luke concerning this notion and was told that Luke was seriously contemplating making that transition, but it couldn't occur for about a month because of the shortage of staff all over and that Luke needed me for fill-in for staff members on annual leave or extended sick leave.

Normally, waiting for a month to pass was always a short time, but the month that I waited to be assigned to the NVCCC seemed to be six months instead of the one. I remained very busy doing my work when Luke approached me on a Friday and said, "Beginning on Monday Linda, you will report to the Northampton Veterans Community Care Center in downtown Northampton! Your supervisor will be Mike Jamison, MSW who is the director of the NVCCC."

I knew that this new assignment would take me off the road and that I would care for patients that come to me instead of my going and visiting them. My schedule will be that I will be working Mondays through Fridays from 8a.m. to 4:30pm. I was excited about this assignment and couldn't wait for the weekend to pass so that I could get started on this new work transition.

Finally, Monday was here and I was very excited as was my mother in seeing me with such motivation to go to work. My car was accustomed to travelling up Route 5 since I had already been travelling it for fourteen years. I think I could have put it on automatic pilot, had a little nap and the vehicle would have brought me to the VA in record time. The only change in my travel is that now I am stopping five miles short of the VA in downtown Northampton and the Center is directly on Route 5. I saw the sign for the NVCCC on the building of Store 24 and it directed me to go behind the store. I parked my car in the back parking lot and walked up the road to the main entrance to the Center, which was all the way back up to the beginning of this single-leveled building. As I entered, I initially saw a kitchen area with seven small square tables equipped with four chairs behind an elongated counter. On the far side of kitchen were two offices; one was for the nurse (Chloe) and the other office was the director of the Center (Mike's office). To my direct left was the employee's bathroom. As I slowly walked into the carpeted lobby, I noticed a pool table directly in front of the partitioned secretary's office. Mike's door was open and he noticed me coming into the Center and he approached me, shook my hand and welcomed me aboard. He then gave me the five-cent tour and showed me where my office would be after we toured through occupational therapy and the CWT (Compensated Work Therapy) programs.

I kind of snickered along with Mike when he showed me my office because my so-called desk was a slim counter because there was just enough room for me to sit. In reality, this tiny room was the electrical closet that housed all the phone connections and the circuit breakers for the entire Center. The small single window in this room looked directly at the walkway to the front door and the front parking lot where I noticed several patients stood smoking their cigarettes. Some of the patients appeared familiar to me, but many I didn't know at all and the only thing that was constant was the parade of patients and employees that entered and exited the door which was right next to my office door. There was no temperature control in my office and as a result, I had to constantly wear my jacket in the winter. In the summer, it was hotter than a hooker in an Army barracks with a duffel bag full of fifties! The building had heat and air-conditioning, but neither of these ever reached my office. I came to believe that my office was on the outside of the complex, but like everything else that I did, I was able to acclimate myself to my new surroundings and dig my heels in and learn the new job that I was hired to do.

Mike started me off by having me attend several groups which gave reports of the patients that were attending these particular groups. I heard of patient's progress in occupational therapy, compensated work therapy and substance abuse group. Several of these Veterans were involved in more than one of these groups and were also collecting Supplemental Security Income (SSI) or Social Security Disability (SSD) while others were receiving Veterans benefits from the Veteran Representative in the city or town that they lived in. The CWT program was a work program and Veterans earned monies from working on the projects in the back room. All projects differed in pay and the Veterans were paid every other week. As a result of the projects being paid differently, the techs would rotate the assignments on a daily basis because it wasn't fair to have one patient earn $400 pay and another who worked the same amount of time earn only $80. There were always those few patients who only wanted to work the high-paying jobs and said "no!" to the low-paying jobs because they wanted to make the big money. Every Veteran is told when they get assigned to the back room (CWT) that they have to be open to every job assignment and if they refuse to do any job assigned to them, then their name is dropped from the rotation list and more than likely they never return to CWT because they know that they will never be assigned a high paying detail until they agree to do a low-paying one.

Claudia was the nurse and her office was next door to Mike's. She was pleasant enough, although it seemed like she was sizing up new employees and new patients while she stood in the doorway of her office sporting a slight grin and both hands in the pockets of her slacks. Claudia was also a very sociable person, but also very cautious because when I initially met her she was stand-offish, thus giving me the impression that she was a tad paranoid and didn't want anyone treading in her little area of the world. These thoughts of mine quickly dissipated when Claudia explained each patient to me that was discussed in the meetings. She also assisted me in assigning five patients that she had on her list to me. Mike approved of these patients and remarked that they were easy cases to follow and by lightening Claudia's load, she would have more time to do her medical assignments such as giving injections, filling pill boxes and assisting the doctor who was there for one day each week. Claudia turned out to be a great person and she really stood her ground when it came to Veterans being intoxicated and then showing up at the center. Most of the patients that became intoxicated were the ones who worked in the CWT program and received pay every two weeks. Claudia had informed me of these happenings because they always occurred on pay days. On Friday of my first week, I had noticed Claudia standing just outside the entrance door smoking a cigarette and I joined her at the doorway to smoke my cigarette and to inquire why she was smoking so close to the building when we were told to smoke thirty feet away. Claudia stated, "This is payday and you will see all the ones that drink will show up half-in-the-bag! I'm standing here to block their entrance into the building because they know the rules, but they continue to push their way through so that they can get their pay, regardless of the fact that they should not be on Federal grounds in an intoxicated state!"

Claudia had no sooner finished explaining the reasoning of her stance when around the corner of the building appeared Stewart in an extremely inebriated state. He was a little man and he was talking to himself and pointing his index finger in the air. He was staggering as he walked jacket draped off one shoulder and in a slurred speech was daring the birds to shit on him as he squinted one eye at them. Stewart's face was flushed and he had no idea that Claudia and I were watching him as he talked to the birds. He appeared to be angry and was verbally threatening the birds when he lowered his eyes and spotted Claudia and I at the doorway. He smiled at us and said, "Oh Hello!"

As he stood there and swayed, Claudia lit into him with the rules and regulations of the Center. He continued to smile through the whole lecture and before turning around to leave, he gently and softly stated to Claudia, "You still like me!"

I couldn't help myself to smile and turn my head because he struck me as being very cute. As he left and disappeared around the building, Claudia had to smile herself and remarked to me that "he is one of the cutest Veterans here and he is in his mid-eighties, but every pay day it is a guarantee that he shows up "pickled"! After Stewart's departure, Claudia and I went back into the Center and got back to our work that was waiting for us.

On Thursday, there was another staff meeting and it was at this meeting that Claudia suggested that a patient named "Arnie" would possibly benefit more by being assigned to me than being assigned to her. Since I was new to the NVCCC, I was willing to take anyone that was assigned to me. The following day Claudia introduced me to Arnie and I sat him down in my office to do an intake on him. Arnie had informed me that he lived in a boarding house in the Florence area of Northampton and that he had lived there for about seven years. His appearance could be frightening to someone who didn't know him because he had shoulder-length black hair that was so dirty that the strands were caked together and a full beard that looked to be ten inches long and still held the remnants of egg yolk and toast crumbs from his breakfast. He was sociable and would only speak if spoken to, but the area that needed immediate attention was his personal hygiene. He was a profound smoker and would light his next cigarette from the cigarette he was about to extinguish. I believe that Arnie could smoke a whole pack of cigarettes in a half hour and while he smoked he would march in place as if he was trying to get circulation down in his feet. Arnie reminded me of the "Wild man of Borneo" because of his appearance and the initial impression that he gave to people. His appearance resulted in having him not allowed on a bus and not allowed in a few stores around the area of the boarding house he lived in because he not only looked bad, but his body odor was extremely pungent and offensive. Two days after I did his intake, I summoned Arnie back to my office to discuss his personal hygiene and the benefits of showering, doing laundry, dental care and grooming. I explained that his lack of personal hygiene skills is the result of his being banned from stores and the bus. I also informed Arnie that he has to wear socks and to tie those worn-out sneakers that were flapping as he walked because he had applied scotch tape to hold the soles in place. Arnie informed me that he didn't have any socks, underwear, laundry detergent, toothpaste, deodorant etc. He is 50% service-connected and only receives $679.00/month. This money had to pay his rent, food, clothing and hygiene essentials. His rent alone was $450 a month and the only time he ate was down at the Center because he would borrow money from other Veterans so he could eat breakfast for fifty cents. As a matter of fact, Arnie was even bumming cigarettes from other Vets as well. His fingers were dark brown from nicotine stains from smoking and I learned that he had an extensive bill from the drug store across the street from his residence because of charging many packs of cigarettes. The drug store put a lid on his charging because he wasn't paying his bill. With all this information, I told Arnie that I had no choice but to do an inspection of his room in the boarding house and that I would be doing it tomorrow. He made no affirmative or negative gesture, just turned around and exited my office.

I arrived at Arnie's residence at 10 a.m. the next day and he was standing on the porch smoking a cigarette when we arrived. I was accompanied by a male nursing assistant who was there to assist Arnie with laundry and checking his room for anything that might be broken and needed to be replaced. Arnie's room was on the third floor and there was no elevator, just three levels of wide stairs that Arnie ascended every day. When the three of us reached the third floor and Arnie opened the door to his room, I was horrified and apprehensive to even cross the threshold. Junk yards and pig stys were cleaner than this room and I was shocked to believe that a human-being was living in such filth and squalor. There was one window in this room which was small and the curtain rod and filthy curtain on the rod was attached on only one hook. The window pane was heavily-stained with nicotine, making the room to remain in a dark state even though the sun was shining brightly outside. There were piles of dirty clothes all over the floor and about twelve two-liter coke bottles that Arnie had filled with urine and placed back on the floor of this room. The bed was not made and the brown sheets, which I was told were originally white, were piled messily on the mattress of the bed along with a flimsy blanket that was draped from the bed to the floor. There were dust balls everywhere and I found it very hard to breath in this room and feared that my asthma was going to get the best of me. I told Arnie to empty the cola bottles into the toilet and then to throw the bottles into the trash. When he had completed that task, I instructed him to fill the laundry basket that was in his closet with all the dirty clothes, strip his bed and put those in the basket as well. I trekked him across the street to the laundry mat with the male aide that was with us, purchased a box of laundry detergent and told him to wash everything. He filled seven washers and seven dryers and I told him to fold his laundry so that it could be put away neatly in his closet and bureau. While the washers were going, we returned to his room, asked the landlady for a broom and dust pan and window wash and proceeded to clean his room. It was unbelievable that one room filled four large trash bags which included about thirty Styrofoam food boxes that some still contained foods that he didn't like. He just threw them in a corner in his room where they were stacked up for months and had a great deal of mold in them which probably gave off some of the rotting stench that permeated the room. We opened the window after it was washed just to let some fresh air in and alleviate the stench of mold and urine. Arnie was schizophrenic and it was now obvious that he was incapable of taking care of himself. His whole world consisted of smoking cigarettes. He had no interest or thought of food, clothing, or cleanliness of his room or person or managing his finances. When I returned to my office at 3:30 p.m., I sat for a minute to ponder every aspect of Arnie. I realized that he needed supervision and he needed more money to function in an environment that is structured. He needed to be told to take a shower, report for meals, wear proper clothing and to purchase essentials to maintain good personal hygiene. The only way that these things could be achieved for Arnie was to get his service-connection increased and to have him placed in a residential-care home. So I started inquiries into residential homes in the Northampton area and also started the paperwork to increase his service connection to 100%. I knew that Arnie could not manage his finances, so I was also inquiring if he had a family member who would be willing to be his conservator.

It was Friday, the end of the week and I couldn't believe that the week had passed so quickly. I guess it's true when they say that when you are busy, time just passes by because I realized that I had never been this busy in my life. It was one heck of a week between home visits, writing letters to services and lawyers and phone calls to various institutions and individuals.

I sat Arnie down in my office to ask him some questions about appointing a conservator to handle his funds and that the best appointees were family members. He told me that he had a sister and a brother and had another brother who passed away many years ago. His sister was in a wheelchair and lived in a care home in Maine. His brother lived in Connecticut and Arnie was only aware of his work phone number and wasn't too sure if he could actually recall the exact number. As far as an address, Arnie stated that he knew his brother lived in Simsbury, CT but didn't know the street. He informed me that his brother would visit him about twice a year and that never in those visits was Arnie ever invited to his brother's home in Connecticut. I could well understand why his brother didn't invite him to his home because of Arnie's gross lack of personal hygiene and his total disregard of laundering his clothes and bed sheets and towels. Arnie told me that when his brother would visit him he would take him out to eat, but in the last two to three years his brother would stop at a Subway or McDonald's and get him a takeout order on his way up to visit him. Again, I believe his brother was embarrassed to be seen in public with Arnie because of his Rasputin-like appearance. I told Arnie to go and smoke a cigarette while I tried to get hold of his brother by phone.

I dialed the Connecticut phone information number and requested the number of Marvin Goulet in Simsbury. Without hesitation, I was given the number from the operator and quickly thanked her for her assistance. I dialed the number to his brother's house. The phone rang about seven times when the answering machine came on and informed me that Marv was not there. I left my name and number on the answering machine and requested that he please call me as soon as possible and that this call was in reference to his brother Arnie. I sat back and realized that I have done everything possible in contacting Arnie's family member and would just have to wait and hope that Marvin would return my call.

I observed Arnie smoking just outside my window and I allowed him to finish the cigarette he was smoking. As I spotted his fingers taking out the cigarette pack from his shirt pocket to smoke another cigarette, I quickly intervened and told him to come into my office and that I was going to cut his hair and trim his beard. He had showered the night before and had used a half cup of shampoo on his hair to make sure it was clean enough to cut. I told Arnie to go over to the kitchen sink to wet his hair because I only cut wet hair which allows the hair to layer better when it is cut wet. When he returned to my office, I noticed that he had some shampoo that wasn't rinsed out the night before. I brought

Arnie back to the sink, grabbed a towel from the table and rinsed his hair with warm water from the hose at the sink. I handed him the towel and told him to dry his hair so that it no longer drips. We returned to my office where I used all of my haircutting skills to shape Arnie into an acceptable being in society. When Arnie emerged from my office neither staff nor patient could recognize him. I instructed Arnie to go and stand in the doorway of Mike's office and not say a word. Arnie was never one for words, but he did as I instructed him and stood at the doorway of Mike's office. Although his clothes were wrinkled, they were clean and he looked like a totally different person from what he had been. I noticed some Veterans giving him a double-take as Arnie walked by and when Mike finally noticed that there was someone standing in his doorway, he dropped his pen, rotated in his chair and slowly rising from his chair in total disbelief at the person he was seeing, stretched his hand out to Arnie and said, Arnie, I can't believe this is you! You look fantastic!!"

As I stood by my office door, I was thoroughly enjoying hearing the compliments given to Arnie and watching his reaction to these compliments because he really didn't know how to handle them. He had been ostracized from society for several years and I now realized that my biggest job was still ahead of me. It is easy to clean somebody up and make them presentable, but now I had to write a treatment plan that Arnie would follow on a daily basis just to maintain. I hesitated in informing Arnie about this plan because I wanted to discuss the plan with his brother first whenever he returned my phone call.

It was about 10:30 a.m. the next day and as usual my phone had been constantly ringing since the start of my shift. But this call was the one I had been waiting for because it was Arnie's brother, Marvin. I expressed my gratitude in the quickness of his returning the call and then I informed him of all that had been done for Arnie, such as his laundry being washed, room clean and getting his hair and beard cut. After hearing these pleasantries about Arnie, I inquired if there was a possibility of Marvin coming to a meeting with me that concerned some legal issues for his brother. Marvin was highly cooperative and stated that he would plan to meet with me and his brother the following Tuesday in my office. I thanked him again for quickly returning my call and would be looking forward to meeting him on Tuesday.

I was sitting very comfortably in my small office after finishing all my paperwork and phone calls and was just sitting back in my chair relaxing for a minute, when suddenly everything was shaking and moving slowly on the desk and window sill. The first time that happened, I seriously thought that we were having an earthquake, but we were not. The railroad tracks abutted the parking lot in the rear of the building and the train runs at least once a day and there were times that it ran three times in one day. If it's a short car train there is barely any shaking that takes place, but when you get a train with thirty-five to sixty cars on it, it feels like a 7.5 or better earthquake. Several Veterans have labeled it "The Shanghai Express"! There are also many homeless that live in tents or some hand-made hovels along the tracks and they usually cut through our parking lot looking for handouts from the various restaurants along Main and King Streets. In the summertime, we plan several picnics for our Veterans which usually consist of hamburgers, hot dogs, potato salad, coleslaw, chips and soda. It's a well-rounded meal and any leftovers we gave to the homeless that are on the tracks. This is easily done because all the provisions are purchased from the staff at NVCCC and not the VA. The homeless smell the meat on the grills cooking and they line up across the tracks and wait patiently for their turn to eat. A few Veterans would give their first dishes of food away and then would return to fill a plate for themselves. These are the Veterans that had experienced homelessness and hunger so they empathize more towards the homeless.

Having weekends off was a complete pleasure, or so I thought, because it was a normal work-week for the general public and now I was experiencing a normal work week. The only trouble with this is that I had to cram my house cleaning, shopping, laundry and ironing into the two days off, along with any social plans with friends. I realized that there was just not enough time on the weekends to get everything done that I needed to get done, so I had to improvise and started to alternate and separate my responsibilities to every other weekend.

Finally, the weekend was gone and Monday arrived along with a multitude of Veterans coming to the Center. There were Mondays that were so busy and crowded with Veterans that it seemed like Ellis Island was opened again and we were processing an abundance of Veterans to be registered for treatment in the VA system. It was hectic, but we were proud of the fact that we had registered so many new numbers for the VA. I started to wonder why we were getting such an influx of Veterans interested in the Northampton Veterans Community Care Center and after interviewing seven Veterans and seeing the line forming outside my office door, I ventured to ask the question, "What gave you the incentive to seek treatment at this Center? "

Upon eyeballing me and a bit puzzled by the question I asked, many of the Veterans expressed the same or similar reasons why they came to the NVCCC, "I was told that you don't have to wait long to be seen!"

"The staff is much nicer and care more than the staff at the hospital!"

"The NVCCC is not as crowded as the waiting room at the hospital and the appointments are scheduled within a week and not three months down the road!"

These were the major reasons that the Veterans gave me, but I also realized that the NVCCC was in downtown Northampton and it was very convenient to the patients because many lived in boarding and rooming houses in the area and everything was within walking distance from their homes. Another major reason was the fact that the NVCCC was directly on the bus route and the bus stopped right across the street from it. Patients appeared to be happy and they welcomed the opportunity to engage in treatment on an outpatient basis instead of an inpatient basis because they had more freedom and they also had access to doctors, alcohol techs, compensated work therapy, social workers, and occupational therapy. The Northampton Community Care Center was a microcosm of the hospital that was neatly tucked into the fast-paced life of the city, allowing Veterans an escape haven that they could enter and leave the pressures of society outside the door.

Bright and early Tuesday morning as I was looking out my single window in my office and dreaming of the day's activities that were ahead of me, I spied Arnie standing by the corner of the building and lighting his cigarette. This was the day that his brother was coming to see me and to have Arnie sign the papers for his brother to be his conservator. As I was watching Arnie smoke his cigarette, I was wondering if Arnie's brother resembled him in looks or if he was an individual that looked so different that one would wonder how this different individual fit into the family. I had come across family members that had been adopted and therefore, it is understandable that these members bore no resemblance to the family, but in Arnie's case, he had specified that his sister and brother were his full blooded siblings. As I continued to watch out the window, I could see that the buses had arrived because the front parking lot was filling up with many more Veterans waiting for the front door to open so that they could dash over to the thirty-five-cup coffee pot to get their kick of caffeine to get their day started.

It was about 9:15 a.m. and I was in Claudia's office just talking about generalities with her when suddenly Arnie was standing in her doorway with a man who was not familiar to anyone and being that I was sitting in the chair directly by the door, I didn't notice anyone other than Arnie standing in the doorway. Claudia looked at me and stated, "Linda, I believe there is someone here that you are scheduled to meet with today!"

I immediately stood up and looking past Arnie I noticed a very pleasant, well-dressed and well groomed individual who was introduced to me as Arnie's brother. I stuck out my hand in Marvin's direction and inquired if he had any trouble finding this center. He smiled and stated that he appreciated the good directions that I gave him along with feeling that he wanted to leave earlier because he wanted to avoid the heavy traffic through Hartford which has a bottleneck effect every day. Traffic will back up for miles and goes at a snail's pace. As Marvin was making this statement, Mike came out of his office and approached me and told me to take his office for the meeting because it is bigger; three people would be more comfortable in his office than they would in mine. The meeting was great and Marvin agreed with all the treatment plans and the conservatorship papers for his brother. Marvin asked if it would be alright to take his brother Arnie out for lunch. As they were departing, Marvin thanked me again for the wonderful care and concern I gave to his brother and told me that he didn't recognize Arnie when he pulled into the parking lot. As Marvin left, he stated very definitely that he would stay in touch with his brother on a weekly basis and would also stay in touch with me to be assured that Arnie was following his treatment plan.

The patient population was increasing in their visits and involvement at the Northampton Community Care Center. I noticed that there were many Veterans that I was very familiar with from the inpatient days at the VA that were now interested in coming to the NVCCC. What was not surprising is the fact that they were seeking me out! As these Veterans started to trickle in, Mike was starting his transfer to the Springfield Community Care Center. He lives in Hampden and this transfer would make it easier to commute to work because Hampden is right next to Springfield and it would certainly give him a big break in his gas consumption. He wouldn't have to use as much gas as he did when he commuted to Northampton. This move of Mike's to Springfield would leave an opening for the director of the NVCCC and I wondered who would apply for it from the VA.

Sophie "Scrappy" Lindstrom had returned to the Northampton VA from the Providence VA about ten months ago and was assigned to the mental health clinic. I had maintained contact with Scrappy while she was in Providence and continued our communication in the MHC. I was familiar with her because I had worked with her before on the Post-Traumatic Stress unit and she was an excellent social worker and I was seriously contemplating asking her to apply for the director position at the center. I was a little hesitant in calling her, because I didn't know how she would react to my suggestion or even if she had an interest in the position. My office may be small, but it is a great place to think and I was thinking what would be the best way to approach Scrappy with this proposal. I knew one thing, I had to wait until Mike vacated his office before I could even suggest anyone to apply for his vacated position and we were already looking at six weeks before he would be a permanent fixture at the Springfield VCCC.

Three weeks had passed and catching up with Scrappy was always a difficult task being that she was constantly on the go running everywhere and doing everything that she could for the Veterans. I happened to catch her talking with a Veteran in the hallway of building 1 when I was on my way to the credit union. She agreed to meet me in the canteen for coffee in ten minutes. After completing my business in the credit union, I moseyed down to the canteen to get a cup of coffee and sat at one of the tables when I spotted Scrappy walking through the door to the canteen. I waved at her to let her know where I was sitting and after she got herself a cup of coffee, she happily joined me at the table. Initially, we discussed missing each other and the things that had transpired in our lives since she transferred to the Providence VA right up to this point. The conversation between us was going very well and sometimes we would reminisce about the past and we would find ourselves laughing a lot. When we talked about any up-to-date news, Scrappy stated that she liked working in the mental health clinic and felt very comfortable there along with being very happy to be back at the Northampton VA. I wanted so much to address the soon-to-be vacant position at the NVCCC, but I didn't want to burst her bubble or upset her realm of contentment. So, I buried the thought until there was a more appropriate time to address it with her.

CHAPTER TEN

Late spring is a beautiful time of year in New England. Everyone remarks about the beauty of the foliage in autumn which overshadows the other seasons, but believe me when I say that the springtime in New England is equally as beautiful. The crocus, daffodil and tulips are the first flowers to break through the thawed ground, standing erect and making their presence known. As you drive along any road or highway, forsythia bushes line the front lawns of every other house or establishment displaying their radiant yellow-colored coats in full bloom, hiding the small green leaves of the bushes as if protecting the bushes from the elements. These exquisite displays of nature were everywhere and as far as the eye could see into woods, near rivers/ponds, hospitals, and private homes. The Center was especially beautiful because nature had wild plants that were scattered along the railroad tracks behind the Center that would make one think that it was taken from a "Thomas Kinkade" painting. The only thing that was disappointing about this beauty was that it only lasted for a short period of time, which was usually two to three weeks.

Mike's final day at the NVCCC had arrived and the staff and Veterans were setting up a going-away party for him in the back parking lot. He had vacated his office earlier in the morning and placed the last box of his papers and books in his car so that he wouldn't forget them. Everyone shook his hand and wished him the best and told him that he would surely be missed. Some Veterans asked him if he had any idea who his replacement would be, but like everyone else, Mike had no idea who would follow in his footsteps and be assigned there. At 3 p.m. the festivities were dying down. Mike got in his car, was saying his final goodbyes to everyone, exited the parking lot and turning south on King Street, headed to Springfield and his new assignment as the director of the Springfield Veterans Community Care Center.

Everything at the NVCCC continued to stay on course for several weeks after Mike's departure. The director's position was finally posted and it was at this point that I decided to convince Scrappy Lindstrom to apply for it. As I was communicating with her over the phone, I could tell by her hesitancy in talking that she was interested in the position. I didn't want to sound like I was trying to cram it down her throat, so I just expressed to her that there was a deadline for the application to be filed and if she was interested in it, she would have to get the paperwork to Human Resources (HR) within two weeks. We talked a little bit more of general conversation and before she hung up, she confirmed that she would get the application that very afternoon, fill it out this evening and get it filed in HR tomorrow. When I hung the phone up, I sat back in my chair and smiled about the way that Scrappy is so thorough and complete in her affairs, the only thought that came to mind was "SHE'S a SCRAPPER!" I thought this just by knowing and working with her in the past. I knew that she would do exactly what she told me she would do.

I wasn't surprised to hear that Scrappy got the position at the NVCCC as the director because she was more than capable of handling and fixing any situation that she encountered. It never took her long to acclimate to any new environment, staff or clientele. She had worked inpatient and outpatient and even transferred to other VA facilities, but her main objective was to do her job to the best of her ability and to assist every Veteran who walked through the doors. This was also the expectation she had of every staff member that worked with her. She wanted everyone to do their job to the best of their ability and if anyone needed assistance with any Veteran who might be considered a complex case, she told them that her door was always open.

One of the details that I was assigned when I first came to the NVCCC was to drive the van to Greenfield to pick up seven to eight Veterans and bring them back to the NVCCC so they could work in the back room in the compensated work-therapy program. There were three stops in Greenfield where these Veterans would wait for the van. At 3p.m., I would announce that the van was returning to Greenfield and the riders would gather their belongings, climb into the van and enjoy a tired, quiet ride back to Greenfield. When my workload increased to doing groups and several interviews, Mike had assigned a dependable Veteran to take over this assignment. Earl was the patient assigned to this detail and on my last day of doing this run, I had Earl accompany me on the van so that I could show him the stops and the Veterans that he was to pick up. Earl did so well at the driving that he was asked to do other driving assignments such as going food shopping for the center, picking up donated furniture and clothing and monthly trips to the food pantry for Veterans who had no income. The patient pickup in Greenfield was increasing as a result of the placement of Veterans from the VA to several halfway and residential care homes there. Thus, their follow-up appointments and outpatient care was to take place at the Northampton Community Care Center. Girard was one of the new patient's to the NVCCC. Although I did not do his intake, I heard of his medical and psychological problems at a staff meeting on Tuesday. I was informed that Girard had some dementia and was very forgetful and his wife was concerned about his well-being and in his being home alone when she went off to work. He had some weakness in his arms and hands and it was presumed that he might have also experienced a mild stroke which caused this weakness. Earl took a likeness to Girard and it was reported from other Veterans from Greenfield that they were never allowed to sit in the front seat because that was the seat reserved for Girard. It was also noticed that every time Earl left the center to do shopping, pickup or whatever, he would always haul Girard with him. Other Veterans would ask Earl if they could go on these trips, but he always refused them outright. Upon hearing these complaints from the Veterans, two staff members approached me and asked me to talk to Earl about these complaints and concerns of the Veterans. I nodded my head and stated that I had no time today, but would talk to him tomorrow immediately after he returned from the Greenfield-run in the morning.

I was looking out my office window watching the Greenfield van that just arrived and parked directly across the lot from my window and view. The seven patients disembarked from the van and in single file entered the Center's main door. Earl and Girard were always the last to enter the Center because Earl had to lock and secure the van and make sure all windows and doors were secured. I was standing in the doorway of my office when Earl came through and I asked him to see me after he returned the keys to the cabinet. Earl knocked on my door and I invited him in and told him to have a seat! I began the conversation by asking him "how he liked driving the van". Earl stated, "I love it! There are many more Vets to pick up and I have about five stops instead of three! I used to start the stops the way that you showed me and my last stop would be at Girard's house which was on the other side of the city near the Gill/Greenfield line."

"What do you mean you used to do the stops the way I showed you?"

"Well, I now do them in reverse, I start at Girard's house and my last stop is at the Greenfield/Deerfield line"!

"Why did you change the pickup stops? That will confuse the Veterans! Earl, I've also noticed that the van is not here when I come into work at 7 a.m. Do you have any idea where it is or who has it?"

"I have the van! I get it early so that I can go to Girard's house where his wife makes us a big breakfast every day, then I pick up Girard and then travel to other stops and pick up the rest of the Veterans and return to the NVCCC by 9 a.m.! Is there a problem with this?"

Leaning back in my chair and letting out a small sigh, I looked at Earl and said, "There is a big problem here! To begin with, the van is a Federal vehicle and is not to be used for personal use. When you take the van early and eat at Girard's house, you're using it for personal use! THIS IS NOT ALLOWED! Your permit to use that vehicle starts at 7:30 a.m. and not before! Secondly, many Veterans have stated that you are showing preferential treatment to Girard by reserving the front seat for him; by taking him with you on every detail you do such as shopping, running an errand or dropping something off at the main hospital. They have also told staff members that they have asked you if they could go with you on some of these outings and that you have outright refused them. Why? What are your reasons for refusal?"

His demeanor had changed from curiosity to a guarded anxiety. It was very obvious that his microcosm plans had been discovered. Earl stated, "I'm not taking anyone else with me but Girard because I get along well with him and the others drive me crazy!"

"Earl, your favoritism and partiality to Girard is blatant in the eyes of the other Veterans and is unacceptable with the staff. Girard is in treatment here and he has been assigned to occupational therapy doing crafts and when you constantly take him with you on every detail, you are interfering in his treatment plan and depriving him from the care he desperately needs which is the whole reason for his being here to begin with. You are very good at driving the van and doing the stops in a timely manner, but if this behavior continues, I will be forced to relieve you of the permit and will assign it to somebody else. Before you leave, I have one more statement to make…the staff wanted me to inform you that Girard is to no longer go on trips with you. If you do not want to take others Veterans, then you will have to drive alone on your details. You look like you're in shock about the statements I just stated to you, but realistically, you knew and expected this moment to come. So now, the ball is in your court Earl, are you going to play or quit? It's totally up to you!"

Without giving comment or uttering a word, Earl rose from the chair and exited my office in silence.

I felt that I was the royal "badass" because whenever somebody did something improper or wrong, some staff members would come to me and ask me to talk to them. For the most part I don't mind, because most of the patients that I end up verbally correcting are already assigned to me. But there is that rare occasion that another staff member has a patient that is difficult and unapproachable and when that Veteran needs to be corrected for whatever, I am the staff member that they ask to talk to them.

Census was increasing almost on a weekly average. We were getting daily attendance of 100-135 Veterans a day. That's a lot of patients for a staff of eight to care for on a daily basis, but we were a team and a well-functioning team in which we could anticipate the moves of each staff member and we were respectful of each other as well. I sincerely believe that there were two staff that knew me better than I knew myself and would predict exactly what I would do. These staff members that could predict the moves and techniques of other staff members were staff that had worked together for well over twelve years. We were like a family and as predictable as yelling "heads" in the toss of a two-headed coin.

Things were getting back to normal and Earl was driving the van properly without bringing his sidekick Girard with him on every run. Earl was slowly getting over his being corrected by me because for the first two weeks after talking to him about the van incident, he sulked and wouldn't talk to any staff. I suppose he felt that he was punishing the staff by not talking to us, but truthfully, he was giving us a break from constantly asking him to run errands or take the van to get it washed or filled with gas. This also allowed staff access to the van if they needed it because the van was now available to them and it also allowed Earl to do the rest of his assignment which was to load the kiln so that it could fire overnight and decrease the backup of patients ceramic projects that were ignored when he was constantly driving all over the place with Girard riding shotgun.

As the patient census increased so did the need for more groups. The groups would have to be increased to meet the demands of the Veteran population. We had groups for substance abuse, interpersonal groups and occupational therapy groups and compensated work therapy groups. But Scrappy Lindstrom, who was the newly-appointed director of the NVCCC, was always looking for any improvements in care that would benefit the Veterans. At the Tuesday staff meeting, Scrappy had informed the staff that she had noticed a huge increase in angry attitudes coming through the doors of the Center and threw it on the table to discuss and get feedback from other staff to see what information or techniques the others could mention to alleviate this situation. I was seated at the end of this meeting table and was doodling on the pad and was thinking about an anger management group. I did these groups on the PTSD unit and they were very successful. I continued to doodle, but never mentioned these groups in the meeting. I knew that there would be a big difference in doing anger groups on an outpatient basis because there would be close to twenty-five people in the classroom. On an inpatient basis, these groups were limited to ten maximum in the class. I was so deep in thought trying to figure out if any of my unspoken ideas would come to pass when Scrappy spoke up and said, "Linda, are you here with us or are you out there in "Angerland" somewhere?"

Lifting my head and looking directly at her, I said, "What do you mean by that?"

"I happen to see the pad you're doodling on and you have the word ANGER written all over it! There are small ones, big ones, cursive ones and printed ones and boxed letters as well, but the entire piece of paper is covered with the word anger! I'm not being offensive, I was just wondering!"

"Oh no, it was the last word that I heard before I went into deep thought so I was just doodling it. I didn't realize I was in such deep thought!"

I turned the pad face down, put the pen on the table and rested my chin in the palm of my left hand. I turned my attention to the staff's conversation that suggested resolutions in an attempt to solve or decrease the strong anger attitudes at the NVCCC.

The following day was Wednesday and the staff at the NVCCC always referred to Wednesdays as "Hump day" because it was the middle day of the week and we were going over the hump and heading back downhill to Friday. I was in my office writing notes when there was a knock on the door and without looking, I bid the individual to enter. Scrappy entered the office and sat in the vacated seat that was next to me and in a somewhat low voice said, "Linda, there is something I would like to discuss with you if you have a few minutes to spare!"

Sitting back and grinning at her, I knew in my heart what she was there to discuss with me. It had to do with the anger issues and attitudes at the center. Before she could utter another word, I calmly and directly faced her and stated, "I'll bet that you are here to discuss the high levels of anger that prevails over this center and you have seriously contemplated asking me to do an anger management group just as I had on the PTSD unit. You figure that if I could handle teaching angry Vietnam Veterans, then the mixed clientele at the center would be a piece of cake! Well you are four-fifths correct with your logic, but there is one prevailing problem. The anger groups that I taught comprised of no more than ten individuals. With our daily census of one hundred or better, I'm looking at groups of twenty to twenty-five in attendance. The classroom at this center cannot hold that many!"

I noticed Scrappy listening intently to everything I said and as her eyes made direct contact to mine she uttered, "Use the conference room! It certainly is large enough and I'll have some of the guys in CWT place extra chairs in there!"

Rising from her chair, Scrappy left me to think of the proposal of the conference room for an anger management group. The room was long and I could picture chairs lined up along the walls. There was also a fifteen or eighteen-foot table that took six-to-eight men to carry and set up in that room as well. On the far wall, opposite the entrance door was a five-foot-wide eraser-mate-board that I would need for the anger management classes. Everything seemed to fit into place and everyone was cooperative with the planning, but I continued to have that gnawing question. How am I going to handle twenty-five individuals in an anger management group when I was used to teaching no more than ten?

Monday arrived and I felt a little anxious about doing this group, so I took a walk from my office to the conference room to check out if the chairs had been placed in there. Opening the door, I saw that the chairs were placed right next to each other which made me think that it looked more like fifty chairs, but I knew there were only about twenty-five. Chairs were placed against three walls and the only breaks in the placement were at the door and in the front where the board hung on that wall. I was asked what days and time would I like to do these groups and I came up with Monday and Wednesday at 9 a.m. or Tuesday and Thursday at 9 a.m. I settled on Tuesday and Thursday for the initial start of these groups and if the days needed to be changed for whatever reason, I had the other option available to do so.

I was sitting at my desk, drinking a cup of coffee that I picked up at Dunkin Donuts on my way into work and was just mentally focused on how I was going to start that anger group at 9 a.m. with heaven knows how many Veterans in there. I decided to go into the conference room about fifteen minutes early so that I could write on the board the exact way that I planned to teach this group. Veterans started to filter in as I was writing and I asked them to please sign in on the sign-in sheet that was on the table.

When I finished writing on the board, turning around and facing the class, I was surprised to see that there wasn't one vacant chair in the room and the door was closed. All eyes were riveted at me and everyone's face displayed a moderate amount of curiosity about this group. Just as I was about to start speaking, there was a knock at the door and Jesse who was sitting next to it, opened it to four more Veterans asking if they could attend. Seeing that there were no more chairs available, these Veterans took four chairs from the tables in the kitchen and placed them around the conference table so that they didn't get in anyone's view of the board, but most of all they didn't want to squish together the Veterans sitting around the wall. As I began this group, I introduced myself and then asked everyone to introduce themselves because there were a few new faces that I was not familiar with, but the majority I did know and they knew me.

With the introduction completed, I was standing up by the board and when all was quiet you could hear a pin drop. I proceeded to introduce this program, "This is an anger management group! Everyone in this group, including this speaker has anger issues that we have to change. Some of our anger is passive and some is aggressive or I could phrase it as being "black and white," but that is a fallacy because so many people ignore the huge grey area that exists between the black and white. I will introduce the issues we will discuss in each class, but all of you will participate in each class. You will have fun and you will learn a great deal about anger, but even more, you will learn about yourselves!"

I held these groups in three-week sessions comprising of six one-hour class periods for two days each week. As I completed one rotation, I would invite anyone to attend as many sessions as they wanted because having a group as large as a classroom, there is bound to be something that someone will miss.

My anger groups were becoming extremely popular with the Veterans because they were passing the word around town and around the VA. Veterans that were involved in the Northampton court system had conversed with their probation officers and part of their probations were to attend my anger management group. These new probation orders were activated after I had a few meetings with officers from the Probation Department and their inquiring about these groups and to see if they would be beneficial to the Veterans they were assigned to probation. I also explained that the first six sessions in the rotation is mandatory attendance and any subsequent rotations are voluntary by the Veterans. A couple of the Probation Officers inquired if they could mandate their clients to more than one rotation. I told them that if it is written in their rules of probation then I would respect that order, but it has to be written, it cannot be verbal. All agreed that written was the proper procedure to follow and that it would be proof that the client attended because his/her names would be on the sign-in attendance sheet that is required for every group.

I thoroughly enjoyed doing these groups, but more so, I enjoyed taking these Veterans for a trip down memory lane. I would ask them, "Who was your favorite cartoon character?"

I had twenty-eight Veterans in attendance for this group when I asked that question. Amazingly, everyone gave me a different cartoon character for their favorite. One Veteran had a mustache and beard that went down to his naval and hair that went down to the small of his back. When the question finally got around to him, he mentioned that his favorite cartoon character was "Yosemite Sam" which brought the classroom to their knees in laughter. When things quieted down, I told everyone to think about the cartoon character that they stated was their favorite and how much in common they had with that character. They were amazed to see such similarities between themselves and their favorite cartoon character. These similarities went beyond just features as was the case with Yosemite Sam, but these Veterans recognized behavioral similarities and anger similarities and noticed that these cartoon characters had tremendous anger issues that they solved solely by reacting. It was at this class that I explained the difference between reacting to a situation and thinking about it. As my eyes circled the room and seeing that all attention was focused at me, I stated,

"Anger is highly contagious! Oh, you're wondering how anger can be contagious; well let me give you a scenario! We have all been in situations where we were at a party or picnic with family and friends and there is always someone who has to be the last to arrive for whatever reason. Over time this has been acceptable from the others because even though they arrive late, they manage to fit in and socialize with everyone as if they had been there from the start. But this time it's different! This "arrive-late" individual comes to the gathering and has a face on like half past six. When he was greeted at the door with "Welcome" he remarked, "I don't need a god-damn welcome!

Others heard him say this. Suddenly the laughter and conversations stop, others cease their eating and drinking and everyone's attention is directed at the angry individual who just made a grand negative entrance to the party. There is complete silence except for the ranting angry individual who is yelling and cursing at everyone in his eye's view. Some approach him to inquire why he is so angry and he tells them to get the " f—k out of his face"! Before you know it…..everybody is arguing with each other, the pleasant gathering is now in shambles and as everyone starts to depart, they still wonder why that asshole was ever invited to the party! This is a made-up story, but I can certainly tell from the looks and expressions on your faces that each one of you has experienced something similar to this situation."

I would ask other pertinent questions that dealt with their past, such as, "How many remember your first day of school? How did you feel going to school for the first time?"

This was another question that became quite comical in the answers because some of the answers were, "My mother took me and I was kicking and screaming all the way!"

Another Veteran stated that he had wet his pants because he was scared. Still another one stated that he would not let his moth-

149

er's hand go when they arrived at the school and when a teacher asked him his name; he just stared at her and never uttered a word. I explained that we all deal with change in our own way. Some of us can roll with it, while others cannot deal with any change at all. I asked this class the following question because I knew that I would get an immediate answer from each one of them.

"What is it that every time you see it, hear it or read about it that sends your anger right over the hill because it is a major trigger for your anger?"

Seeing that there were twenty-seven Veterans in this group and the writing board being small, I was forced to arbitrarily select individuals at random for their answers. I limited the selection to twelve, but I was pleased with their answers because every one of them had a different response for the trigger that highly-activated their anger. Some of the answers mentioned were, prejudice, injustice, abuse of any kind, government, bullying, lying, irresponsibility, incompetency, sarcasm and hatred, just to name a few. I wrote these anger triggers on the board and then asked the Veterans the following question, "How do you respond when your anger is triggered?"

Carlos was looking a bit bewildered when I asked this question and said, "What do you mean?"

"What I mean is what is happening physically, mentally and emotionally to you when your anger has gotten the best of you?"

Carlos, for a moment, just sat there and then he shrugged his shoulders and said, "I guess I just go berserk! What are you doing when you go berserk?" It depends on how mad I get! Sometimes I'll throw something, or I might verbally mouth off, or scream at everybody in my eye sight or it may even be a combination of all these things."

"Carlos, upon completing this display of personal chaos, did you feel satisfaction…were you still agitated…was your mission accomplished when your anger triggers were activated and your response to them?"

"I'm asking this question because what you just described was a reaction to a situation. There was no thought involved, it was purely physical response. In situations like this, we gain nothing and lose a lot! To begin with, we lost our temper and in losing our temper, we lost control. We lose control of rational thinking and lose the possibility that perhaps we could have avoided this situation and never have gotten involved in it. There are many other possibilities that we could try before we react to any situation."

When I finished this statement, I don't believe I could have even heard a pin drop as my eyes surveyed the room and noticed every Veteran sitting stoically and mentally processing the statement in their minds. I permitted this quiet-time for three minutes before I decided to inquire, "How many times have you found yourselves in this situation?"

Not surprisingly, every one's hand was raised high in the air upon hearing this question. I placed the dry- erase marker on the board and removing my glasses from my face, began to explain that everyone has patterns of anger that we develop on an individual basis. When everyone raised their hands, I knew that most of them responded to their anger by reacting. There was little to no thinking involved and that that was the main reason they were sitting in this classroom. I then asked the following question, "Why are you in this class? Did you volunteer for this class or were you told to attend?"

As I went around the room, I was receiving many answers to these questions. Many responded that they were ordered by the courts to attend this group or a probation officer wrote it in their probation requirements. Others that had no court records stated that this had been the pattern that they had maintained all of their lives to deal with their anger. Surprisingly, many of the Veterans that were mandated to do one complete rotation of this group, cheerfully signed up for two or three more rotations because they felt that one didn't really get to know oneself through just one rotation along with the fact that they were enjoying the group…

completely! It was a mixed group of personalities, of aggressive individuals and passives, of draftees and enlistees, combat Veterans and ones that were never stationed outside the continental United States, as well as a spattering of female Veterans. In front of these varied-personality individuals, standing erect and having full control over all is me. I believe the most difficult ones to work with or teach were the aggressive individuals because you had to tone them down so that they did not occupy the entire class with their constant questions and their demands of being more important than anyone else. I also realized that Passives were equally difficult to handle because they had to be built-up with confidence so that they were able to express their feelings in group. It was at this point that I established the Passive/Aggressive line and re-named it the Anger Line.

Anger Line

Passive									Aggressive
1	2	3	4	5	6	7	8	9	10

I would only use the numbers one to ten with one being extremely passive and ten being extremely aggressive. I would follow this up by writing down characteristics of both extremes. After completing the writing of the characteristics, I asked everyone in the class,

"Where do you think you belong on this scale at this moment? I want complete honesty! I don't want to hear you say where you would like to be, but rather where you are right now!"

Everyone gave an answer to where they fit on the scale, but there was one individual, Dane Benjamin who stated that he was a fifteen because his anger goes right into rage. I had to snicker because there is always one individual that will mention the word RAGE in every class. I turned to Dane and asked him, "What is the name of this class?" He answered, "Anger Management!" "That is correct!"

We are all here to manage our anger, to learn new techniques in dealing with it, to understand it and to realize that the old ways that we have dealt with our anger in the past, no longer works for us. You will never find rage on an anger line because there is no way of controlling rage. There is no memory with rage and for those that have been arrested and placed in jail as a result of rage, they usually inquire to the guard or officer on duty, "how did I get here!" or "What am I doing in jail?" They simply cannot remember anything and are horrified when they learn the reason behind their arrest. You have all read stories about women that have taken tractors off of their husbands or fathers that have manually removed a vehicle from atop their child because the last thing that these mates and parents remember was that they literally saw life quickly leaving the bodies of their loved ones. These occurrences were rare, but they most definitely existed and when the wife or father was asked how the vehicle was removed, they had no idea and couldn't even venture a thought of how it happened. They were in a state of rage and had no memory. Many times during war, combat soldiers will experience rage reactions because the only time that rage can be listed as semi-beneficial is in a life-and-death situation, such as war or accidents where individuals are pinned under a vehicle. I mentioned that these rage stages are semi-beneficial, but only in the cases that I just mentioned. "In the case of a combat soldier who experiences a "flashback" as a result of a word said, a commercial, or a simple situation that triggers him back into combat-mode resulting in his destroying his home, hurting someone, fighting police etc. is a very sad situation because this is the individual that cannot understand why he is in jail because the last thing he remembers is that he was sitting in his living room drinking a cold beer and watching TV."

When I finished my definitions and examples of rage and why it was never on an anger line, I could see by all the serious faces looking back at me, that they fully understood the meaning of rage. It was getting towards the end of this group, so I told the class that there was only five minutes left and that I wanted them to think of all the information that was discussed in today's group as they slowly left the room, one by one. I felt proud of each and every one of these Veterans. I knew that their ways in dealing with their anger was definitely going to change. Many of the other staff noticed that there was change in these Veterans and they complimented them for their efforts in changing their lives for the better. But, the ones who definitely deserved center-stage were the never-smiling, constant-growling about anything, hardcore Veterans with the perpetual pissed-off angry attitudes. These were the Veterans who displayed the greatest noticeable change. These are the Veterans that approached me in private and stated that they never had to look at themselves before this class. They never realized that they owned their anger and were responsible for it, no matter what the outcome. But, the biggest lesson learned was that they could change and wanted to change so that they were more acceptable in society and no longer felt like a misfit or an outcast. They now realize that society did not make them an outcast or misfit, but that they chose to be misfits and outcasts themselves. They were getting respect and were giving respect. Their demands went to requests and if some of the requests were denied, they no longer bolted out the door, slamming it and cursing all the way, but now understood why a request could not be fulfilled because they were patient enough to listen to the explanation as to why it was denied. These Veterans allowed me to do my job which was to work for them, not for the administration. After all, it is titled VETERANS ADMINISTRATION MEDICAL CENTER and I served these Veterans with honor and pride and to the best of my ability and many came back to tell me that I did just that!

In September of 1997, several Veterans stated as they were coming through the entrance door of the NVCCC, that there was a fancy special bus that was parked across the street at the Northampton Hotel. The bus didn't have any writing on it, but it was painted in shades of purple, blue, white and black. It was obvious that this vehicle belonged to someone of importance. Sherry worked in the occupational therapy department at the NVCCC and apparently her curiosity was getting the better of her. She ventured across the street and inquired with the bus driver on whom this bus was transporting. She wasn't there very long when she came back to announce that the bus belonged to Kris Kristofferson and he was checking out of the hotel. He had sung at a local popular tavern the night before and was scheduled to do another gig in New Jersey. A few staff and some Veterans, including myself, crossed the street to see if we could get an autograph from Mr. Kristofferson. He was very charming and cooperative with the signature requests and when he was asked if he could drop into the center for a few minutes to see the Veterans and the work and treatment that they were getting, he threw his overnight bag on the bus and crossed the street and as he entered the door I announced to all, "Staff and Veterans…it is my pleasure to introduce to you and to welcome to our Center…Mr. Kris Kristofferson!"

Mr. Kristofferson greeted everyone at the center and was impressed with the Veterans and their accomplishments. A Veteran who was assigned to crafts presented Mr. Kristofferson with a ceramic fish he had made there. This wonderful celebrity posed for some pictures with staff and Vets and being on a tight schedule thanked everyone for the invitation to the center, particularly the Veterans and at a quick pace exited the door to catch his bus.

Another autumn in New England was upon us and all Veterans were told not to smoke near piles of dry leaves because one spark or hot ash would quickly ignite a good-size fire in the wooded area near the railroad tracks. Usually, the fall season is very picturesque with the bright red, yellow and orange leaves adorning the trees, but around the Northampton Community Care Center were oak trees and their leaves did not turn colors. They just turned a mousy greyish-brown and fell along with the acorns that you heard popping under the tires of every car that parked in the back parking lot. These were the days to take a pleasant walk at lunchtime or a break just to enjoy the nice weather before

Old-man-winter started to blast us with his cold winds and frigid temperatures. More and more Veterans were mingling outside just trying to absorb any of the nice weather and to avoid any unpleasant thoughts of winter. I had just arrived back from my pleasant walk down two blocks and as I was walking into the parking lot, I was confronted by a Veteran from the compensated work program who informed me that Scrappy was looking for me! As I entered the center, I was immediately met by Scrappy, who directed me to her office where she closed the door and holding an envelope in her hand stated, "Linda, this is an invitation for you and me to attend a seminar at the Northampton courthouse involving substance abusers that have been incarcerated in the Hampshire County House of Correction. Many of these abusers have been Veterans and several are Veterans that you and I have dealt with over the years. We have been personally invited by a judge who is the major figure in sentencing these repeat-offenders. This invitation was at the request of the probation department who had spoken very highly of the anger management course which you do. As your supervisor, I was also invited to attend. It is a full-day-seminar at the courthouse, so I will notify Social Service at the VAMC to let them know of the date and time of this seminar for both of us!"

"Are we invited to see the process that substance-abusers undergo when they go to court?"

Scrappy had an almost blank expression on her face and turning to me stated, "I'm sure we will find out when we get there!"

When I left her office to return to mine, I still had a bit of confusion and inquisitiveness rolling around in my head because the mere thought of knowing that I was going to be spending a day in a courthouse made me think that I had done something wrong. I started to think that the invitation was a subpoena because even when I was on jury duty, I was either dismissed by 11 a.m. or my section number in the jury pool was called and told that we were excused. Pulling jury duty was basically the only times that I have been in court. I attended court for my brother's divorce in 1980, but it was strictly for support of my brother during his divorce proceedings.

I started to get a spattering of Vietnam Veterans at the Center who wanted to know where I was working. They had inquired at the hospital and they were told that I was at the Northampton Veterans Community Care Center in downtown Northampton. We had moved from King St. to Pleasant St. to a brand-new building and I now had a plush-carpeted office and was able to fit all my seventeen plants in very nicely. My office also had a six-drawer file cabinet, bookcase and a new desk that appeared as big as a small dining room table that held my very own assigned computer, mouse and keyboard. I was in electronics heaven because I was in want for nothing. My office was the second to the last down a long hallway and the secretary would call me on the phone to inform me that there was someone present in the waiting room who wished to see me. As I walked down the hallway, getting closer to the waiting room area, I noticed Ginzo and Eamon sitting in the waiting room and quickly rising from their seats as I rounded the corner. These were two of the Veterans from the PTSD unit that I had had in group when I was working there. They accompanied me back to my office and after pleasantries and feeling totally satisfied and pleased that they had located me, I decided to ask them, "Why did you want to find me? It has to be seven or eight years since I worked the PTSD unit and like you, I have moved on!"

Ginzo spoke first and being a little hesitant stated, "Linda, we were talking the other day about the PTSD unit and the staff that made an impression on our lives and we all agreed that you were top on the list along with Sophia Lindstrom. We felt very comfortable to walk in your office and tell you anything because you showed an interest in each and every one of us. We also realized that you have heard some horrific stories and you never displayed any shock or disgust or expressed any opinion in hearing them. Well, we are no longer able to express our feelings and problems because we are now told that there is no time to get into anything that has occurred recently and we get shut-off and are told to bring up items next time we meet. In the mental health clinic the sessions are limited to no longer than fifty minutes and many times the sessions are thirty minutes because of phone calls or interruptions. It's almost useless to make these appointments because we feel no different after the session then when we walked in. Sometimes, we have even felt worse when we left."

Noticing the lost and saddened expressions on their faces, these two Veterans felt that they were going backwards instead of forward. Looking into their pleading eyes and hoping that the answer I would give them would give them some solution to their predicament, I sat back in my chair and said, "I thoroughly understand what you are saying to me, but unfortunately, there is nothing I can say or do to rectify it. I do not work in the mental health clinic, nor am I qualified to work there. I am a caseworker not a therapist and as such, I am limited in what I can do! The only thing I could tell you is….if you are not satisfied with your therapist, you have a right to request a different one, as well as to request any professional whether doctor, social worker, nurse etc. The ball is in your court!"

I saw a slight smile forming on Ginzo's face and turning to Eamon, I noticed the same grin on his face and I suspected that there was a little more to this visit than just to see and visit me. They were up to something! So I turned to them both and stated, "I'm sensing that you did not come here just for a visit, but rather that there is some other ulterior motive in mind! Do I need to brace myself in this chair just to cushion the impact of what you are going to say, or is it strictly a suggestion?"

The smiles on their faces became wider and they even chuckled at my statement because they were well aware that I knew them so well. At this point, Eamon spoke up and said, "The bottom line is that we are bored and we want something to look forward to, we want something to do! We go to our appointments, we pick up our meds, we call each other on the phone and we sometimes go out for a sandwich or pizza. There are about twelve Vietnam Veterans that meet in twos or threes at a time because it is too difficult to have all gather at one place. I guess what I am asking is if you know any place that we can all be together to meet and talk."

The smiling faces that I saw a minute ago had now turned into very serious pleading expressions of need to be with their comrades. I also felt that there was a very strong need for a social-type group for combat Veterans because in war they were all members of groups, whether it was a squad, search and destroy or just guarding the perimeter; no one did any combat duty alone. I told these two Veterans of war, that I will do my best to see if I could assist them to find a group room where they could all meet. They thanked me and as they exited my office, they appeared to be a little reassured that something would be done and that some place would be found where they could meet as a group.

The following day I confronted Sophia Lindstrom with a proposal for a group for these Vietnam Veterans. I explained the entire visit to her and stressed their concerns and a deep need to meet with other Vietnam Veterans, not in a therapeutic group, but more like an interpersonal group where they can talk about their own issues. Scrappy Lindstrom was very understanding and asked me if I would be interested in doing a group for these Veterans. I gave her an affirmative nod that I was more than willing to do this group and she further told me that it would have to be late in the afternoon because there were already too many groups occurring during the day. I chose Mondays at 3:30pm for this group and returned to my office to call Eamon and Ginzo to let them know that their problem had been solved. I asked them to notify the other Vietnam Veterans and inform them that there will be a group at the NVCCC and that it would be led by me. I also told these Veterans that this group will start on the following Monday and they were thrilled that their request was accomplished so swiftly. All of these arrangements occurred in the last week of June

1997 and their first meeting was going to take place on the follow-ing Monday which happened to be on July 3rd, the day before the holiday. I thought of the symbolism of starting the new group of combat Veterans the day before Independence Day because here we are in the late twentieth-century with men willing to continue to fight to defend the Constitution of the United States. Men who were equally as young as the boys who fought in the Revolutionary War and were exposed to the extreme elements of hot and cold with only their uniforms for protection. These brave men of the past had muskets that had to be reloaded after every shot. There was no such thing as a repeating rifle and when their musket balls were gone, they used their swords and fought in open areas. I'm sure that these old soldiers had post-traumatic stress disorder, but unfortunately, there were no established VA hospitals for them to receive any treatment for their wounds or psyche, thus many died in the very fields that they fought in.

Several average citizens of this country (USA) are against wars. The individuals' who are constantly griping and complaining about the rules and regulations in accordance with the Constitu-tion do not know our national anthem or the words and do not know the "Pledge of Allegiance"! This is pathetic! They cannot comprehend that it was the diligence of fifty-six men who gath-ered in Philadelphia in 1776 to compose and sign the Declaration of Independence. This is the document that allows them to freely speak their feelings and to state their opinions openly without any threat of reprisal or vindication. They're not even thinking about the soldiers who have fought and died so that we can continue in this manner. There are also some American citizens that I have heard say, "There has never been a war in this country!"

This kind of statement will make me put my glasses at the end of my nose so that I'm looking over the brim and I continue to listen to the follow-up remarks these same people continue to say, "The United States has fought in Europe, South Pacific, Korea, Japan, Vietnam, Mexico, Cuba, Kuwait, Iraq and Afghanistan, all over the world. So I don't fear there will ever be any war in this country and there never has been!"

At this point, I have fully removed my glasses from my face and gently swinging them in my right hand, I turned my attention to the individual who was just talking and I stated, "Excuse me! But I have overheard what you were saying and if permitted I would like to ask you one question! You have stated that there was never a war fought in this country and if you truthfully believe this, where was the American Revolutionary War fought? Where was the American Civil War fought? They were not fought in East Tasmania, but rather they were fought here on our own "terra firma"!

I would usually excuse myself at this point and would hope that I left the individual with a little more historical information about the United States than what they had displayed in the last fifteen minutes. It never ceases to amaze me, the conversations that one can hear from sitting in an outdoor café or at a bus stop or sitting on a park bench.

CHAPTER ELEVEN

The interpersonal Vietnam Veterans group began with only five in attendance. I asked Ginzo and Eamon about the others who were slated to be in this group and was given various reasons for their non-attendance. Some of the reasons were, "Too short a notice for when the group was to start; not enough time to make plans, some were working until 3:30 or 4 p.m. and still others weren't even home to receive notification of the group."

This group was held weekly and some members informed me that they were unable to attend it weekly, but could attend it monthly or at most bi-monthly because of their work schedules or the fact that they live forty to fifty miles away and traveling that distance on a weekly basis would be too difficult. Some came in from the Albany area of New York, while others traveled from Brattleboro, VT or Hartford, CT, but in the long-run, it didn't matter where they came from because this group developed itself into the close-knit-comradeship group that these combat Veterans needed.

Jesse is the Veteran who would travel from Albany NY. He was very apprehensive in the beginning because he had no idea what to expect along with not knowing many of the other members. Jesse was a tall, robust, pleasant Afro-American who sported a silver grey pigtail that extended halfway down his back and a grey goatee. He had a very distinguished appearance as he stood erect and proud accompanied with a strong sense of self-dignity that would camouflage any insecurities from the general public in ever knowing that he was a combat Vietnam Veteran. Jesse became a prized addition to this group and the times that he was unable to attend, the others would inquire about his absence.

In the second meeting of this group there were seven Veterans present. In keeping this group low key, I decided to introduce a topic of discussion. As I observed the faces of the Veterans who were staring back at me and waiting in anticipation for the topic I was going to choose, I couldn't resist smiling at them as I began to speak, "I have heard every story of war that could possibly be told. War is dirty, bloody and sometimes

Second guessed, but I believe that it wasn't like this all the time. There were some very comical moments in each of your combat tours and it is these moments that I would like to discuss in this meeting."

Although everyone was relaxed, they became more relaxed and some even started chuckling as they were mentally recalling the rare comical happenings during war. Jesse was the first to tell his story.

"I was stationed in the jungle in III Corp and my squad was sitting on the log at the bottom of a hill in a friendly village. The village chieftain was on the top of this small hill cooking food in a huge cauldron for the people of the village and he was singing his heart out in Vietnamese as he stirred the cauldron. The aromatic smells of his cooking were hitting our noses and started to bother me. The other guys were content to eat their K-rations, but I was getting very fed up with lima beans and ham. You reach a point where you had enough of the same old cold meals, so I grabbed my tin plate and fork and headed up the hill to join the villagers in a hot meal. The cauldron was filled with vegetables and a big block of meat and it smelled absolutely scrumptious, so I sat on the ground with the villagers and waited for the food to finish cooking. Being a guest, the chieftain offered the first helping to me so I stood up and I couldn't wait to taste hot meat. The chieftain put some vegetables on my plate and then he set to cut the block of meat and as he pierced the block of meat it gently rolled over and revealed that the meat was a monkey. My eyes rolled back and I signaled the chieftain that I didn't want any meat because all I could think of is that I didn't want to eat anything that looked like one of my relatives. I quickly returned back down to my squad and after seeing boiled monkey, lima beans and ham didn't seem so bad!"

Needless to say, Jesse had everyone in stitches because you could just picture the entire situation, but a story is always funniest when the individual experiencing it is the one telling it. The group started to settle down from their laughter when Graham decided to tell his story. Graham was an Army medic and was attached to a MASH unit and as soon as the helicopters would land they would quickly get the wounded and place them in the Quonset huts for treatment or surgery. It was one of these landings that Graham told the following story, "We were running back and forth all day long, loading and unloading the helicopters with stretchers of wounded soldiers. It was about 3:30 p.m. when another helicopter landed with wounded, but there was an extremely difficult situation for a wounded RVA soldier. We were told by the pilot that this soldier was unconscious and imbedded in his eye socket was a live grenade that hadn't exploded yet! As we scrambled to get him in the hospital and being very careful not to jar him so as to protect ourselves and him from the grenade going off, the doctor seeing what the situation was, directed us to put him back on the helicopter. We headed back to the helicopter and the pilot would not allow him back on the chopper because of the danger of the live grenade so we headed back to the hospital. We must have run back and forth five times between the hospital and the helicopter as if we were in a Max Sennett comedy. Finally, a doctor checked out the vitals and stated that this soldier was dead and the pilot was told to take this soldier and to dump his body in a safe place for the grenade to explode and where no one would be hurt or injured. It wasn't comical concerning the condition of the soldier, but it was comical with the running back and forth and never putting the stretcher down."

Graham was one of three medics that were in this group, but he was the only one attached to a MASH unit. The two others were lovingly called "bush medics" because they were out in the jungle with the troops. Sydney was a tall, bearded Afro-American and a member of the first cavalry who spoke often of the dangers of bush vipers who were also referred to as "two-steppers" because if you were bit by one, you only managed to take two steps when you collapsed and died instantly.

"Not much a medic can do when a soldier is bitten by a viper other than bagging the body and shipping it home!"

This tiny group of soldiers became very close with each other and it didn't matter what branch of the service that each served in because they functioned as a single unit of combat Veterans who fought in the Vietnam War. Sydney Wells and Lane Sullivan were two combat soldiers who were very close and the best of friends who met each other in this group at the Community Care Center. Sydney was the Afro-American medic who hailed from the State of Rhode Island and Lane was a Caucasian marine who was raised around the Boston area who sported a strong Bostonian accent. One was never seen without the other and some of the funniest situations happened to them after the service and not during. Both of these Veterans wore glasses and many weekends Lane would go over to Sydney's apartment for a meal and watch TV. Sydney had a good size television and he bought several sized speakers because he wanted surround sound and he placed these speakers at specified places in his living room. As the meeting was ready to convene on Monday afternoon, Sydney decided to tell of a funny thing that occurred to him and Lane over the weekend.

"Yesterday afternoon Lane came over to my apartment and we both pitched in and made ourselves a delectable roast beef dinner.

After we ate, we went into the living room to watch a comedy movie on the TV and without intending to, we both fell asleep. I was in the recliner and Lane was on the couch. We had no idea that a war picture was scheduled after the comedy and we also didn't think that we would zonk out as long as we did. Well, what woke me up was the sound of grenades and gunfire which bolted me out of the chair and covering my head with my hands, I hit the floor. At this same time, I noticed Lane diving off the couch and heading under the coffee table for protection. When we realized that it was the TV, Lane looked at me through his crooked glasses that were hanging on to one side of his face and slowly getting up stated, "You black son-of-a-bitch! Are you trying to give me a heart attack or what! That scared the shit out of me!"

I was just as shook up as Lane, but I couldn't help laughing at the situation because it was a total surprise. I guess old habits are hard to die and once a soldier, always a soldier!"

Sydney was laughing as he was telling this story and for a good part of it, had acted it out by taking his glasses and placing them exactly the way that he had seen them on Lane. Everyone was laughing and I feel that the acting accentuated the comedy of the story as well as displaying the frightful flashback that brought these two Veterans back to the war-torn jungles of Vietnam, if only for a moment.

On another occasion when there was a torrential downpour and some of the Veterans had arrived early to the center to avoid the rain, Lane and Sydney were a little late because they had to take the bus from the VA where they had late afternoon appointments. The bus stop was directly across the street from the center and when we heard the door open to the center and in walked "Frick and Frack" as I lovingly called them, looking like two drowned rats. The squishing of the water from their shoes and the puddles that were forming from their soaked clothes let us know just how hard the rain was coming down. Both stood there with grins on their faces when suddenly Lane stated,

I told the guys to stay right where they were and I headed into the kitchen to get them some towels. They were soaked to the skin so I gave them three towels each so that they could at least put one on the chair they were going to sit in. The meeting was going on for ten minutes when I noticed that the sun was shining, so I instructed the group to go outside to the picnic tables so that Lane and Sydney could dry faster in the sun. Several of the Veterans remarked that the downpour reminded them of the monsoons in Vietnam with the one difference, the monsoons lasted weeks and months and this was just a rain burst that lasted no more than half an hour.

Greg Keizer was an active member in this group and was an extremely quiet individual for a Marine. Greg enjoyed this group and he found that it brought out some release of his stress. He was usually the last one to talk about any of his war exposure and experiences, but we were all respectful of this fact. Thanksgiving was around the corner and the group discussed the possibility of celebrating Thanksgiving with each other here at the center on Monday of Thanksgiving week. I told the group that I thought that this was a great idea so we made the plans and inquired what item of food each would bring. When Greg was approached with these preparations for a feast he stated, "You guys go ahead and celebrate because I will not be here for your celebration. I have not celebrated Thanksgiving since my return from Vietnam. Every Thanksgiving I eat fish heads and rice because that is what I ate in Vietnam. I was stationed in Hawaii and my MOS (Military Operational Code) was embassy guard. That code was a front to what I actually did because they had to put something down and my entire record is sealed for fifty years. My job was to be dropped over the borders of Cambodia or Laos and to observe for any downed American aircraft. I was to get the pilots and crews back over the border of Vietnam because we were not supposed to be in those countries. I was dropped in alone, there was no one else with me with little to no equipment and I had to survive on my surroundings. So I ate fish heads that were discarded and floating in streams and raw rice from the rice patties where I would go quietly at night so that I wasn't seen or heard. Now you all know the reason why I celebrate Thanksgiving in my own way and alone."

Everybody's mouths were hanging open and I'm sure that some were wondering if they had just heard a horror story or if they heard the truth. I assured them that Greg had spoken the truth because he came to me to try to get his records and when the records returned to him from St. Louis, MO, the only document that was intact was his DD214 and his job description in the military stated that he was an embassy guard. His total records were blacked out, a clear indication that he spoke the truth no matter how unbelievable it sounded. Lane ventured to ask Greg the following question, "Greg, are you going to be celebrating Thanksgiving by eating raw fish heads and raw rice just as you did years ago?"

Greg turned to Lane and with a small smirk on his face stated, "I no longer eat these things raw, rather I eat cooked fish heads and cooked rice and truthfully speaking, I am looking forward to it! Some things you just don't get out of your system."

There seemed to be a generalized sigh of relief that went around the room knowing that Greg had advanced his taste buds to cooked food and an element of respect was extended to him as the other member continued on with the planning of their Thanksgiving feast.

On Wednesday, I was going through the mail in my mailbox and came across an order that I was scheduled to do a drug inspection at the VA for the following day. Mike Jamison had put me on this assignment when I first came to the center and also told me that this inspection falls under the director of the hospital. I haven't done an inspection in over a year and a half and I would be assigned with another inspector. The inspections are only for narcotics and all have to be counted, both in the pharmacy and on the wards and clinics, which takes about four to five hours to do.

I arrived at work on Thursday, but I didn't report to the main VA hospital, instead I came to my office at the NVCCC to check my mail and to see if there were any phone calls or cancellations. Realizing that nothing had changed, I bid farewell to Scrappy and informed her where I would be if she needed me and said that I would hopefully see her after lunch if everything goes smoothly for the inspection. In my experience, I have learned that things can change in the blink of an eye and that is the reason I tend to use the word "hopefully" when I spoke of my return because you just don't know.

I was driving leisurely to the main campus of the VA hospital and was wondering who my partner would be for this drug inspection. I parked my car behind building 1 and entered the police office to pick up my inspection packet. As I entered the office, I noticed Wilson Harry sitting there talking to the police chief. The chief handed me and Wilson the packets and informed us that we were to go to the pharmacy first, so we headed down the hallway to the pharmacy and without any notice we knocked on the door and said, "We're here to do a drug inspection!"

We could hear the commotion and almost panic behind the door and it was understandable because everybody just started their work shift and they weren't even ready to take prescription orders, let alone to have two inspectors come in for a surprise inspection. When the door was opened to us, we walked over to the other side of the pharmacy to the "cage" which is the locked metal door to a large closet that contains all the narcotics in the hospital. One of the registered pharmacists had to be in the cage as well, just in case we had any questions about anything. We started with "A" and worked all the way down to "Z", counting pills and making sure that our numbers added up to the numbers on the packet. It gets very hot in the cage because there are no windows and there is only the one door that is always locked. When Wilson and I finished in the pharmacy, we looked at our packet to see how many wards and clinics we had to go to that had narcotics on them. It wasn't too bad, because it was one ward and two clinics and I looked at Wilson and stated that there was a good possibility that we would be done before noon, which pleased us both. The ward that we went to had three injections of morphine that was used for a patient with terminal cancer and the three that were left matched up with the number on my sheet. From the ward, we headed to the clinics where we were met by Kyle Rohan RN, who had worked these clinics for many years and I knew him very well. The narcotics in the clinics also matched up and then Kyle went over to another refrigerator and turning to me with a very serious expression on his face stated, "Linda, write this down anywhere, on your hand, the cover of the folder, a scrap piece of paper, the clinics have seven vials of epinephrine!"

"Kyle, that's not a narcotic!"

"You know it and I know it, but please report the epinephrine! It is extremely important that you do so!"

I stood there bewildered and wondered why Kyle was so adamant about my recording epinephrine when my inspection was only concerned about narcotics. I looked at Wilson and he just shrugged his shoulders, so I noted that the clinics had seven vials of epinephrine and this was also noted in the final report that I submitted to the VA police department. I felt strange to report epinephrine on a narcotics report, but I did so because Kyle was so pleading in his request and I was never one to ask any questions on "why" someone made a certain request. But, I found out the reason a few months later, when the horror story was printed all over the front pages of the local papers and beyond.

After finishing up the narcotics inspection and submitting the report, I bid farewell to Wilson and returned to the Community Care Center in downtown Northampton. Scrappy looked surprised to see me back there before twelve noon, but I informed her that there was only one ward that I had to report the use of any narcotics, so it made the process go quicker and that was why I was back so early. I asked Scrappy if she wanted to go out to lunch to get a sandwich and just to get a change of environment for a half-hour. She went back into her office to get her sweater and purse and out the door we went to enjoy lunch without any interruptions of phone calls or individuals. It was a rare occurrence when we were able to go out to lunch because we often worked right through our lunch and breaks without blinking an eye or even thinking about eating. We went to a sandwich shop that was around the corner and after ordering the sandwiches we wanted, we sat at a small table to relax and to catch our breath, if only for a minute. Looking at Scrappy, I asked her the following question, "So! How was your morning?"

Without turning in my direction and just looking straight ahead, Scrappy stated, "Well, it was different! I guess I was used to you being there early and with knowing that you were doing the drug inspection, I just felt a little lost because I approached your office three times to talk to you, forgetting that you were up at the VA hospital."

"Did any of my patients have any problems while I was up doing the inspection?"

"No not really! Burt approached me early asking if I could write a letter of referral for housing and I told him that you would be back this afternoon. So you are expected to meet with Burt when we return from lunch."

"No problem! It's only about the seventy-fifth letter that I have written for Veterans applying for housing, both here in Northampton and in the surrounding areas."

It was at this point that our sandwiches were delivered to our table, so we just stopped talking to enjoy a delicious sandwich, as well as the company of each other and a leisurely walk back to the center.

When we entered the center, Burt was standing by my office door patiently awaiting my return. I unlocked my door and bid Burt to enter and have a seat and I also informed him that I was aware of the reason for his visit. I asked Burt some pertinent questions concerning the housing that he was applying for and his reasons for making an application to that particular housing. I completed Burt's letter in twenty minutes and informed him that I also made a copy of it in case he needed to apply to other housings if this application did not pan out for him.

The staff was getting ready for our typical weekly staff meeting that was going to commence at 2 p.m. We all sat around the conference room table waiting for the last straggler who was waiting to close up the CWT area after the last Veteran left. Scrappy led the meeting and stated that there wasn't much to discuss or report, so she decided to ask the leaders of the different areas such as Occupational Therapy/Recreation, CWT, Substance Abuse, Medical/Nursing and Volunteer Service to see if there was any problems in these areas that needed assistance. The only area that had a little concern was the Occupational/Recreational area because they felt that some of the Veterans were losing interest and appeared to be bored and wondered if there was some kind of group project that these Veterans could do. Not one staff member came up with anything that was new, rather there were many repeats of projects that these Veterans had already done. The nurse, Claudia, was sitting with a shit-ass grin on her face and knowing her the way I know her, she was thinking of a real butte! Without any hesitation and breaking the silence of everyone thinking, Claudia uttered, "I've got an idea that would be a challenge to the Veterans and would also be a lot of fun, but I need the cooperation of the entire staff!"

As everybody's attention was directed at Claudia, she continued to express her plan and how she expected it to be run.

"It is said that the Veterans are getting bored doing repeat projects and the same old things day in and day out. We all know that the patients are interested in this staff and like being here, so the project that I am thinking of involves the entire staff. We can set it up like a contest and the winner will have free meals for one week. My plan is this! Every staff member will bring their baby picture in and give it to me. When I have everyone's picture, I will post them on the wall with numbers on them. The Veterans will be asked to identify the staff member's baby picture and the one who has the most correct will be the winner. What do you think?"

As everyone's heads rotated around the room looking at each other with smiles on our faces, it was easy to know that we all agreed to this baby picture project.

The cooperation that the staff gave was 200% because everyone thought that it would take about a month to gather all the baby pictures. Some of the staff was raised in the eastern part of the State or in another State all together. So, it was felt that these people would have difficulty getting their pictures. Surprisingly, everyone had their pictures within a two-week span, so Claudia started to number each picture and put them all on a big piece of corkboard and placed the corkboard on the wall next to the kitchen at the NVCCC. It was quite comical to see so many Veterans stopping and looking at the pictures. They were so interested in this project that some would stop at the board before they would even get a coffee or go to their assignment in the back room or in group. Some Veterans would ask some staff if a certain picture was them, but of course the staff member couldn't confirm or deny if it was their baby picture because it would spoil the results of the contest. One factor that every patient agreed on was that these baby pictures were pictures of very cute and adorable tots. They had a sincere interest in this contest. They also felt that it would be very difficult to figure out which staff member was which baby. We included the doctor and secretary's baby pictures as well, just to make it more challenging for the patients.

The day of the contest had finally arrived and the secretary had printed out fifty papers that had numbers listed from 1 – 15 on them. As each patient came through the door, he/she immediately approached the secretary and asked for the paper for the staff baby-picture contest. I was sitting at a table drinking a coffee and couldn't help smiling at the swarm of Veterans going into the secretary's cubicle. There weren't any basic rules to this contest other than stating that the stop time was at 2 p.m. This gave everyone time enough to attend any groups or appointments that were scheduled without any interruption in their daily activities.

The line was forming and it was extending into the kitchen and there was respect given to all, as well as consideration for each other and the kitchen staff who were attempting to get breakfast prepared for those who wanted it. As I sat there, I couldn't help wondering which Veteran would be the winner of this contest by getting the majority correct. I also thought, "what if there is a tie", two or possibly three Veterans that have the same score! The reward is a week of free breakfasts and lunches at NVCCC.

Would both get the same award or would the award be split between the two by giving each 2 ½ days each of meals! These are questions that I have a tendency to think of after the fact. I was told one time by a supervisor that I have a concrete-thinking ability and at the time, I didn't know if this was a blessing or a curse. I was attending an in-service at the Hotel Northampton and she started the session out by writing seven colors on the board. She did not use the same color chalk to write the name of the color. For instance, if she wrote the color "red", she wrote it with green chalk and this was true for all seven colors that she wrote. Not one was in the same color as the word. I happened to be the very first one that she asked a question and her question to me was, "Linda, what colors do you see on this board?"

As I looked at the board, I quickly named the colors that I saw, not the words, just the colors. It was here that she stated that I was a concrete-thinker. She further asked me why I didn't say the name of the colors that were written and turning to her I stated, "Words are not colors! You asked me what colors did I see on the board and I told you the colors that my eyes were seeing as they scanned down the board!"

These thoughts were coming back to me as I was trying to figure out which one or two of these ambitious and determined

Veterans would walk away with the grand prize of free meals for a week. I was also thinking of the next project that these great Veterans would have an interest in doing because they were entirely involved in this staff-baby-picture-project.

At 2 p.m., the official time for the contest to end, every Veteran who had taken part in the contest had submitted their forms to the secretary. Claudia collected these forms and was correcting them in her office and at 2:30 p.m. announced that there was only one grand winner who had correctly identified nine out of fifteen baby pictures to the right staff member. I had to laugh because Claudia informed me that many of the patients thought that her baby picture was me and that my baby picture was her. As we sat there and laughed at a few of the choices that these Veterans made in this contest, I had a thought for the next project for them. Smiling, I looked at Claudia and I stated, "These patients had a great time doing this baby-picture-project because they were able to know the staff a little bit better. In keeping with that idea, I thought that the staff should put their initials down on paper, all three of them and ask the Veterans to identify what they think the middle initial represents?"

Claudia felt that this was a great idea and knew that some of the staff's middle names would be easy, but there were quite a few who had family surnames or their maiden name for their middle name. She knew that it would be equally problematic as the baby pictures, but she further agreed that it keeps the Veterans thinking and using their logic. Similar to the baby-picture-project, no Veteran was allowed to ask any staff member if they knew the middle name of another staff member. This project was set up to take place in two weeks and the prize was going to be the same for those who scored the most correctly.

I was experiencing one of my rare moments of just sitting back in my chair and thinking of the years that had passed so quickly and everything that I had been involved in, in those passing years. My eyes were fixed on the brown oak leaves that were gently falling from the branches of the tree as if the mild autumn wind were rocking them slowly to the ground. Some leaves appeared to be temporarily suspended in air because it seemed to take them forever to reach the ground. So many thoughts were crossing my mind as I watched the leaves falling. Those leaves were reminding me of the many Veterans that I cared for over the years and also of the many that had passed away over the years as well. I started to dwell on thinking of the Veterans that had passed and I knew that I had to snap myself out of it because I had living Veterans that needed my assistance and who were eagerly awaiting their next challenge that the staff was going to set up for them.

Two weeks had passed and it was now the day of the challenge for the Veterans to try and figure out the middle names of the staff. Each patient was given a paper that listed every staff members name and their middle initial. Some of the Veterans sat at chairs in the kitchen and decided to finish this project before they started their groups while others folded the paper and chose to fill names in when they felt comfortable to do so, but they were very aware that they were limited to completing these papers by 2 p.m. on that day. I realized that some of the staff's middle names would be easy, but the majority of names, the Veterans would have some difficulty figuring them out. Bart, who was a staff member from CWT, had a middle initial of "E". I knew that the patients would probably think it was Edward, Ernest or Earl, but I knew that his middle name was Eustis. I would say that the Veterans were going to have a harder time figuring out the middle names then they did in figuring out the baby pictures. Many middle names were old family names from the past being a given name or a surname. Many of the Veterans handed their papers in well before the allotted time of 2 p.m., so Claudia and I decided to check some of the names out on the early arrivals. We were laughing hysterically at some of the answers because it was as if the Veterans were giving names by association. For instance, Chaz worked in the Substance Abuse Program and his middle name was a "C". One patient wrote down that "C" which he thought stood for "Champagne"! When all the papers were in and corrected, the winner with the highest score of correct answers was only one Veteran who correctly answered five out of fifteen middle names. This sadly was the last project for the Veterans for this year because the holidays were swiftly coming upon us and we had to ready ourselves for them.

Holiday time at the NVCCC is very festive and Veterans and staff work together on decorating, cooking and baking. It was my turn to do the baking of apple and pumpkin pies and I must say that the baking of pies was very tricky in electric ovens because the top crust of the pie gets burned and the bottom crust is raw or vice versa. I decided to regulate the oven so that both the top and bottom of the ovens were heating equally and I was not going to place one pie into the oven until it was regulated. It took me about an hour to be sure that the oven was cooperating with my fine intentions of baking the pies completely. There were several Veterans sitting at tables and at the central counter who were very busy peeling apples and chopping them up so I could fill the pies. Others were peeling potatoes, winter squash and turnips, while others were stringing Christmas lights around windows and doors and a few were busy setting up the Christmas tree. There are always the clowns who make everybody laugh when they parade around wearing garland like a boa and singing a Christmas song as if they were the major celebrity in a Broadway hit show. Amazingly, they never stopped until they finished the song! The funniest character was Fred who came out entirely covered in red, green and silver garlands and sang "Silent Night" like Marilyn Monroe when she sang "Happy Birthday" to President Kennedy in 1963. With total cooperation from everyone, it was very obvious that the spirit of Christmas had touched each and every individual that walked through the door of the NVCCC and this spirit was taken home to their families to continue the joyful holiday celebration.

As we entered the year 1999, we were thinking that we would all be trudging through the final year of the twentieth century. It was fearful, as well as exciting because nobody ever thought about the end of the century in which we all were born. This is January and in March I roll over to the grand old age of fifty and there were many that were going to turn fifty along with me that also worked in the VA. We didn't have time to think about ourselves because when we were on the job, our thoughts and concentration were entirely on the Veterans or I can at least speak for myself in this manner.

It was around July 1999 that there was a rumor about the Northampton VCCC closing and the possibility of it going back up on the hill. The staff was letting this rumor run like water off a duck's back because there always seemed to be rumors running all the time about something in the VA, so no one was getting excited about another rumor and we just ignored it. We were self-sufficient and I couldn't understand why the rumor started that the NVCCC was going to close or be relocated back on the hospital grounds. We were paying our own bills and had our own budget. There was no financial assistance coming from anywhere. Why did the director want to close something that was working? I started to think of the way the VA did things in the past and it started to make sense to me. You see, I learned a long time ago that if something is working, the VA has to fix it and if something is broken, the VA ignores it. This is sad, but true, because I have seen it and experienced this on more than one occasion.

In September, Scrappy Lindstrom informed the staff that there was a meeting scheduled in the conference room at the NVCCC with the hospital director, the director from the United Veterans of America shelter, the area newspapers and several staff members from senator's and congressmen's offices to discuss the fate of the Northampton Veterans Community Care Center. Two Veterans, Ginzo and Eamon had heard about this meeting and decided to wait and plead their case to keep the center open. They were calmly sitting at the table in the kitchen area and watched different delegates going in and out of the conference room. I noticed Scrappy walking down the ramp from CWT and asked her how things were going on in there! She looked at me strangely and said, "How are things going on where?"

"You're in the conference room with all the big wigs. What's going on?"

Ginzo and Eamon reconfirmed their faith in Scrappy and told her that they were assured that she was putting a good word in their defense to keep the center open!

Hearing these statements and questions, Scrappy who was looking perplexed stated, "I'm not in that meeting and I have not been invited to it either!"

I looked around and noticed that there was not one single staff member that worked at the NVCCC who was present in that meeting that was determining our fate. They were all strangers who knew nothing about the accomplishments and successes of the NVCCC. I stood there speechless, when suddenly the conference room door opened and Dr. Bart and the medical director approached Scrappy with a question.

"How many people are employed at this center?"

"There are 6.4 employees working here! Why do you ask?"

"Because the hospital director just told the news media that there are thirteen employees working down here!"

Scrappy was livid and turned to Dr. Bart and said, "You have to go back in there and straighten this out! He doubled the count and he's lying to everyone!"

Dr. Bart looked like he was caught between a rock and a hard place because he responded with, "You cannot correct this director because what he says…goes! That is also the reason that you were not invited in there, because he knows that you are a truthful person and he didn't want you bucking him!"

Scrappy stood there with her mouth gaped open as Dr. Bart retreated back into the conference room to rejoin the cutthroats that were deciding the fate of the staff and Veterans attending the NVCCC! I sat down in a chair in the kitchen and instinctively knew that the center was going to close. After all, it was the only thought that made any sense to me. Not one employee of the center was in the meeting and Scrappy who is the director of the center was specifically shunned from the meeting. The two Veterans who were patiently waiting to go into the meeting to plead their case of the need for the center to remain open saw my quietness as I sat there thinking that the center was doomed. One of these Veterans and I'm not clear which one, inquired if they were being allowed to plead their case in the meeting. Slowly turning my head in their direction, I stated, "I highly doubt it! If the director of the center wasn't invited to the meeting and we all know that she would have convinced everybody in the conference room that this center should remain open and viable to every Veteran that crosses the threshold of this center, then I must say that your chances are nil to be summoned to the meeting. You know, I heard this particular saying years ago and I quote, "No good deed goes unpunished in the VA!"

I think this situation describes this saying very well. We are being closed because we were Self-sufficient, independent from the main campus and Veterans were treated with respect and compassion and easily accessible to any staff at the center which also includes the secretary."

Eamon and Ginzo were starting to get a little hot under the collar and I could fully understand where they were coming from. It was only recently a group was formed so that eight to ten Vietnam Veterans could gather and discuss issues that concerned them. They started to make some comments about writing to their congressmen and senators and slowly shaking my head, I told them,

"That is a very good suggestion and normally contacting your representatives would work, but the representatives from Kerry, Kennedy and Neal's offices are already present in the meeting room along with the newspapers and other media officials and guaranteed you will read of the impending closure of the Northampton Veterans Community Care Center in tomorrow's paper."

These Veterans looked very depressed and I reassured them that the move would not be in the immediate future because it takes planning and arranging the movement of furniture and records and this process takes several months to figure out. I also assured them that their groups will continue until the move and then when we were settled wherever on the VA grounds, I will find a room so that the group can continue with little to no interruption.

CHAPTER TWELVE

The Center managed to stay solvent for five months before the gavel was dropped and we headed back to the VA compound in Leeds. The date was January 18, 2000, a day that would live in infamy to the staff and more important, to the Veterans who committed themselves to the NVCCC. This was a community center which was set up to serve Veterans in the community, not for a hospital-based program. But, like everything else if something works in the VA the "powers to be" have to fix it and if something is in total chaos and running amuck, it is totally ignored! It was at this point, when I started to realize that not every director is for the Veterans. I experienced a few that were only interested in their own well-being.

All the staff was present and their furniture was in the offices that Scrappy assigned them. We were assigned to the South section of Ward 4L and some offices in the hallway. The nurse and the doctor had offices in the hallway and OT staff, Sophie (Scrappy) and I had offices in the southern section. Our offices were next to each other and mine was directly in the corner and was very spacious with three windows. I was able to hang several plants from chains in each window. All the rooms were very large and could accommodate several tables and chairs in the Occupational Crafts room for the Veterans to do their projects comfortably. The kiln room was at the opposite end from our offices and was well aired with five windows. The storage room with the craft supplies was between the kiln room and the OT crafts room. After I took my own personal tour to see where everyone was situated, I returned to my office and began to place my furniture that was basically piled in the middle of the office at appropriate and balanced areas in the office. I was glad that the place was closed for three days so that the staff could acclimate themselves to their new surroundings. But, you always get the few Veterans who get curious about something new and stop in for a visit just to see if they are able to find it appropriately and to inquire if any part of the program had changed. Even in the midst of setting up our offices, we always had time to answer a Veterans questions and give them a tour of the new Northampton Veterans Community Care Center now situated on the grounds of the VA Medical Center.

It was strange when the patients started to return to the NVC-CC now that it was back on the hospital grounds because many of them had a problem with the center being on the hill and not in the community. I fully understood their dilemma and hesitation in their return because some of these Veterans had recently been discharged and wanted nothing to do with returning to the environment that they felt imprisoned in for over a year. They loved the independence of residing in the community and resented the fact that the NVCCC was moved from the community back to the VA grounds. When the community center was downtown, the Veterans were coming in in droves and now there was only a trickling of Veterans that crossed the threshold of the on-VA-ground community care center. This move was highly counter-therapeutic for the Veterans because Veterans that attended the center on a daily basis when it was downtown, now only attended once a month, or at most, would attend once every two weeks. This move was the start of the destruction of the Northampton Veterans Community Care Center.

The program was slowly getting back on course and Scrappy made sure that the only change was going to be environmental and she stated that the guts of the program would continue just as it was downtown. The staff meeting was always held on Thursday afternoons and all the staff at the NVCCC was always present at this meeting in which all patients were discussed about their progress or lack of progress in the program. Scrappy had started our typical meeting and was sitting at the head of the conference table when in through the door, briefcase in hand, came Barney Judson MSW. Barney was the director of the Pittsfield VCCC and as he approached the top of the table he announced, "Hello people! I have just been appointed head of all the VCCC's and starting today, I will be attending and heading all the staff meetings every Thursday!"

We all sat there completely dumbfounded and looked at each other for some kind of an answer. Some thought that Barney was pulling a prank just to see the reaction of the staff, others looked to be in shock and still others believed that anything that came out of an administrator's mouth was true. Scrappy sat there in complete silence staring at the note pad she had placed on the table in front of her. I broke the silence when I inquired, "Barney! When did all this take place? I never saw a promotional notice posted for that position? What is going to happen with Mike Jamison and Sophia who are presently the directors of the Springfield VCCC and the Northampton VCCC?"

Barney had smugness about him when he walked into a room. He expected everyone to bow down to him and praise him which some did, but I could only snicker to myself because he didn't have one-third of the knowledge that Scrappy or Mike had at being a director of a Community Care Center. As a matter of fact, Barney often received the praise and credits that Scrappy, Mike and the rest of the staff in the VCCC's should have received because he never specified that it was the efforts of Scrappy or Mike that accomplished these earned kudos, rather he claimed all their efforts for himself. These were the thoughts that were in my head when he took his time answering the questions that I had just inquired of him. He pompously looked at me and stated,

"Dr. Dabbs informed me this morning that she appointed me head of all the VCCC's! So now, I am the supervisor/director of all the centers and your immediate supervisor. I will be evaluating all staff members who work in the mental health service line in the three VCCC's and I am sure that we will all get along together."

Upon hearing this half-baked answer to my question, I was not satisfied with his explanation because it sounded like a fib. I held direct eye contact with Barney when he made this statement and he quickly turned his attention to the matter at hand which was the weekly patient report meeting. It was obvious that the staff was in no mood to speak about anything, let alone the progress of the patients because of the wave of shock and depression that had swept over the meeting. It was also an uneasy feeling to have Barney heading the meeting that Scrappy had held for several years. This was the second downfall for the Northampton Veterans Community Care Center and knowing that many things come in three's, I wondered what the third attack would be. This is just another example of "if it works, then they have to fix it!"

Molly Pascek was the secretary on ward 4L. She was the main secretary for the substance abuse unit which was on the opposite end of the hallway from the community care center. Molly worked a short time on BX back in 1977 which is where I first met her. Molly never limited herself to only the staff of the substance abuse unit, but would assist any staff member or patient if she was able. Everybody loved Molly because she was personable and knowledgeable about many things and could multi-task while just sitting at her desk. She made and cancelled appointments, supplied every staff member with stationary requests and calendars, made sure that the copier and printer were in working order, recorded group and individual meetings with the counselors and she was ever present when I would lose some document or note on the computer by hitting the wrong key and didn't know how to retrieve it. I would call Molly and explain the situation over the telephone; all the while I'm calling myself every bad name under the sun for losing the note. Molly would laugh every time I called her and would assure me that the small problem was easily fixable. She also had the knack of calming me down so that my blood pressure would return to normal. Molly was one of those rare individuals that someone meets once in a lifetime. I'm thrilled, honored and blessed to have been one of those that knew her and took her to heart because of her availability to everyone regardless of their status. She is the true definition of one who is fair and equitable to all.

As a result of Scrappy being usurped from the directorship of the NVCCC with the replacement of Barney in her position, the staff was again answering questions to the Veterans about this situation. Many Veterans could not understand why there were so many changes to the Center. They were very comfortable with Scrappy as the director and many stated that she was easily approachable, but Barney they did not know and many stated that they didn't trust him because they didn't know him. He also didn't appear to have any interest in the Veterans' needs, but rather was more comfortable sitting in his office talking with the staff members. Guess it takes all kinds to make the world!

On September 11, 2001, as I was getting out of my car and heading up the ramp to the ward, I noticed a familiar Veteran waving at me as he was crossing the parking lot. He yelled out, "Linda! I haven't seen you since we were downtown and today is my birthday!"

I expressed birthday greetings to him and further stated that he continue to be healthy and happy and to stop in and see me whenever he could. He had a big smile on his face as he continued his trek towards Building 6. I arrived at work between 6 a.m. and 6:30 a.m. every day. I had a small refrigerator and a coffeemaker in my office and would always make a pot of coffee first thing before I would even attempt to start any work. I heard Scrappy unlocking her office door and knew that she would be joining me shortly for a needed first cup of coffee. Gradually, we could hear the rest of the staff in their offices and some Veterans who enjoyed being the first to greet every staff member that were present in their offices. Aaron was one such Veteran who always greeted each staff member with a smile on his face and politely knocking on the door even if the door was open. He would then head down the hall to the occupational therapy room to make crafts which he was very talented at and enjoyed doing.

At roughly 8:50 a.m., I was headed down the hallway to the copy machine when a staff member from OT came out of the VCCC shouting, "The World Trade Center just had a plane crash into it! It's unbelievable!"

I turned around in the hallway to see who had made this announcement when I noticed her duck into the doctor's office. I stood there for a moment and thought that it was a freak accident and that the pilot miscalculated his instruments. I continued down the hallway to Molly's office and to the copy machine when I observed three or four staff members from the substance abuse program standing in front of the television in the group room. I walked in and noticed that the news was doing a replay of the plane crash. Everyone was silent, including myself as we watched that horrific crash and black smoke billowing past the tail of the plane that stuck out of the WTC wall. It was then that I noticed another plane flying low near the WTC and I figured that this plane was sent to survey the damage done by the plane that crashed. In complete horror, my mind was void of any thought when that plane crashed into the other tower of the WTC. My mouth dropped open and I realized that these crashes were no accidents. They were purposely planned! Betsy who worked in the substance abuse program became enraged and stated, "This is the work of that goddam Osama bin Laden!"

I had no idea who Osama bin Laden was because that was the first time that I ever heard his name! Everybody was very edgy and slowly dispersing from the break room back to their own offices. They could only shake their heads and wonder how something such as this could happen on our own soil. I headed into Molly's office to make copies and then headed back down the hallway to my office. I walked down the hallway slowly and as I passed Dr. Hussein's office, I noticed that he appeared to pace nervously in there. I knocked on his door and stated, "Doctor Hussein! Are you alright!"

He beckoned me to enter and he sat down at his desk and was wringing his hands together, and talking in a soft voice and Middle Eastern accent, Dr. Hussein uttered, "I was born and raised in Afghanistan and I have been a US citizen for over thirty years. I have several siblings that still live in Afghanistan whom I have not seen in over two years. Now that this has happened, I may never see them again! The last contact that I had with my family occurred six months ago and my sister stated that Osama bin Laden was creating chaos in Afghanistan! I love and miss my family and I'm fearful that I'll never see them again!"

There wasn't much I could do, but listen to him and allow him to vent. I placed my hand on his shoulder and told him that I would keep his family in my prayers and he turned and thanked me for my consideration. I realized that Dr. Hussein was Muslim, but any prayer is just a different road that leads to the same place. At this point, I exited his office and returned to my own office and my own work which I had a great deal of difficulty doing because of the horrific sight of the Twin Towers engulfed in flames. It was a permanent image in my mind and deprived me of any concentration on my work.

As a result of the attack on the Twin Towers, high security was immediately in effect throughout all government buildings and facilities. Evacuation drills were practiced on a monthly basis and in one instance, there were medical helicopters that were used to medevac anyone injured in a bombing. These helicopters came from Barnes Air National Guard base in Westfield, MA and also Westover AFB in Chicopee, MA. There wasn't one detail of high security that was ignored at this time and everyone from the director to the kitchen aide was responsible for their part in maintaining the care and protection of the Veterans. Everyone was also mandated to complete the training for high security so that everything would be accomplished smoothly and properly.

It took several months for everyone to relax a little from alert status, but like everything, it takes time to heal and more so, it takes time to calm down and quell the nerves from every suspicious sound. Sounds that were normal before and you wouldn't think twice about are now resulting in staff doing a double-take and questioning where it originated. It seemed forever that no one smiled or told a joke; they were very serious and we had to be serious and concentrate on the care and treatment of the Veterans that were in the VA at this time.

In April 2002, Dr. Dabbs approached me in my office and stated, "Linda, Mike Jamison MSW, needs help in the Homeless office and I thought that you would work well in that setting so I'm going to assign you to the Homeless office to work with Mike!"

I sat there thinking that she had no idea that I had worked with Mike in the downtown Northampton VCCC and if she did, she never would have made that decision to place me with him. So, with this secret being kept in my mind, I inquired, "When is this change to take place?"

Dr. Dabbs sat in the chair next to my desk and she was quietly thinking of the entire situation when she uttered, "It is a bit difficult because you are still needed here in the VCCC, so I would suggest that starting next week you are to begin to slowly turn some of your cases over to other staff members in the VCCC so that you will be able to work in the VCCC in the mornings and in the Homeless office in the afternoons. I calculated that in three months you will have completed a full transition to the Homeless office and to have terminated all your cases in the Veterans Community Care Center."

When Dr. Dabbs finished her grand oration in telling me what she expected me to do, she slowly stood up and quickly exited my office without allowing me to ask her any questions about the new assignment, but then again, she never allowed anyone to ask questions because she enjoyed having the last word. I sat there thinking that it would be good to work with Mike Jamison again and the convenience of just walking down the hallway to the homeless office was very refreshing. Mike was moved to the hospital campus from Springfield and was placed on ward 4L with the rest of the programs that were outpatient programs.

A week had passed since Dr. Dabbs informed me of my new assignment and I had already re-assigned a few of my cases to other staff members and this was my first day that I was going to enter the homeless program in the afternoons. I was aware that Mike didn't come into the office until the afternoons because he was on the road in the mornings visiting several homeless shelters in the area. As I approached the homeless office, I saw that the light was on inside so I gazed through the door window and observed Mike busy on his computer. I gently knocked on the door and Mike turned around from his desk and beckoned me to enter. As I entered, I started to sing, "Together Again!" from the sound score of the musical "Annie" and Mike couldn't help laughing as I sang. When I finished the song, I sat at the desk across from Mike's and asked him a question because my curiosity was killing me, "Mike, did you request my presence in this office as you did years ago when you were the director of the Northampton VCCC? No, I didn't request any particular individual, I only stated that I needed help and that there was too much work to do it all by myself! Why do you ask?"

I always felt very comfortable with Mike and we never lied about anything to each other. I felt the same way with Scrappy because these individuals had respect for me and I reciprocated the same respect to them. So, as I smiled at Mike, I described the entire approach that Dr. Dabbs delivered to me last Monday. He listened intently and then shook his head in disbelief as he picked up a paper packet on his desk. Mike told me that the form he was holding was an S form and that these forms had to be filled out on every Veteran living in a homeless shelter or in the woods. Mike was very thorough and further explained, "There are several forms that are required by NEPEC (New East Program Evaluation Center) for homeless Veterans. One of the reasons that I arrive at work in the afternoon is the result of being on the road every morning visiting shelters, vacant buildings and hobo camps down near the railroad tracks! Homeless Veterans are an increasing population and it is the job of this office to search them out and to offer them the care and treatment that they deserve. Many do not want anything to do with coming into the VA because they want nothing to do with the government and the VA is part of the government. I have seen Veterans that haven't had a shower/bath in over a year and their clothes are rags and falling right off their bodies. They make campfires to try to stay warm, but there is little to burn to maintain the fire. Their tents are pieces of plastic or canvas that was found in a trash bin. Many have even been found in metal clothing bins because the clothing makes a comfortable bed and the lid prevents any snow or rain from falling on them. It is an extremely sad situation to see a Veteran who defended and fought for the United States of America, get ignored and mistreated as if they were the dregs of society!"

I could see that Mike was standing on his soapbox, but he was absolutely correct in saying what he said because in the past year I had referred several Veterans to him. Mike had so many projects going for the homeless Veterans such as a blanket program (acquired 1000 blankets to be given to homeless Veterans), some pup tents from sporting goods stores for the Veterans that wished to remain in the woods, thousands of personal hygiene kits that consisted of a comb, shampoo, toothbrush, toothpaste, socks, shaving cream, disposable razor, bar of soap, face cloth and deodorant. I knew that I would be in my element being with Mike and the homeless program and I was excited to begin this new phase of my employment at the VA because I'm sure that the word had spread that I would be working with Mike and the Veteran's grapevine passes information like wildfire.

When I completed the training and learned everything about the homeless program that Mike was able to teach me, it was also at that point in time that I made a total transition from the VCCC to the homeless program. Here I was in a new office, a new program and a new supervisor. It was confusing to several Veterans who would stop by the homeless office to ask me a question concerning something in the Community Care Center which was located at the end of the hallway. I assumed that they could not get used to the fact that I was no longer working in the VCCC. The Veterans even enjoyed seeing Mike again and would often stop to talk to him as well! I had one problem in the move to the homeless office and it had to do with the size of the office. My office was big and had three windows in it and now I was sharing an office with Mike that was half the size of my other office and the only window was on Mike's side which maintained a pleasant temperature through-out the seasons. My side was stifling in the summer and frigid in the winter because of the lack of air circulation in that cramped room, but I made the most of the situation because I never stayed there for any length of time. Some of the determents were making copies of things, or I was on the road picking up some of the slack that Mike couldn't get to or conversing with many Veterans in the hallways or outside in the parking lots/tunnels.

Mike explained that I would be on the road visiting shelters and missions three days each week and he also stated that the area of our travel realm extended as far East as Worcester, as far North as southern Vermont, west across the New York State line and South into Connecticut and Rhode Island. The Northampton VA received many Veterans from Connecticut VA's that were initially placed in the UVA Shelter on the grounds of the VA. This place-ment in the shelter of these Veterans was beneficial to all, but the initials UVA shelter was confusing to the Veterans and staff from Connecticut because they thought that VA of UVA meant Veterans Administration and that the shelter belonged to the VA. I explained to the staff and Veterans from out of state VA's that UVA stands for United Veterans of America and that the shelter has nothing to do with the VA, but rather is a privately-owned program that is only based on the VA grounds. My back was against the wall feeling that I was obligated to define the differences between the homeless program which is a new VA program that was established within the last ten years. The UVA was established by a Vietnam Veteran in the late 1980's for homeless Veterans, and was originally established in Building 20. Since then, it has moved to a larger building, namely Building 6, which is right next door to Building 4, which is where Mike and I have our office. Mike was well aware that I was opposed to having the shelter on the VA grounds because I knew that there would be a great deal of confusion over the initials. VA Medical Center and UVA are complete opposites. Even people in the community thought that the shelter was staffed and established by the VA. I was really getting fed up with explaining to everyone that they were two separate organizations and that the UVA was housed on the VA campus grounds. It seemed that there was a burst of attitude from several Veterans from the shelter in that they would approach Mike and me and state, "You have to help me out! I'm in the VA!"

Not knowing who these Veterans were that abruptly burst through the door and made their demands to me, I pleasantly invited them to sit down so I could get some information on them.

"You stated that you are in the VA! Could you tell me what ward you are on?"

"I'm in building 6 and the staff told me to come here and see you and that you would help me because I'm in the VA!"

As I sat there thinking "Oh! Here I go again!" and without uttering one word, I slowly turned my head towards the Veteran and smiling said, "I am employed by the VA I do not work for the UVA. I know it is confusing to you considering that both have VA initials, but the UVA is the shelter and the VA is the Veterans

Administration. I have explained the difference to so many people that I feel like a travel agent going nowhere. Oh! By the way, you are not in the VA, you are in the shelter!"

The Veteran had a crooked grin on his face and apologized for rudely entering the door the way he did and settled back to answer the questions from the homeless registration form that I began to ask him.

The month of April is very pretty on the VA grounds because it is hidden from the general public and the buildings are completely surrounded by tall trees as well as some very thick forest areas that extend deep into the hills. I was busy in my office, or shall I say, my half of the office, in the mornings doing a variety of forms with Veterans from the shelter as well as walk-in Veterans. Mike was always on the road in the mornings, so we agreed that he would be on the road in the mornings and I would do the afternoons and in that way everything was covered. This schedule made everything roll as smooth as possible and we both agreed that managing the office and the work was running much easier. I was disappointed to leave Sophia (Scrappy), but I was elated to be working with Mike once again, after all, he was my first supervisor when I transferred to the Northampton Veterans Community Care Center in 1990.

As long as I have known Mike, he never worked on his birthday and being back with him in the homeless program was no different. I was only working the homeless program two months when Mike informed me that he would be going on annual leave the week of his birthday which was at the end of May. Mike was considerate and didn't want to leave me overwhelmed with work so he finished most of his work before he went on vacation because he knew that I was new and only there for an extremely short period of time. On Friday, Mike left me a list of phone calls that he was expecting returned to him as well as some paperwork that had to be completed by the following week when he would be gone on leave. The week went smoothly and there were several

Veterans that would knock on the office door, greet me "Good Morning" and inquire about Mike's absence, which many were aware that he was on vacation.

The following Monday arrived and as I was sitting at my desk interviewing a homeless Veteran, my phone rang so I excused myself to the Veteran and answered the phone. The call was from the secretary of the mental health service line, who stated, "Linda, Mike Jamison will not be in today! Apparently, he was in an accident and broke his ankle in three places and is presently in the hospital having surgery!"

I inquired, "Do you have an estimate of time on when he will be back to work?"

"No, I'm sorry! That was the only information I was given and instructed to relay it to you!"

As I gently replaced the receiver to the phone, my thoughts were focused on Mike in the hospital and his requiring major surgery on his ankle. I was well aware that there was no possibility of his return to work in the near future. Even though I was new to this position, I would have the total responsibility of maintaining the homeless office. Leaning on my elbows and closing my eyes to mentally picture this dilemma that was just presented to me I heard a gentle voice say, "Linda…. are you alright?"

Turning my head, I noticed the Veteran that I was interviewing prior to the phone call was looking at me with great concern. I apologized to him and proceeded to complete the interview because the Veteran was my prime concern. I felt that my dilemma could wait because I needed time to reason how I would manage the office alone.

The following day I was surprised to have received a phone call from Mike. He stated that he was going to be in the hospital for about a week and that they placed five pins in his ankle just to hold it together because the bone was so badly shattered. Mike also reassured me that he would call me on a daily basis once he was home to assist me on what to do to maintain the office in his absence. Mike is a real sweetheart and was considerate of the fact that even though he had instructed me on many things in the homeless office, there were still many more things to learn. We conversed for about ten minutes more and before Mike hung up the phone, he gave me his home phone number and told me to call him for anything that I was unsure of or if I had any questions concerning the office.

Arriving at work in the mornings was no different than usual. It was the afternoons that I found confusing until I could acclimate myself to Mike's schedule and to be the only one running the homeless office. I could understand why Mike requested assistance in this office because there was too much for just one individual to do. As a matter of fact, I had my doubts that two people could cover everything that needed to be done. Between the paperwork, interviews, phone calls and traveling to the various shelters seeking and interviewing homeless Veterans was an impossible feat for any one person to accomplish. So, I sat at Mike's desk on a Tuesday afternoon with my elbow on the desk and my chin resting in my hand wondering "where do I start". I knew that I would be covering this work on a solitary basis for at least three months.

The phone calls that I received from Mike were extremely helpful and beneficial both to me and the Veterans I was serving. Dr. Dabbs was the supervisor of the homeless office and she would frequently, at the beginning, visit me and inquire how things were going. She was aware that I was new to this position and her words of encouragement were, "Just do the best you can!"

In conversation with Dr. Dabbs, I made the following request, "Winnie, as you see Mike has several boxes underneath the counter and his desk that he hasn't even been able to unpack from his move to here from Springfield. I'm assuming that he just didn't have any time to empty the boxes! I have already conversed with Mike about the box situation and he told me to go at it when and if I had a slow day that would enable me to do this task! This

Friday will be a slow day for me because the shelter has scheduled an outing and all the Veterans over there are going to attend the outing as well as the staff, so I was wondering if Friday would meet with your approval for me to clean this office and get things in their place!"

Dr. Dabbs took a long look at Mike's side of the office and observed about six to eight boxes crammed under the counter and under his desk. She also noticed that there was no room for anyone's legs under the desk as well. Slowly turning towards me, she gave a smile and nodded her head and exiting the office she wished me luck in my cleaning detail that was definitely going to occur on Friday.

Many Veterans would step in the doorway of the office to greet me or to inquire if there was anything I needed from the canteen and these friendly, sociable and considerate behaviors from these Veterans made me feel important, loved and appreciated by them. My office door was always open and any Veteran that needed to talk or had a problem was invited in and I would immediately stop what I was doing and directed my full attention to the Veteran. I had to laugh at many of the comments from some Veterans when I was sorting out the papers from the boxes. I was completely surrounded by stacks of papers and with the door open, interested Veterans would give the following comments, "Linda, you look like you're the survivor of an explosion in a paper factory! I know you are from Holyoke and it is known as the "Paper City", but this is ridiculous! If I didn't know you like I do, I would think that you just jumped out of a paper recycling bin from someplace downtown."

I had to laugh along with these Veterans because it looked the same as they described from where I was sitting too! I couldn't believe some of the papers that Mike was keeping! There were some receipts from the purchase of groceries for the Northampton VCCC when he was the director, years ago. There was no longer any kitchen connected to the VCCC since it was re-located to the hospital grounds three years ago. He had letters (copies) that he wrote for various Veterans that had either moved away or were deceased. There were a few discharge papers (DD214's) of Veterans from World War II and one from World War I. I was getting scared to view any more DD214's because I thought that I would come across a DD214 for Julius Caesar! Mike threw nothing away and as I called him three or more times a day to inquire if he needed certain papers that I was coming across, he informed me that he literally just dumped all paperwork into boxes because he had to be moved out that day and receiving short notice, he had no choice, but to dump what he felt was his into boxes for the move.

It wasn't easy, but I managed to hold things together in the homeless office for the three months that Mike was recuperating from his injury. His return was a complete surprise because no one warned me or even gave me a heads up that he was coming back to work. As a matter of fact, Mike never mentioned it in the many phone calls that we shared during his absence. It was a Wednesday morning and as usual, I was sitting at my desk recording my day's activities/appointments in my scheduling book when I noticed through my peripheral vision the stature of a man standing in the doorway. Without lifting my head, I just assumed it was a patient who was there to greet me "Good Morning" as they did on a daily basis because I always had the door open so that it made it easier for anyone to enter without knocking. The quiet, motionless individual standing in the doorway broke the silence with, "Am I in the right place?"

Turning my attention to the individual in the doorway and feeling my jaw drop as if it was going to fall on the floor, I slowly rose from my chair and was delighted to see that it was Mike standing there leaning on a cane for support. As I approached him I inquired, "Is this a visit or are you back?"

Mike smiled and stated that it was a little of both. He walked with a limp over to his chair and as he looked around he sat in disbelief to see the office so clean and organized. After a few seconds of just looking around the office, Mike who was pleasantly pleased with everything said, "Linda, you have been busy in this office while I was out! Everything looks great! My doctor cleared me yesterday to come back to work for a half day for six weeks. After that he will re-evaluate me and decide if I can return on a full-time basis. I'm getting very bored at home and I'm looking forward to coming back to work."

"Soooo, how have things been going for you?" he stated as he continued to gaze around the office!

I couldn't believe that I was really staring at Mike as he sat there across from me. He looked wonderful and had good color even though he had to rest frequently as a result of walking slowly and not placing too much weight on his ankle. Mike sat back in his chair and was delighted that he was able to stretch his legs under his desk which was impossible in the past from all the boxes that were stuffed under there. I instructed Mike just to take it easy for the rest of this week and to check out where things were in his desk and file rack because it would be difficult to get back in to the swing of things if he didn't know where things were to begin his job.

Chapter Thirteen

Mike came back to work on a full-time basis in October and although he possessed a slight limp, he was walking at a quicker pace and without the cane. He was back in stride with his old schedule by traveling to shelters and halfway houses in the Springfield/Chicopee area in the mornings and entering the office by 1 p.m. It was just after Halloween when Mike entered the office taking short steps looking very much like a Hopi dancer. He had a huge grin on his face as he made his way to his desk. I couldn't help my eyes following him and wondered what that soft friction sound was that emanated from him. He continued to stare at me and he knew by the expression on my face, that I was aware that there was something that was not right. I couldn't resist or hold my tongue anymore so I ventured to inquire and said, "Mike, you were ambulating very well and now you appear to have trouble walking and your feet are shuffling! There is definitely something wrong, did you have a set-back? What's going on?"

Still smiling, Mike answered my inquisitive questions promptly and directly to ease the concern and worry that he saw in me.

"No, I don't have a set-back and the reason I am walking like this is because I am wearing ankle weights to strengthen my ankles. They are five-pound weights on each ankle and they are sand-filled which probably describes the sound you were hearing when I walked into the office. I wore them from my house to work, but they are beginning to feel like they are twenty-five pounds each so I am taking them off before I overdo it!"

After Mike removed the ankle weights, his gait was funnier than it was with the weights on because he now was able to lift his feet without them being held down. As he supposedly was walking normal, he appeared to be high-stepping as if he was attempting to get over a fence that didn't exist. I began to pack my bag and clipboard so that I could go out on the road to the Pittsfield/Greenfield areas. Turning to Mike I instructed him to take it easy and not rush off to anything because he could very well end up on his face. He smiled back and bid me to have a good afternoon so I reciprocated the same wishes and headed down to the garage for a government car for my road trip.

I always had a sense of freedom whenever I scheduled a road trip. It wasn't a freedom from my job or any minute' aspect of my job, but rather it was a freedom that made me reminisce about the many patients that I was exposed to over the years. It didn't matter what route I took or what destination I was headed in because my thoughts and memories were always inclusive to the Veterans. Many times, I would think back to the year I started my employment in the VA and wondered how the Veterans were that were discharged to their homes or to nursing facilities and I would mentally question if they were still alive or if they had passed on. These were my thoughts as I traveled up Route 5 to the Greenfield/Orange area, passing cornfields of tall and erect stalks that reminded me of a battalion of soldiers standing at full attention as a general passed by. I rarely put the car radio on because the music would frequently interrupt these trains of thoughts of the Veterans. If someone ever asked me to count on my fingers and toes the number of Veterans I have encountered, I would have to tell them that I would need a thousand arms and a thousand legs and even then I would wonder if that was enough to include all the Veterans I met and assisted in their care. As my thoughts started to slow down, I relaxed and just enjoyed the rhythm of the motion of the car rolling along the road. Observing the first of my stops, which was just down the road, my thoughts switched to the new Veterans that I would be meeting and the services and care that I could assist them with.

There was a great deal of construction going on in the ward above me, which was ward 4Upper. Many renovations and structural changes were taking place and there was a vent directly above my desk in which several minute' pieces of plaster and dust would fall. Frequently, when I would enter the office in the mornings, I noticed these dust and plaster elements covering my desk, computer and chair and it irritated me because this was not the condition I left my station in yesterday when I departed after my tour was done. Several times, I could feel the debris falling down on me as I was working at my desk. I began to cough on a daily basis, but I figured it was just my allergies acting up. The following day there were several other VA workers who were complaining of breathing problems, burning eyes, burning throats and reports were made and presented to administration concerning these health hazards. A quick investigation ensued and it was reported that there was asbestos removal occurring on 4U and that was the result in the physical effects of the VA workers on 4L. The entire staff that worked on 4L was relocated to other buildings that had vacant offices and we would remain in these offices until the construction on 4U was complete.

Mike and I were assigned to room 1058 which was in building 1. When we first viewed this office, it appeared to be a good-sized office, but there were five cubicle sections and it would make it difficult to communicate with each other and extremely difficult to interview homeless Veterans. Looking at Mike I inquired, "Are those sectionals permanent or can they be removed?"

Without looking at me and without any hesitation Mike stated, "They are not permanent and they will be dismantled and removed! You know, this is just our luck! I just returned to work about six months ago and you cleaned and organized the office and now we have to go back to putting everything in boxes and starting all over again! It just doesn't end!"

Slowly closing the door and walking down the main hallway of building 1, I turned to Mike and issued an invitation to lunch in the canteen. He readily accepted and I hoped that lunchtime would calm both of us down from the thoughts of the impending move to building 1 and room 1058.

We were barely settled into our new office when we were notified that we had to undergo several tests for asbestos exposure. Times were given for respiratory clinic and x-ray therapy for all the staff that had worked on 4L and there were usually two to three employees at any given lab during these tests. Some staff had notified their lawyers prior to taking these tests, while others just went along and cooperated with the entire process. We were all informed by the technicians that it takes a long time for symptoms of asbestos poisoning to occur. In many situations, it could even take years, but that was only in severe exposure cases and not in mild or slight exposure cases.

At about this same time, Mike had informed me that he was seriously contemplating resigning from the VA. I didn't react or respond to this statement because he stated that he was only thinking about it and there wasn't a day that went by that I didn't hear someone saying, "I've got to get out of here!" Retirement or resignation statements were usually the result of some confrontation with a boss or supervisor. Too many times, the lowly-working staff member had been put down, falsely accused of something they didn't do or been set up by a co-worker who ran to the supervisor and the supervisor accepted the first opinion without the decency of hearing the employee's view who was set up. It's just typical VA politics where they attack the individual at the bottom of the totem pole when everyone is aware that the problem started at the top. It seemed that Mike would make these resignation statements right after he met with his supervisor. He would remain quiet when he returned to the office and I figured if he wanted to

203

talk about it he would introduce it, but he chose to remain silent and I would mind my own business and never ask him anything about the meeting.

The day arrived that we were moved into room 1058 and all the sectionals were removed and the room appeared much larger and roomier with the sectionals gone. My desk was right near the door so I was the first person anyone saw when they opened the door. Mike was on the other side and if we wished to talk to each other, all we had to do was to swivel our chairs around. Christian Robbins, MSW was the social worker on 1West and he was also the social worker that had started the homeless office with Mike when they were in Springfield. Chris was told that the position was only for two years and when he was approaching the two-year limit, he applied for a permanent social work position in the VA and was appointed to the vacancy on Ward 1West. He was in the homeless office more than Mike or I because I think he was avoiding the staff on 1 West. They seemed to be constantly looking for him to do the social work duties on that unit. After two months of Chris's constant visitations to the homeless office, I felt obligated to ask him a question, "Chris, do you like your job on 1West? You seem to be here more than on the ward you were assigned!"

Chris sat there with a smile on his face and said, "Oh they can get along without me, besides there's not much to do up there!"

I was surprised to hear that statement come out of his mouth because I had covered on that ward and being the admission ward there was plenty to do. I turned my gaze in Mike's direction and detected a smirk as his head slowly turned back to Chris and uttered, "Chris is hiding out! It's his pattern and it's nothing new to me because he did the same thing when he worked with me and I am using the word "work" very lightly!"

Chris wasn't bothered at all by the comments that were delivered to him from both Mike and me. He continued to remain seated in the chair making idle conversation and ignoring the fact that Mike and I were extremely busy with our work. We continued our work and even ignored whatever Chris was talking about. When I had had enough, I picked up the phone and dialed his ward without him knowing it. When the ward secretary answered the phone and after friendly greetings I made the following inquiry, "Are you missing your social worker up there because if you are looking for him, he is sitting right over here in the homeless office downstairs in room 1058! "

As I was making this call, I noticed Chris starting to rise from the chair and looking at me with hate in his eyes, he placed the chair back up against the wall and turning to me as I was hanging up the phone receiver said, "You're a bitch!"

Mike turned around and looking at Chris appeared to be pleased that Chris was finally removing himself from the office as I returned a comment to Chris to his statement, "No, I am not a bitch and you left me no alternative because you were ignoring all the other hints we were dropping on you. So you see, I had no choice but to call your ward and inform them of your where-abouts!"

Amazingly, Chris didn't show up in the homeless office for a lengthy period of time and Mike and I thought that Chris must have found another place to hide in.

I was surprised to learn that Mike was actually going to resign from the VA and that his resignation was going to occur at the end of June. Here it was the end of April and I would only have two more months to work with Mike which didn't settle too well with me because I wondered who would take his place. Like everything else, I just had to wait my turn to see who would be the chosen one for Mike's job. It could only go in two directions, either I would be pleasantly surprised or I would be in total shock at the choice and at the way that things were going, I anticipated being in total shock. Knowing that I had only two months left to work with Mike, I dropped the thought of who might be his replacement and concentrated on working with Mike which I always considered a pleasure.

On the morning of June 27, 2004, Mike walked into the homeless office with the biggest smile on his face and was totally relaxed in every way. He had good reason because this was his last day of work in the VA. He had gradually cleaned his desk up and he packed up all his personal papers and items over the last month. His desk and area was vacated of all his things and for anyone who didn't know that he was resigning would have perhaps thought that he was moving in instead of leaving. I watched Mike plop down in his desk chair and putting his crossed feet up on the desk and his arms behind his head, he sat there gently swiveling his chair and smiling at me. I couldn't resist returning a smile and shaking my head I uttered, "I'm going to miss you! This office will never be the same without you. After all, you were the one who started this office and whomever they appoint they will never fill your shoes!"

Mike continued to smile and swivel in the chair and raising an eyebrow stated, "We'll stay in touch, Linda, and I feel that I am leaving this office in good hands. You know a great deal and have done a great deal in this office when I was on extended medical leave in the past. As far as anyone filling my shoes, we both know that they will get somebody of their choice."

I know Mike well enough that when he shrugs his shoulders and continues to smile that he knows something, so I squinted my eyes at him and stated, "You know who's going to take your place, don't you?"

Mike's demeanor changed slightly as he sat up straight in the chair and giving me direct unblinking eye contact said, "I was informed by our supervisor and when she gave me the name of my replacement, I requested that I be the one to inform you! My replacement is Chris Robbins!"

As my jaw dropped and sitting erect in my chair, I remarked, "YOU HAVE GOT TO BE SHITTING ME! They could have just left me to run this office alone because he'll be off hiding someplace and avoiding work! Besides that, he will expect me to do all the work, along with the supervisor telling me to teach him about the homeless program. This is damn typical of the preferential treatment that the "favorites" get around here from administration! You see…Mike, you and I will never be favorites around here because we speak our minds and when we see that there is something wrong, we question it! Certain supervisors don't like that and we happen to have one who is in that category."

Mike appeared to feel that with this appointment of Chris Robbins to his vacated position that it was going to be a big mistake and readily agreed with everything I just said. He told me not to chase Chris around to do his work because there were several forms that only Chris could complete as the director of the homeless program and if these forms were not filled out in a timely manner he would be the only one held accountable.

"Let the supervisor jump all over him because those forms are his responsibility, not yours!"

Mike always had a knack for calming me down with explaining truthful situations that he had experienced himself in the past. At this point, I decided to return to doing my work and Mike stated that he was going to the canteen to get a coffee.

Monday was June 30th and this was the day that Mike was clearing from the VA. Chris had already plunked himself in Mike's chair just gazing around the office as he talked incessantly about nothing. I was on the computer attempting to do my work, but was interrupted several times as Chris asked me question after question. Chris was slowly transitioning to this position because he had to continue doing work on Ward 1West until a replacement was appointed to that social work position. Chris had shown me his schedule and the days that he picked to be in the homeless office and the other half of the week was to be the social worker on 1West. I taped his schedule on my computer so that I could arrange my own schedule to meet the needs of the homeless office and to make sure that there was someone present at all times. Chris's schedule was as follows, Monday – 8am – 12 noon only,

Tuesday – 8am – 4pm, Wednesday- all day on 1 west, Thursday – 12noon – 4pm and Friday – all day on 1 West.

This wasn't a bad schedule, but it only lasted for one week because Chris started to spend every day in the homeless office and very little time on the ward. It never took him long to start his antics and I am sure that he was hiding out in the office to avoid any work on 1West. I swiveled my chair around to inquire why his schedule changed so suddenly and I asked, "Chris…did they get a replacement for you on 1 west?"

Turning to me and looking very serious at me, stated, "NO… they haven't"

"Well you are in this office every day and your schedule states that you should only be here part-time!"

Chris didn't say anything more, but about five minutes later he left the office and I assumed it was to return to the ward. I learned two hours later that my assumption was totally wrong because I received a call from Molly Pasek, the secretary in mental health asking me to meet with Dr. Dabbs at 2:30 p.m., in her office. I arrived at Dr. Dabbs office five minutes earlier than my scheduled time so I went into Molly's office and chit-chatted with her until I was called into the office. When I was summoned, Dr. Dabbs bid me to sit down as she closed the door of her office. She returned to her own chair and looking at me inquired, "Why are you not helping Chris in the homeless office?"

This statement took me by surprise as I stated, "Winnie, I'm doing my job, I have no idea what his job consists of!"

"Linda, Chris came to me this morning complaining that you were not helping him at all and that you were isolating."

It was at this point that I realized that Chris came to Winnie when he left the office this morning and never returned to the ward. He was setting me up as a fall guy so that there would be no blame on him if anything was to go wrong. Looking at Winnie, I stated, "You know…I didn't put in for that position, Chris did and he was appointed to it! He worked with Mike in the homeless office before I did. As a matter of fact, I believe I was appointed to the vacancy that Chris left when he was appointed as the ward social worker to 1 West! Chris worked with Mike for two years and has a Masters in social work. He must have learned what Mike's position was all about because he applied for it. If he didn't learn anything from Mike, why is this burden placed on me to teach him about a position that I would never be qualified to do?"

Winnie just stared at me all the while I was talking and when I finished, she turned in her chair and with her eyes on her computer said, "Chris is the head of the homeless program and you WILL assist him in everything that he needs! You will not isolate or abandon him and when he asks you to do anything in that office, you WILL do it!"

There was a veil of silence that draped over the office as I sat there in total disbelief at the demands she just placed on me. I continued to hear Mike's voice echo in my ears as he warned me about Chris and Winnie and that Chris was one of her favorites. Speaking softly, I asked Winnie if this meeting was concluded and without looking in my direction, she softly stated that it was over and I could return to the homeless office. I rose from the chair, opened the office door and after closing it, I proceeded down the long hallway of building 1, back to room 1058 and the homeless office.

When I opened the door to the homeless office Chris was sitting at his desk and swiveled his chair around to see who had entered the room. My desk being just inside the door allowed me to take a seat immediately as Chris turned his chair back around without uttering one word to me. I opened my computer and started to do some work to calm my nerves and to get the thoughts of choking that asshole out of my mind. I could never understand how some people could be such slime-buckets, especially when two people share the same office and he never asks you for assistance, but instead runs off to the supervisor to complain that you never help him. It is true that Chris didn't get a thumb's up from me at his appointment to Mike's position, but that doesn't mean I couldn't work with him.

As time passed, Chris began to tolerate and understand me and I did the same concerning him. He was definitely no Mike and didn't even come close to Mike's shoe strings and his dependent trips to the supervisor to complain became less frequent as well. It seemed that Chris would complain about me when his work was in question. Apparently, the paperwork that Chris was responsible to complete on a monthly basis was being done incorrectly and the entire packages of homeless information was being sent back to him. The supervisor was receiving the reports that the paperwork was completely wrong and unacceptable, so when she had to confront him about this mess, he would tell her that I wasn't helping him with it. I became very familiar with the phone call from the department secretary on a Friday morning informing me that Dr. Dabbs wanted to see me at 3 p.m. in her office. I would chuckle with the secretary after she informed me of this meeting and stated, "Well, here I go again! This is to be corrected for something that Chris did wrong and it is no trip down the primrose lane!"

"What are you talking about?" asked the secretary.

"Everybody has patterns and a pattern that I am very familiar with is Dr. Dabbs. Whenever I get a phone call asking to meet with her at 3 p.m. on a Friday afternoon is to tell me that I am not cooperating with my co-worker in assisting him with his work or to give me some form of verbal rundown of my so-called negative behavior that is supposedly obvious to everybody and to instruct me to rectify it immediately!"

I was surprised that I was able to describe the discussion that would ensue in Dr. Dabbs office when I went to meet with her, but it was always the same thing because there was never a change in the place, day or time. Even if Chris was corrected on Tuesday, Dr. Dabbs would always make the meeting with me on Friday afternoon, my last day of work for the week and was probably hoping that I would have a lousy weekend as a result of this end-of-the-week meeting.

In August 2005, Hurricane Katrina hit New Orleans and devastated the entire city. There was constant news coverage of the horrific damage to homes, business's, personal lives, pets and life as they knew it. It appeared that Mother Nature tore into New Orleans with a vengeance. Different groups of employees were deployed to Louisiana to assist and to do anything they could to the displaced people of that State.

On September 28, 2005, I was attending a conference in the Teleconference room at the VA that was about to start at any minute when Shelby Parsons, the secretary for Dr. Dabbs, came into the room and tapped me on the shoulder and requested me to join her in the hallway. I followed her out and when we reached the hallway, Shelby turned to me with papers in her hand and told me to go down to Travel because I was being deployed to Louisiana for two weeks to assist with the Katrina victims. This was 1 p.m. and the clerk in Travel made the flight arrangements for me and three others who were going there as well. I was one of three females and one male that would be heading South on a 7 a.m. flight that was scheduled for the following morning.

CHAPTER FOURTEEN

We were all on time at the airport for our flight on Delta Airlines to the Atlanta Georgia airport where we waited almost two hours for our next flight that would bring us to Louisiana. The Delta flight was fine and quite comfortable, but when we boarded the flight to Louisiana we boarded a sixteen-passenger crop-duster that was packed with all government employees that were headed to Louisiana. I looked around the plane and I noticed that the others were from the Federal Animal Rescue Team and that we four were the only ones from the VA. I started to feel like the odd man out because there were twelve people from the Federal Animal Rescue and Darren, Abby and Lydia worked in the medical field as nurses and nursing assistants. Here I sat being the only one on the plane working in social work and dealing with the homeless. At one point, I had to smile at Darren because he was sitting sideways with his feet in the center aisle and his arms resting on his knees and muttering, "Where did they get this plane...out of a matchbox set? This is the most uncomfortable contraption I have ever been on!"

One of the guys from the Animal Rescue joined in the fun and stated, "I think they resurrected this plane from Kitty Hawk, NC!"

It seemed that comments were going back and forth up the aisle and everyone smiled and enjoyed each other's company. We hit a great deal of turbulence as we flew from Georgia to Louisi-ana, but the flight was short and we all engaged in conversations which distracted us from the discomfort of the plane.

The plane landed in Alexandria, LA and as we disembarked from the plane, the tarmac was steamy and the humidity was sti-fling and it felt like we were inhaling water into our lungs as we walked into the concourse. We retrieved our bags and we were told that there would be a van from the VA that would pick us up at the airport. We only waited about five minute when the van pulled up in front of the door and a pleasant man in cut-off jeans ap-proached us and stated, "Are you the people from the Northamp-ton VA? If you are, then I am here to pick you up and bring you to the Alexandria VA to be processed. My name is Harry and if you can gather your things, we will be on our way."

As Darren, Abby, Lydia and I stood up and grabbed our gear, we followed Harry out the door to the van that would take us to our destination. None of us were told what that destination would be. In the van, we all introduced ourselves to Harry on a first-name basis and inquired where exactly we were going. The trip from the airport was short to our destination at the Alexandria VA Medical Center. Harry instructed us to follow him and he was going to show us where we would be sleeping. We walked about thirty yards across the campus to a building. We were told to take the elevator because we would be staying on the second floor and our bags were too heavy to haul up the stairs. The four of us stood behind Harry who had entered a huge auditorium that was void of any furniture and near the stage there were five to six piles of mattresses that were stacked six-deep. Harry instructed us to take a mattress and to place it anywhere we wished on the floor of the auditorium as he bid us "goodbye" and exited the doorway. You could hear the echo of our silence as we stood there for a moment in total disbelief. Darren broke the silence by saying, "So, this is home for the next two weeks!"

We snickered at his comment and then proceeded to haul mattresses to our point of interest on the floor. Abby was clever because she decided to take three mattresses and stack them up to make a more comfortable bed for herself. After we noticed her doing this, we joined her and also stacked mattresses for our beds. I had to agree that it was much better than just one mattress and it was a great deal easier getting in and out of bed with the mattresses stacked. We were the first crew to arrive, but we soon discovered that there was a steady traffic of deployed VA personnel that were coming in every hour through the night. We also realized that our comfort beds were short-lived because as people came in there were others that needed a mattress. I can truthfully say that I got little to no sleep that night because of the constant relay of people coming in and by morning there wasn't even a walk-space between the mattresses covering the floor. It was wall-to-wall mattresses with barely a nine-inch space between them. I felt like I was playing hopscotch just to go to the bathroom, but at least the ladies room was on the second floor. The men had to go downstairs if they needed to shower or bathe. The night was long, especially when there was hourly interruptions and noise. I stared at the ceiling of the auditorium all night long and at times wondered just how high the ceiling was from the floor. I even imagined that if they had painted florescent stars on the ceiling it would make one think that they were camping outside in a wide-open field, but unfortunately I ended up staring at the metal beams that supported the ceiling. I laid there with my hands under my head for most of the night when I noticed a purplish hue coming through the window and knew that the sun would be rising within the next hour. I pressed the light button on my wristwatch and saw that it was 5:15 a.m., so I decided to get up and shower and get dressed before the line formed at the shower door. After putting my socks on, I stood up and quietly walked between and around the scattered mattresses and being careful not to wake anyone, I heard someone whisper, "Good Morning!"

Stopping immediately and turning my head to the right, I noticed an Afro –American man sitting on his mattress with his back up against the wall. I returned his greeting and whispered back, "I see that you are also an early riser!"

"Not really" he said. "I've been awake all night, just like you!"

He noticed my bundle of clothes in my arm and knew that I was heading to the shower. I noticed his clothes in his arm and stated that he was headed downstairs to do the same thing. When I returned to the auditorium after showering, I noticed that there were many others starting to rustle from their beds and one by one headed to the showers. I thought that if this was my first night experience…what would be the result of the next two weeks!

As Darren, Abby and Lydia headed for the showers, I told them that I would be outside sitting in one of the metal lawn chairs in the front yard and would wait for them there. I was surprised that I was sitting in the smoking area and after being surrounded by five or six smokers and inhaling their smoke, I politely excused myself and walked over to the doorway where the air was smoke-free. I had quit smoking ten years ago and I find that since I was diagnosed with asthma I have a breathing problem around smokers. It wasn't long until Darren, Abby and Lydia joined me in the front yard in which we all simultaneously mentioned getting a cup of coffee. We headed over to the canteen to have breakfast and coffee before we met with personnel service to find out where we were going to be assigned.

The personnel office was crowded with deployed people and the line went down the hallway. We waited in the waiting room for each other after we received our assignments. Darren, Abby, and Lydia were all in the medical field so they had to report to the chief nurse for their assignments. I was in social service and more particularly, the homeless program, so I was assigned to the homeless program at the Alexandria VA. After we received our assignments, we were instructed to return to the auditorium and gather our belongings because we were being assigned beds in a vacated ward at the far end of the Alexandria VA.

I wasn't joking when I mentioned the far end of the VA campus because that was exactly where we went. The auditorium was at the extreme south side of the campus and we trekked to the extreme north side. When we reached our destination, we were told that we were being housed on the third floor and that we had a choice of taking the elevator or the stairs. We gazed at each other and then observed the bags and suitcases that we just hauled clear across the campus and in unison we stated that we would take the elevator. The elevator was small and was only able to carry two individuals and their belongings at a time, so the two that were closest to the elevator door boarded it first and the other two had more time to sit and relax and await the return of the elevator to the ground floor.

Lydia and I were assigned to the same room which was a three-bed room with a bathroom. Abby was assigned the next room down which was also a three-bed room with a bathroom. Darren was assigned a room on the other side of the ward which was a private room with a TV and complete bathroom with a shower. There appeared to be a steady stream of traffic passing each other in the hallway as we were checking out the living quarters of each other. Everybody was thrilled at the fact that we were sleeping in a bed and not on the floor. There was a community room with a 42-inch screen TV and a small kitchen for anyone who wanted to cook popcorn or to warm up some food. We all felt like kings and queens in our new surroundings compared to the auditorium which had no conveniences.

My first day in the Alexandria VA homeless program was slow and consisted more of introductions to the single staff member of that program and to two other deployed VA employees. Deana Tripper came from the Battle Creek Michigan VA and Tina Lynne was an Afro-American who was one of the displaced employees from the New Orleans VA. The head of the homeless program was a very attractive Black woman named Meredith who was very busy organizing different Veteran groups to participate in the yearly Veterans gathering known as Stand Down that was scheduled to take place in two weeks. Meredith had assigned Deana and me to check out the packets that she would be passing out at this event and to make sure that these packets were complete with the information she had put together. This task took an hour to do with the both of us doing it and when we finished, we ended up just sitting there and talking to each other because Meredith had to attend a meeting for the rest of the morning. As the three of us sat there when a lull in the conversation occurred, Deana stated with some discouragement in her voice, "I don't know about you two, but I feel that I am getting very bored here! This is not what I came here to be… a paper shuffler! After lunch I am going to personnel to see if they have anything that is more beneficial in assisting the displaced people of Hurricane Katrina. Who's with me?"

I felt the same way as Deana did and knew that I was not being utilized properly and I was definitely not assigned there to do another VA employee's job when it was obvious that Meredith was capable of handling the homeless program at the Alexandria VA alone. I joined Deana for lunch and for the return trip to personnel for a position where we could assist our displaced brothers and sisters who lost everything from Hurricane Katrina.

Deana and I arrived at the personnel office at 1 p.m. and were surprised not to see a line stretching down the hallway, but instead it was free and we were beckoned into the office and told to sit in the chairs in front of the manager's desk. Smiling pleasantly at us, the manger inquired, "How can I help you ladies?"

Deana speaking freely for both of us stated, "The both of us have been deployed here from other VA hospitals and we have both been assigned to the homeless program. There is not enough work to keep us busy and we feel that our time is being wasted. We were wondering if there is something that we could do that would utilize our efforts appropriately and completely in assisting the victims of the Hurricane. We would also like to work seven days a week so that we could utilize our full potential to assist these victims."

The personnel lady sat back in her chair and as she looked at both of us, remarked, "I am impressed! I have never had anyone come into my office and ask for more work!"

She slid forward in her chair and picking up a pen she quietly wrote something on a small piece of paper. She handed the paper to Deana and told us to clear with Meredith in the homeless office for the next two to three weeks. We had to finish that week out working with Meredith and that starting on Monday we were to report to either Tim or Jean-Nanette who were working the Nazarene Campgrounds.

The homeless office was in building D, which also was the home-base for the substance abuse program. I was sitting in the lobby when I noticed a very pleasant Afro-American man sitting there with scrubs on and smiling at me. I returned a greeting and a smile and began to sit down when he uttered, "The beds are a lot more comfortable than the mattress on the floor!"

I felt a little surprised and embarrassed when I realized that this was Cole Lawrence who was the same man that said "Good Morning" to me on the first night in the auditorium. We decided to sit at the same table to catch up on any information about our assignments. Cole was a counselor for substance abuse out of the Indianapolis VA Medical Center and he informed me that he was the only one from Indianapolis VA to be deployed. He was working the substance abuse unit at the Alexandria VA. After talking with him for about a half of an hour, Cole hinted that he was displeased with his assignment because he wanted to do something different from his regular job at the Indy VA. I told Cole that starting on Monday, Deana and I were going to be working at the Nazarene Campgrounds doing hands-on work with many victims from Katrina. He gave me his full attention and when I finished he asked, "I would like to do something like that! Do you think they would have room for me to go with you?"

I gave Cole the information that was given to us and told him to go to the personnel office and then he had to clear it through the substance abuse director and if he did it today there would be a very good chance that he would start with us on Monday. Cole headed up to the personnel office and I ambled back into the homeless office where very little work was awaiting me. I was looking forward to working the campgrounds because I was getting bored sitting in an office and doing little to nothing. The little was an interview here and there and the nothing was just sitting there doing nothing, waiting for the shift to be over and wondering just how long the last two days would be in the homeless office and wishing that Monday was already here.

I was walking slowly back to the ward I was staying on when I had concluded my day in the homeless office and as I was walking the grounds, I noticed a mound sticking out of the sandy ground that reminded me of a miniature volcano. Stopping to admire it and crouching down to inspect it more closely, I wondered what kind of insect had the ability to build this structure. The hole/opening at the top was about a third of an inch wide and the insects blended in with the sand which gave me the impression that it was moving sand. As I was gaping at this tiny architectural structure, Cole approached me and stated, "Linda, don't touch that and don't sit on the ground or put your hands near that! Those are fire ants and don't let their size fool you because their bite is vicious and it feels like you put your hand into a fire!"

I stood up to distance myself, but I continued to stare at these tiny creatures that were so busy doing what they do when Cole directed my attention to the edge of the grass where it meets the sandy area near the ant hole. I could barely see the ants, but they were certainly there because I observed a slow-moving dead carcass of a recluse spider that was being carried on the backs of thousands of fire ants that were heading to the volcano opening. When I observed this, my only thought was that the ants were going to have a feast of that recluse spider and I had made that comment out loud and Cole agreed with me. Cole also informed me that he was cleared to join Deana and me on Monday at the Nazarene campgrounds.

Monday morning had finally arrived and the three of us were sitting in the dining room enjoying a full breakfast when Deana pulled out her cell phone and pressed out a number. I thought that she was calling her husband which is what she did every morning to let him know how she was doing and to find out how he was doing. I soon found out that the receiver of this call was not her husband, but rather it was Tim Cavanaugh, who worked at the campgrounds and one of the names of the contacts that was given to us from the personnel manager. It was 7:30 a.m. and when she closed her phone, she turned toward Cole and me and informed us that Tim would be picking us up at 8:00 a.m.

Tim was very punctual and also very pleasant and he was the main van driver to the campgrounds for the VA personnel who were deployed from other VA's throughout the country. Tim was another New Englander who hailed from the State of Maine and the Togus VA. He worked as an admissions clerk in the Maine VA, but he worked as a little bit of everything at the Nazarene campgrounds. The campgrounds were about four or five miles from the Alexandria VA and they were deep into the woods. Tim dropped us off at the entrance of the community center which was a brick building that contained the laundry room, kitchen, food supplies with refrigerators and freezers and a pantry that consisted of hundreds of large cans filled with fruit and vegetables. Loaves of bread were stored in the freezer because the humidity and wetness would turn the bread moldy very quickly if it wasn't stored in a frozen area. When we entered the center we noticed a huge fireplace on the opposite wall and there were about fifteen to twenty tables that a maximum of four people could sit at and eat their meals. We also noticed a table in the lobby area where a blond-haired woman was sitting and when she greeted us, I detected a strong Bostonian dialect. This lady was also a deployed VA person who worked at the Brockton VA medical center in Brockton, Massachusetts and her name was Jean-Nanette. She was in charge of handing out the work assignments to the deployed VA people. She asked the three of us to sit down so that she could describe the camp surroundings and to the type of details that we would be responsible to do. Jean-Nanette was not only informing us of the surroundings, but she also informed us of the rules and regulations and the respect to the members of the Nazarene Church because they are very devout and many do the cooking and the laundry here. She was very informative about everything and she spoke like a travel agent when she described the setup of the campgrounds.

"There are five bunk houses scattered throughout the woods. They are all within view of the center and they are built to resemble log cabins. Each bunk house has ten sets of bunk beds that can sleep twenty people and each house has a full-bathroom with three showers, four toilets and five sinks in them. There was also a large two-story rooming house that looked more like a motel than a rooming house. The rooming house is the building that is located just across the street from this center. There are twenty rooms in that house in which ten are in the front and ten are in the back and this house is also in log cabin style. The Nazarene Church is the white-wood edifice that stands directly across the way from the center. In the basement of the church is a collection of clothing that they acquired through donations. There are clothes for men, women, teenagers, small children and babies and they also consist of a variety of sizes. The only time that you are not allowed to enter the church basement is when services are being conducted in the church which occur every day for two hours. This is one of the instances where you have to be respectful. The kitchen, laundry room and supply room are in this center. This community center is the heartbeat of the entire campgrounds because this is where all interactions take place. I am not going to assign any details to you today. I just want you to scope the grounds and familiarize yourselves to the daily process of hearing the needs of the displaced individuals who enter here every day. Do any of you have any questions?"

Jean-Nanette was very thorough with the explanations and layout of the campgrounds and I only wondered about one question, so I asked, "What time do the details here start in the morning?"

Jean-Nanette smiled and softly stated, "Everyone reports to the grounds at 6 a.m. Monday-Friday or should I say the deployed VA workers report for 6 a.m. The Nazarene workers arrive at 7 a.m. and they cook all the meals. The weekends are different because the Nazarenes do not work on the weekends so we come in and cook the meals starting at 3 a.m."

The three of us appeared to be pleased in hearing the work that we would be doing at this site and we were content to know that we would be assisting the victims of Hurricane Katrina and doing it in a hands-on manner. We decided to take a walk around the campgrounds to get better acquainted with the layout and to talk with some of the victims that lost everything to Katrina.

At 5:45 a.m. the next morning we were boarding the van that was bringing us to our first work-day at the campgrounds. We were excited and ready to do anything that they needed us to do. We entered the community building with Tim who had the key and we followed Tim into the kitchen. He instructed one of us to get a huge soup pot out and fill it with water and place on the stove to boil which was the job that Deana volunteered for because that pot was going to be filled with grits which I never had or had any idea how to make. Cole had the assignment of getting the four very large (36" long) cookie sheets that were filled with sausage patties and he preheated the ovens and then placed all four sheets in there to cook for about a half-hour. I volunteered to make the scrambled eggs which consisted of powdered eggs and two-dozen real eggs and the pan I used covered three burners on the stove because it was so big. Tim was preparing coffee in two 100-cup percolators. We were all together, but separate doing our details. We were very happy and many wondered what was going on in the kitchen because they heard laughter and singing every time we were in there. There was a sign-up list for the meals and people had to sign in so that the cooks knew how many people were eating for that meal. Breakfast people signed the sheet the night before and this was usually done after they ate their supper.

At 7 a.m. the cooking staff began to trickle in and they were very grateful that the breakfast had been started because it saved a lot of time. So they set about lining up the three five-foot long tables in the dining area and placed three toasters with several loaves of different breads, jars of jelly and jams and peanut butter. Along with these items the staff set up a large container filled with ice which contained bottles of three different types of juices. Another table contained the large coffee pots that Tim had brewed with all the milk, creamers and sugar. We all knew that would be the first thought of every adult walking through the door for breakfast. To be able to taste that first swallow of coffee going down their throat because coffee seemed to initiate their minds into figuring out exactly what they wanted to eat for breakfast or any of the meals for that matter.

At 7:45 a.m. Jean-Nanette was sitting at the small table near the front door of the community center and she had the check-off paper of those that would be eating breakfast. Some people were already sitting quietly in the dining area waiting for the food to be ready. I exited the kitchen with a large pan of scrambled eggs and behind me came Cole with his pan full of sausage patties. Deana was too small to carry the pot of grits so Tim grabbed two pot holders and took the pot to the serving table next to the bowls for the grits. There were boxes of cold cereal with four gallons of milk for the children and there was no such thing as running out of anything because everything was there and the supply truck restocked it daily. The time finally arrived and the food was ready to be passed out and the line formed to my right. I was amazed that this process was so organized and everyone was respectful of each other. My thoughts flashed back to my high school days and even some grammar school days when I was part of the lines of children in the cafeteria. Some kids would be pushing each other; others would cut in line so they could be the first ones out so they could talk more with their friends. There was always the ones that finally made it up to the steam/cooking station and would notice what was being served for lunch and would remark, "I don't want any of that! I don't like peas, cabbage or tomatoes!"

There was no one at these campgrounds that uttered any words of dislike because they lost everything and had nothing. They were grateful for anything and everything, no matter how small it was. I felt total satisfaction just from receiving a smile from an adult or a shy child trying to hide behind his/her father's leg and I know that my co-workers felt the same. We didn't ask for these smiles, they were freely given and appreciated by the staff because we knew we were doing something right and beneficial to our fellow human beings.

After breakfast, Jean-Nanette assigned Cole and me to strip the bunks in bunkhouse #4 and to clean the bathroom and shower room. We hauled a full laundry wagon down the path to #4 and as I stripped the beds, all twenty of them, and placed cleans sheets and a blanket on each bunk, Cole was busy cleaning and scrubbing the bathroom. It was muggy and being in the woods with the over-hanging trees seemed to make everything worse. The perspiration was literally dripping off our chins and our clothes were sticking to our bodies, but this didn't prevent us from doing what we were asked to do. I was in the large room putting new sheets on the stripped beds when I noticed Cole standing in the doorway of the bathroom holding something that looked like a women's nylon stocking as he uttered, "Linda, look what I found!"

After seeing him holding it up in the doorway, I responded, "What female left only one of her nylons here? It must have a rip or hole in it!"

Cole snickered and said, "This is not a nylon stocking, it's a snake skin! Some snake has shed his skin in here!"

I immediately stopped moving and turning slowly to Cole I remarked, "WHAT! You mean to tell me that there is a snake in here! I HATE SNAKES! Where in the bathroom did you find that skin?"

Cole was chuckling at my reaction and then proceeded to let me know that the skin was wrapped around one of the pipes under the sinks. My eyes were rotating all over the place and I was hoping that I wouldn't see that slithery varmint anywhere. We finished by about 11:45 a.m. and headed back up the path with the laundry wagon that was now filled with the dirty sheets that I stripped off the beds. It was very close to lunchtime and Cole and I were looking forward to just something cold and refreshing to drink that would replenish the fluids in our bodies that we lost in the mugginess of the bunkhouse.

The community center was filled with people and there wasn't a table to be had when Cole and I arrived after putting the laundry wagon in the laundry room. So we decided to get a cold drink from the soda machine that was on an open cement platform that was to the right of the main door to the center. Upon retrieving our drinks, we sat at one of the long benches that lined the main walkway to the community care center and simultaneously gave a sigh of relief just to sit down. I put my head back just for a moment and noticed the long strand of Spanish moss hanging from an old magnolia tree that was gently swaying from a soft balmy breeze. It was strange that this nice breeze didn't exist when Cole and I were down at the bunkhouse.

We returned to the VA at 7:30 p.m. and the three of us elevated up to the third floor where Deana and Cole took a left off the elevator and I took a right. When I entered my room, I noticed that Lydia's bed was stripped and her belongings were gone. The same for Darren and Abby which left me puzzled because no one knew anything about where they had gone. When I investigated

Darren's room there was someone else assigned to it and Darren's belongings were all gone. The person that was presently in Darren's room just happened to be the same obsessive/compulsive, narcissistic and egotistical "asshole" that had bugged Darren to switch rooms with him when he was first assigned it. Darren had a single room with a full bath and a TV and when everyone went around checking out each other's room, this jerk wanted Darren's room in the worst way. This was another incident where I had to shake my head in disbelief at the VA and their hiring techniques. This individual came from the Northport VAMC on Long Island, NY and from what I heard from others, he was a registered nurse. Nurses have a tough job and rarely does any ever go home with a clean uniform because of patients vomiting, coughing, sneezing or soiling themselves. This nurse from the Long Island VA would go to work with an immaculately pressed uniform that made one think that he was in a medical uniform fashion show and then he would return with the same clean uniform. I was told that he even ironed his "tighty whities" and he never sat down because he didn't want to ruin the perfectly ironed seam in his trousers. He displayed an attitude as if he was the greatest thing that was ever hired by the VA and it was this same attitude that he used to make claim on Darren's room because he felt that he deserved it.

Still wondering what happened to my co-workers from the Northampton VA, I decided to confront Harry about their whereabouts. Harry was another driver of the van that went to the airport and I thought that maybe he might have driven them to the airport. Harry stated, "Linda, the three were assigned to a nursing facility about fifty miles north of here and they were transported there with six others by bus. They will be there until their time is complete and then will go directly to the airport for the return flight home to Massachusetts. I think the next time you see them will be at the airport!"

I thanked Harry for this information and headed back to my room so I could shower and go to bed because I would be back up at 2:30 a.m. so that I would be on the van to go to the campgrounds and begin my work day at 3 a.m.

Working at the campgrounds was highly rewarding for the three of us because we were doing what we were deployed there to do. We were all working 16-17 hours a day and engaged in every detail from cooking and serving to cleaning and mopping floors and not one complaint came out of anyone's mouth. It didn't matter what VA that each of us came from because the VA ways, rules and regulations were the same throughout this great nation. Tim and Jean-Nanette didn't work weekends so Tim gave the van keys to Cole so that we could continue the processing, feeding and housing of displaced Hurricane Katrina and Hurricane Wilma individuals.

Weekends were exceptionally grueling because on Sundays we were the only staff available to assist anyone with their needs. This was because the staff from the Nazarene Church who did the cooking and laundry considered Sundays their day of worship. They were not allowed to labor in any capacity that would take their attention away from their worship. I was invited to attend their Church by one of the elderly staff members who had overheard me when I was talking to Deana about not being able to go to a Catholic Church. In this section of Louisiana, Catholic Churches were few and far between. This surprised me because their counties are called parishes and this State was originally settled by French Catholics. I was working on the far outskirts of Alexandria and I'm sure that the cities would have several Catholic Churches, but Deana and I agreed that we were doing God's work without attending church. Cole was a Baptist and a church-goer as well, but overhearing Deana and me quoting a statement from the bible, "If you have done it to the least of my brothers, then you have done it to me"

We started to state quotations from the bible and directing these statements to each other, we inquired who said it and in what book of the bible was it written. We would do these trivia games and not miss one beat of helping anyone with cooking, serving, cleaning or just placement in a comfortable bed.

There were some VA workers from the New Orleans VA that were being housed at these campgrounds. One in particular was occupying one of the rooms in the motel house. The other VA people from New Orleans were busy working for the VA in Alexandria, but this one individual didn't want to work and just laid around being waited on and just believing that because he was displaced that he was someone special. That kind of attitude never sits well with me! I didn't bother him for about a week, but when a family came to the campgrounds in an old dilapidated truck with everything they owned or could salvage in the truck bed, which wasn't a lot, I knew that this would be the time that that freeloader was going to evicted. Getting out of the truck was a young father and mother and there were three small children that exited the cab with them. I was sitting on the bench near the entrance to the community center when the father approached me and stated, "Am I in the right place?"

I noticed that his wife and children joined him and looking at them I asked, "Well that depends! Where exactly are you heading and is there anything that I can assist you with?"

They all appeared to be tired and puzzled about the surroundings as they stood there looking at me when the father with effort stated, "My family and I have been riding and sleeping in the cab of this truck for two weeks. We came from Lake Charles down near the Texas border where Hurricane Wilma hit us like a bomb. We barely got out with the clothes on our backs. I stopped at the gas station in town to get $4.00 of gas and to try to wash up in the restroom. When the man at the station discovered that I only had $4.00, he told me to come here and that I would get some help. He also gave me a full tank of gas and didn't charge me!"

I told him that the station manager was absolutely correct as I escorted them into the dining area of the community center and asked the kitchen-help to please get them something to eat because they haven't eaten for quite some time. As this family was eating, I prepared to get into battle-mode and to approach the freeloader and to toss him out of the room that this family greatly needed. Knocking on his door with Deana by my side, he gently opened it and the room was a mess. I informed him that he had a half-hour to move his belongings to the bunkhouse because there is a family in drastic need of this room. He wasn't too thrilled about it, but reinforcements are much more convincing than a 1:1 contact. I emphasized that I meant a half-hour and if he dawdled I would have his belongings thrown on the porch and he could pick them up from there. He was out in that time and Deana and I cleaned everything, stripped the beds and re-made them, cleaned the bathroom and placed clean towels for five people. When I returned to the community center the family appeared to be satisfied from eating and was heading to the door and I informed them to please sit down while I go to the supply room to get some things. I picked up soap, shampoo, tooth brushes, toothpaste, combs, powder and deodorant. I handed the bag of goodies to the father and told him to follow me to where they will be staying until they get back on their feet. When I opened the door to the room all their mouths just dropped open. The father uttered, "I don't have any money to pay for this! I only have four dollars!"

Turning to him I said, "You don't have to pay for it! You are homeless! You are displaced because of Hurricane Wilma! As you see there are two double beds and a full bathroom. There is also a TV and two sets of bureaus to put your clothes in and an open closet with a pole and hangers. Meal times are at 8 a.m., 12 noon and 5 p.m. Laundry room is in the community center where you can have your clothing washed and get clean sheets and towels on a daily basis. It is presently 1:15 p.m. and there will be snacks for the kids at 3 p.m. and dinner will be at 5 p.m. Here's your key and do you have any questions for me before I go and leave you to settle in?"

They just stood there in total disbelief and I know that that room was like a castle to them after they lived out of the cab of their truck for two weeks. I returned to the center and sat down at the table with Deana to share an iced tea and I couldn't help smiling because I felt such joy and satisfaction in my heart and couldn't get the surprised expressions of that young family out of my head.

We seemed to be continuously cleaning up the dining room area because this was the area that the children played and watched TV. I was surprised to see several babies along with their parents that were displaced from New Orleans. With the waters still over their heads in many places, they knew that they would have a long wait before they could return to their homes. They wondered if their homes were still standing there or if they had been washed away by the flood waters. It seems that I could never stop smiling every time I entered the center because the children were so cute. Several had to show me a picture they made or a coloring they did, or best of all, to listen to a story that they made up. These were children who had nothing but love and imagination that they freely shared with others. They had respect and didn't demand anything from anybody. After all, when you have nothing how can you demand anything!

Preparations were beginning for dinner and Cole, Deana and I started to assemble the serving tables for the food to be placed on as it came out of the kitchen. Plates, utensils, napkins, condiments and cups were placed on the first table. An enormous cask that contained Kool-Aid or punch was on the next table along with four gallons of milk sitting in a pan surrounded by crushed ice to keep it cold. A salad bowl that was two feet in circumference adorned the next table along with two types of dressing. The hot pans started to come out from the kitchen and I noticed that we were serving spaghetti and meatballs along with garlic bread or plain rolls. The entire staff manned an area of the serving table and the space that I stepped into was to serve the sauce over the spaghetti. People started to line up at the first table and as soon as the last staff member was ready, the line started to move along the front of the serving tables and everything went very smoothly. It was towards the end of the line that I noticed the young family in the chow line. When the father reached me for sauce, he attempted to hand me his four dollars for the meal so I turned to him and said, "Your money is no good here! Remember, I told you that you do not have to pay for anything here. Put your money in your pocket and sit down and enjoy a great spaghetti meal! "

He put his money in his pocket and he held two plates, one for himself and one for his youngest child. His family looked refreshed and much better than they looked when they first arrived to the campgrounds earlier in the day. Smiling at me and feeling energized this young father said, "We all had a hot shower and then we all took a nap! I guess we just passed out because as soon as our heads hit the pillows, it was the last thing I remember and we have you to thank for it!"

I looked affectionately at this young family and said, "You don't have to thank me because all of the staff are doing the job that we were sent here to do. Our job is to assist people that were devastated from the hurricanes and to give them a chance to get back on their feet by providing food, water and a roof over their heads. In some cases, we have even found some employment for people on a full-time or part-time basis."

The entire family gave me the biggest smiles as they continued down the serving lines and I winked at each child as they passed by. There were those smiles again just as they were when I exited their room in the early afternoon.

Time appeared to be passing very quickly and before I could even think about departing and returning home to New England, Cole mentioned that we only had two more days in Louisiana until the big silver birds flew us back to our home perch. This was the first time that I had ever been to Louisiana and I grew very fond of the people and the culture of that State. The only areas that I had any reservations about were with the critters and the Cajun hot sauces. Every restaurant and every dining table in the VA held several bottles of hot sauces that ranged from mildly hot to inferno. I gawked at some of the VA workers that put the inferno sauce on their scrambled eggs and sausage and devoured it without blinking an eye or washing it down with water just to kill the flame. I had taken the cap off the inferno sauce and took a small sniff of it and I believe that it seared the hairs in my nostrils. Thus I was never going to attempt to allow it to enter my mouth. I found that there was an element of difficulty trying to find a hamburger or hot dog that wasn't prepared in Cajun style. Even the potatoes and some vegetables were cooked with Cajun seasoning. I was glad that I had brought three boxes of peanut butter crackers with me because they came in very handy when I was unable to eat the hot saucy foods.

The critters were the other things that I felt was something that I could have done without. But being that I was in their territory, I soon learned to avoid the recluse spiders, alligators, fire ants and a variety of poisonous and non-poisonous snakes. The campground was crawling with snakes, after all the grounds were in the woods and there were swamps all around it. Cole did find a snakeskin in the bunkhouse. I was told that there were rattlesnakes, vipers and cottonmouths which were all poisonous snakes. The only non-poisonous snake that was in abundance there was the black snake, or commonly called a King snake. I inquired why a non-poisonous snake was called a King snake and I was told, "Because he holds his head erect when he crawls and the poisonous ones crawl with heads on the ground until they get surprised and then they coil up and get ready to strike!"

I hate snakes, but I found this information interesting…bizarre, but interesting! I was further informed that vipers are rattlesnakes without the rattles, so they were more dangerous than the rattlers because they have no means of warning anyone that you are getting too close to them.

We worked at the campgrounds seven days a week for 15-17 hours each day. Having just completed our last day at the campgrounds, the three of us decided to get a coke from the machine outside the community center and to sit on the bench and wait for Tim to finish up and drive us back to the VA. We were exhausted and literally dragging ourselves over to the benches. I was the last one to get a coke and as I put my fifty cents in and heard the can drop, I reached down to take it out of the slot when from out under the machine crawled a large black snake about three inches from my foot. I froze in a bending position and watched the snake go off to the left. I noticed that his head was erect so I knew he wasn't poisonous, but I was so tired that I straightened up after retrieving my drink and said, "Just go your way and I'll go mine! I won't bother you because you're not bothering me!"

When I turned to return to the bench, I noticed that Cole and Deana were sitting there with their mouth's gaped open and wondered why I didn't panic or scream. I assured them that I was just too tired to do any of that when we saw the door open. Coming our way was Tim holding the keys and unlocking the van for our return and last trip to the Alexandria VA. We were all leaving the next morning and Tim told me that he would drive me to the airport. Cole was renting a car and driving back to Indianapolis and Deana was leaving a little later in the morning for her flight to Battle Creek, Michigan. Tim would be returning to Togus, Maine the following week because he volunteered for another week. Jean-Nanette's flight to Boston was scheduled in the afternoon, so she was able to pack that morning instead of this evening as I did. With "goodbyes" in order and wishing each other a safe and healthy trip back home, our departure reminded me of spokes on a wheel with everyone heading off in different directions. We met and maintained some solid friendships and remained in contact with each other after we returned to our jobs in the VA's of our home States.

Arriving at the airport in Alexandria, Tim assisted me with my luggage and as we entered the lobby area, I noticed the three co-workers from the Northampton VA were already there. After greeting each other and getting processed for our return flight home, we started to discuss our experiences and details in Louisiana. Our return flight was no different from our arrival flight because we boarded the crop-duster in Louisiana and the flight arrived in Atlanta, GA. This flight wasn't that bad because we were talking among ourselves and telling the stories of what we encountered and experienced and for the most part, the stories were quite comical. Darren, Abby and Lydia were assigned to an abandoned building that now housed survivors of a nursing home that was washed away from Katrina. These survivors were placed in Shreveport, LA which was about sixty miles north of Alexandria. Darren referred to the setting as "Hotel Hell" because these survivors were from a psychiatric nursing home and there were no medications available to administer to them. He said that the orders for the medications were issued when they first arrived in Shreveport. Even after two weeks, the meds had still not arrived and they were dealing with the raw psychiatric personalities that required twenty-four-hour observation to make sure that they would not hurt themselves or anyone else. The stories continued at the Atlanta airport as we waited two hours in the lobby of the concourse for our flight to Hartford, CT. When we boarded our final flight, we decided to be quiet and rest and nap which were the things that we grossly lacked during the past two weeks.

CHAPTER FIFTEEN

I arrived at Bradley International Airport in Hartford, CT at about 6 p.m. on October 11, 2005. My brother David was there along with his wife Shirley and granddaughter Brooke to pick me up and drive me home. They were waiting in the baggage claim area and after greeting them with hugs and kisses, I retrieved my luggage. We exited the sliding door to the parking lot and I took a long sigh of relief just knowing that I would be sleeping in my own bed tonight. My brother travelled the back roads avoiding the heavily travelled highways. He did not want me to hear the sounds of traffic like I experienced the constant humming of the airplane engines that resonated inside the cabin of the plane. I felt relaxed and pleased that I was on the final stage of my journey home from Louisiana when my brother announced, "Linda….I am a grandfather again! Trent David Leary was born this morning and baby and family are doing fine."

Smiling at hearing the good news, I responded, "That's great! That little boy makes the twenty-sixth great nephew/niece that I have! The family is growing. You blink your eyes and there is another addition to the family!"

Each one of the three asked me about my stay in Louisiana and I told them that I couldn't answer them at this time because I was so tired. But, I promised them that we would get together very soon and I would inform them of my experiences and details and critter confrontations of my deployment to Louisiana.

I returned to work at the VA on October 17th and there must have been over seventy messages left on my answering machine, so I knew that my first day back to work would be consumed with returning phone calls and clearing my answering machine. Not only was my answering machine packed with messages, but my messages in the computer were equally as many. It's times like this that I develop "telephonitis" and I feel that the phone receiver is attached to my ear because they never separated all day long. My arm was numb from holding the phone and my hands and fingers started to tingle as a result of the decreased circulation to them. There were patients that walked in to greet me and welcome me back and as they viewed me on the phone or the computer would gently wave and smile or give me a thumb's up to let me know that I was missed. My office was back on ward 4Lower and situated on the extreme southern side where the NVCCC used to be. My office was now in the old conference room because one of the new employees, an MSW, wanted the office I was going to be assigned to. So of course their rights were favored and I had none at all. The move to 4Lower occurred about three months before I was deployed to Louisiana and knowing that I had been employed with the VA for twenty-eight years at this point, made me think that the longer one works in this system, the more one gets stepped on.

Things settled down after the first day back to work and it appeared that I had multiple free times on my hands. I believe that was the result of the packed days of working in Louisiana and my pace was still in high gear. I started to wander into other offices and inquired if there was anything I could help them with to kill some time that I seemed to have an abundance of since my return. I left Chris Robbins office for my last visitation because I knew that he would definitely have something for me to do and that something was work that he didn't like to do or avoided at all cost. I would wonder "why" he avoided certain elements of his job and I soon learned that it was because he didn't know how to do it or didn't understand the process. It was at this point, that I fully understood Chris's behaviors of ignoring certain employees and patients and the reason why he always left without informing anyone where he was going or how long he would be gone. Everything was making sense to me because he didn't invest any interest into learning his job because he just wanted to collect a pay check and not apply himself to work for it. As I sat there at my desk chuckling to myself and slowly shaking my head back and forth, I also realized that Chris was only one of several "bump-on-a-log" employees, whose only interest was in the pay and basically nothing and no one else.

In January 2006, I was approached by my supervisor who entered my office and pleasantly sat in the chair on the left side of my desk. She sat quietly and politely, waited until I finished the note I was writing on in the computer. When I finished, I turned my attention to her and after greetings she smiled at me and stated the reason she was there, "Linda, there is no social worker on Ward 4Upper and the one that was there is presently out on sick leave and I don't think that he will be returning. So, I thought of you and I think that you would fit in very well on that unit. You will be going from an outpatient service to inpatient service and you will have a new supervisor because I can no longer be your supervisor as a result of you going inpatient!"

Being a little in a shock state, I responded, "Who will be my new supervisor?"

As she slowly stood up from the chair, she said, "You'll be under the supervision of Dr. Victor Garcia MD! He is in charge of all the inpatient units!"

I didn't want to smile with pleasure because I don't think she was aware that I worked with Dr. Vic when I was at the Northampton Community Care Center. He was the doctor or one of the doctors that treated the outpatients on Thursdays. I inquired, "Does the unit know that I will be assigned there and when would I begin this new assignment?"

I like to get my ducks in line and Dr. Dabbs was very aware of this characteristic of mine because she told me that I was an organized, concrete thinker, years ago. She turned to me and stated, "The target date for your transfer to Ward 4U is February 17th and I informed Dr. Krainski and the staff of your assignment to their unit. In the meantime, it would be wise if you went upstairs and introduced yourself to the staff!"

I watched Dr. Dabbs exit my office and disappear down the hallway. I then swiveled my chair around to face the window and stared at the swiftly moving clouds above the trees that were blanketed by a dusting of snow that was melting from their leafless branches. I was surprised and pleased at this new assignment because I would no longer be accountable to the homeless office and knew that the new employees and Chris Robbins would now have to do their jobs. I was no longer the scapegoat of their mistakes or errors, but I knew that I would greatly miss talking and directing the patients to better places to live and receiving monies or acquiring employment because I had to concentrate on inpatients and no longer would be assisting outpatients. The remaining homeless staff would be responsible to assist these Veterans. I also felt that I should approach Dr. Garcia first before approaching the staff on 4U because he was going to be my new supervisor and I needed to know what his expectations of me would be.

I decided to approach Dr. Garcia on February 3rd and to inquire of the goals that he wanted me to achieve or at least attempt to achieve on 4 Upper. The door to his office was open and he was sitting at his computer when I approached his office door and after knocking, I stated, "Sorry for this interruption, but your worst nightmare is standing in your doorway! I was told by Dr. Dabbs that you are my new assigned supervisor and that I am being assigned to Ward 4 Upper and I will start this assignment two weeks from today! I only have one question for you! What do you want me to do on that unit? I have been working outpatient for seventeen years and now I am being assigned inpatient duties and I need to know what your expectations of me are!"

Dr. Vic lifted his head and stared at the wall in front of him and never turning his head to look at me, put a smile on his face and said, "Linda, I want you to place those Veterans in the community!"

Without uttering another word, he returned to his computer and as I stood dumbfounded in the door, I said, "IS THAT IT? Well Boss, consider it done!"

As I turned in the doorway to return to my office, I heard Dr. Vic respond to my statement by saying, "I know it will be done because I know your capabilities!"

I couldn't help but smile as I walked down that hallway on my return trip to my office on 4Lower.

It seemed strange getting back into my job in the homeless office after working sixteen and seventeen hours in my deployment to Louisiana. I felt that I had more downtime here compared to being constantly busy and accountable for every assignment in the campground and recalling several occasions when I worked through meals and so-called breaks. There were no computers to communicate on or even phones to make calls. I wasn't even worried about these instruments because the victims I was working with didn't have them either and didn't express any concern about acquiring them. These are the thoughts that were passing through my mind as I stared at the screen of my computer and listened to the phones ringing in the other offices. I completed my office work and contemplated going to 4Upper and introducing myself to Dr. Krainski and discuss the position that I would be taking as an inpatient social worker in two weeks.

Dr. Beatrice Krainski was a delightful and friendly individual as she bid me to take a seat in her office so that I would be more comfortable. She had a strong Polish accent and stated that she was grateful that I was sent there because they were having trouble trying to discharge patients without a social worker on staff. After we talked for fifteen minutes, Dr. Krainski gave me a tour of the ward and introduced me to several employees who were busy in the nurse's station. Some of the patients and employees were familiar to me having worked with them in the distant past or visited them in the residential homes that they were once placed in. I noticed this one particular Veteran who was sitting in a reclining chair and repeating, very sarcastically, every word that was stated by the newscaster on the radio. He was almost comical because he was repeating in a sing-song manner as he attempted to maneuver within a four square foot area in the dayroom. Initially, he had his back towards me and as he slowly turned around, my mouth dropped because he resembled a Veteran that was assigned to give me a tour of a residential care home back in 1986, in Pittsfield MA. Dr. Krainski had excused herself because she was summoned into the nurse's station to write a medication order. As I nonchalantly gazed at this Veteran who appeared to be so familiar to me, I started to have my doubts that he was one and the same because even though his facial features were an exact duplicate, his physique was no match. The Veteran that I knew was built like a football player and for those that knew him referred to him as "the gentle giant" but for those that didn't know him, would probably find his stance to be threatening. My curiosity was killing me so I approached the nurse and stated, "Excuse me, but some of the Veterans on this unit appear familiar to me! For instance, the Veteran who is singing statements from the radio has the facial feature of a patient that I knew years ago in a residential home in Pittsfield, but his build does not match. This patient is extremely slight and has difficulty ambulating and the one I knew was built like a football player."

The nurse rolled her eyes to my right and inquired if I was referring to the patient in the recliner and nodding my head affirmatively, she asked, "What was the name of the Veteran you knew in Pittsfield?" I responded, "His name was Clifford Franklin!"

Smiling at me while she reached for another chart said, "Linda, that Veteran is Clifford Franklin!"

As I slowly turned around to observe this frail, small individual who was repeating words and comments that he heard from the radio, I just couldn't believe that this was the same robust, cooperative person in the residential care home who gave me a tour of the home and gathered the Veterans for a meeting that I listed on a piece of paper. I ventured near Cliff and called him by name. He didn't budge from his shuffling through newspapers and magazines and the only comment he stated was, "Oh! They're looking for Cliff…Cliff…Cliff…that little bastard!"

He repeated this line over and over again in sing-song style without any interruption in the rhythm in the way he was saying it. This made me feel sad, so I decided to return to my office downstairs and finish up some work in the homeless office before my official transfer to Ward 4Upper in two weeks.

The next two weeks passed quickly and my transition to Ward 4U was smooth and comfortable. There was no office space available for me on 4U so I was assigned an office on the substance abuse end of ward 4Lower. It was on the opposite end from the homeless program and a much smaller office than I had before in the homeless program. I went from an office that was a meeting room to an office that was roughly a 9'X7' space, but I managed to make it comfortable for myself and Veterans and the Veterans were more interested in the candy bowl that I always kept full of a variety of sweets, instead of the size of the office I occupied.

When it was official and I was transferred to 4U on a full-time basis, my first introduction was to the cardex meeting in which every staff that was available, attended to discuss every patient that was on that unit. Along with the doctor, there was a physician's assistant, charge nurse, chaplain, psychologist, social worker and a recreation therapist. Every patient was discussed and their needs addressed for medications or a change of medications, work details on the hospital grounds, upcoming trips were presented from the recreation therapist. But mostly, the discussion centered about the changes in behavior and attitude of the Veterans. I found this meeting to be very informative because the patients that were progressing were the Veterans that I prioritized for placement in the community. I noticed that every time I wrote a name down on my list, Dr. Krainski was looking at me and smiling. She apparently knew what my motive was when I penned a patient's name on my pad. The physician's assistant was Russell Considine whom I knew and was surprised to see on 4U because he was the P.A. (physician assistant) on the substance abuse unit on 4L when I first made his acquaintance. Russ had a quiet disposition and never spoke much unless he was familiar with the employee. Yesterday, Russ approached me in the parking lot and stated, "Linda, whenever there is a new employee on the unit they have to bring bagels and cream cheese to the first meeting that they attend!"

Staring into his eyes I said, "Oh really…and just how many bagels is the new person having to bring to this grand assembly?"

Smiling at me, he knew that I wasn't falling for his request, but I told him that I would buy bagels and cream cheese for the entire day-staff for tomorrow's meeting. The bagels and cream cheese were in the middle of the table and each staff member helped themselves to a bagel of their choice without causing any hesitations or breaks in reporting changes, good or bad, of the ward patient population.

When it became my turn to speak about discharging and placing the Veterans in the community, I specifically asked the doctor and P.A. if I could take three or four Veterans at a time to visit various residential homes so that it would allow them to make the choice of where they would like to reside. By allowing the Veteran to make his choice of residence, it greatly decreased their re-admission process to the hospital because they were where they wanted to be and not where they were just placed because there happened to be an opening. Taking Veterans out and showing them different places was highly beneficial to the doctor and the Veteran because personalities are varied and many times what one Veteran liked another disliked and I started to realize that Veterans were comfortable in placements that closely matched their own personalities. I was not aware that the visitation process was that popular until referrals started to pour in from other wards. Veterans were making requests to be transferred to 4U because they knew that they would have a decent residential placement when they were discharged as a result of their own personal choice. I was asked by several Veterans if they could go to visit many different possible residential homes and it would swamp the doctor and nurses with discharges. I was asked to slow down the discharges by the staff because there were too many at one time. Along with the discharges, they were also admitting Veterans from other wards and they couldn't keep up with the paperwork. Dr. Garcia would visit the ward once a week and would smile every time he saw me. Dr. Garcia stopped me in the hallway and stated, "You're doing a terrific job!"

I wasn't surprised by his compliment and remarked, "I'm only doing what you asked me to do and sometimes a little bit more, but then again you know me!"

As an inpatient social worker, I was not assigned patients on a caseload basis as were the psychologist, physician assistant and some nurses. I had a caseload on the PTSD unit, the Community Care Center and the Homeless Program, but I never had a caseload as an inpatient worker because there was an MSW available to do that. My job was to place patients in the community, inquire of benefits from Social Security, VA and various Veteran Benefit Counselors throughout the New England area. There was rarely an hour that passed that there wasn't a Veteran approaching to inquire about benefits that he might qualify for or the possibility of placement in the area or out of State.

I enjoyed this assignment and even though my office was downstairs, there was a line-up of Veterans to see me as I entered the ward after climbing the rear staircase. I also started to report to work at 6 a.m. because there were patients that were given 8 a.m. appointments with doctors outside the VA or they had interviews with landlords or managers in the community. I would make a weekly schedule for these Veterans and would tell them the exact day and time that we would go for their interview or appointment and would also tell them to clear everything for that day and if they already had an appointment with someone in the VA, I would change their day to one that was open with no appointments. On occasion, I would be confronted by a Veteran who demanded that I drive him to an appointment in West Haven, CT or Boston and I would remark, "I'm sorry, but that is out of my jurisdiction! There is a shuttle bus that goes to Boston and West Haven every day from this VA garage with a designated driver. If you need a ride, you have to tell the nurse and she will call the garage and put your name on the list for transportation to these other VA hospitals."

I could see that this Veteran was confused by my statement when he stated, "I see you driving many patients from this unit to appointments I don't understand why you can't bring me!"

Smiling understandably at this Veteran, I said, "Any Veterans that have appointments with other VA's have to be transported by the shuttle. I bring Veterans from this unit only to various residential care homes, nursing homes and social security appointments in this area. Sometimes, I go out of State into New York, Vermont, New Hampshire and Connecticut, but it is strictly for community placement of these Veterans or the possibility of a placement for these Veterans."

This situation didn't occur often, but there always was a patient or two who would make demands for a ride to another VA or even better, to a court hearing in another State and when they were told that I didn't do that, they'd think that I didn't like them and complain to the staff. Most of the time, I would explain the reasoning behind my unavailability for their request, but the staff knew what my job entailed and would explain to these Veterans the difference between my transporting and the shuttle's inter-VA transportation system.

I met several Veterans that were unfamiliar to me because they were transferred from other VA's or were an admission from a public or private hospital. There were also the Veterans that were hard to place because of their psychiatric diagnosis of paranoid schizophrenia which when approached about community placement, they would relapse and become assaultive. Fred Baganelli was one of these patients with assaultive behavior. Many of the staff would avoid him when he was in a mood, but he was generally cooperative with the ward milieu. Fred was an inpatient at the Northampton VA for close to two years and I was told that it took him a while to acclimate himself to the facility. He hailed from Connecticut and I was told that his family had totally disinherited him because of assaulting anyone he came in contact with, be it verbal or physical. I would observe Fred from the nurse's station and noticed that he didn't communicate with other Veterans and always sat in the corner of the dayroom alone. I approached Fred in a slow and easy way because he was suspicious of everyone and being fairly new to the unit, I wanted the more difficult Veterans to get used to my presence as a staff member. Several times, I would sit at a table in the dayroom talking with a Veteran in general conversation and would purposely sit close enough to Fred so that he was able to hear our conversation which consisted of teaching the patient a new way of playing solitaire or answering a clue to a crossword puzzle or maybe just answering a Jeopardy question on the TV. The chair that I would sit in was getting closer and closer to Fred's chair and when I saw that the only seat available was the chair right next to him, I stood a little hesitant to sit in it. Fred noticed me standing there and stated, "Linda, you can sit there! I like hearing you answer questions!"

I was shocked that he addressed me by my name, but pleased and honored that he invited me to sit down which I readily did in the chair right next to him. Fred was listed as unapproachable and difficult and with this invitation to me by him, broke the ice for other staff to approach him. He appeared to soften in speech and association and started to communicate with other Veterans on the unit as well as other staff members from other shifts. He really had a pleasant personality and a great smile and with the benefit and maintenance of medications, Fred became an active and involved Veteran on the unit.

Things appeared to be running smoothly on 4U and Veterans and staff appeared to be content with everything. This situation lasted about five months when I was approached by the day nurse and was told that Fred Baginelli was bumming money and cigarettes off of other Veterans and that he had no more money in his account. Looking at this informant, I inquired, "Doesn't he get social security? How long has he been bumming from others? Lastly, how long has his patient funds account been void of monies?"

The nurse gave me an expression that told me she was completely confused with the questions I just asked her. She related little to no information about these questions and I knew that she was requesting my service to talk to Fred and retrieve this information from him. I smiled at her as my mind was saying,

"I love how people pass the buck around here when they don't want to do their job!"

When I exited the nurse's station it was 6:45 a.m. and I noticed that Fred was one of several patients heading to the nurse's office for his morning meds. Fred was not a morning person, so I informed the office nurse that I would talk to Fred sometime today, but not this morning because it takes him time to wake up.

The morning progressed in the usual fashion with patients attending their details or scheduled appointments and the staff had their usual meetings that they had to attend. At 11 a.m., I noticed Fred sitting in the dayroom watching TV so I approached him and said, "Fred, do you receive any benefits?"

I didn't want to approach him in the respect that I knew he had no income or finances, nor to let him know that a staff member informed me that he was bumming cigarettes and monies from other Veterans. If he had known, he would have reacted like a canon and exploded at everyone. I finally got him to a point of trusting me and I didn't want his paranoia to overwhelm him and put him back on the defensive. Upon asking Fred this question, he looked at me and said, "Why are you asking me this?"

Sitting in the chair next to him, I responded, "Fred, you used to go to the canteen for coffee and you also would attend different events and trips through the recreation hall. At times, I would notice you sitting on a bench in the smoke shack between Bldgs. 4 and 6. Now you're spending more time sitting on this ward and I was just wondering if there was anything wrong with your finances because you are not involved anymore in these past activities of yours."

His eyes were looking at the floor and slowly raising his head and looking at me, he uttered, "I get a social security check, but all of a sudden they stopped and they don't send me them anymore!"

"When did they stop sending you a check FRED?"

"It's been a long time, said Fred."

I felt like I was trying to pull teeth out of a tiger getting him to give me specific answers and questioning him in short questions appeared the only solution. I inquired, "What's a long time?"

Fred appeared comfortable because he was leaning on the arm rest of the chair in my direction when he informed me that he hadn't received a check in over a year and a half. I couldn't understand how he survived without any money and that's when he informed me that some of the other Veterans had lent him money and he owes it back to them. I asked Fred if he could meet me in my office at 9 a.m. tomorrow morning so that we could call social security and find out what happened to his checks and why they stopped. Fred agreed to these arrangements.

At 9 a.m. the following morning, Fred was true to his word as he arrived at my office in a punctual manner. As he sat down in the chair next to my desk, he noticed my coffee-maker and a full pot of coffee and inquired if it was possible for him to have a cup of coffee. Smiling at him, I swiveled my chair around, grabbed a mug and poured him a great cup of coffee, asked him what he has in it, then handed him the mug prior to my inquiries to him of his SS (Social Security) check. I needed some more information from him before making a phone call to the Social Security office in Holyoke. After I received the information from Fred, I explained the process and the questions that the social security representative would ask him when I dialed that office. Fred appeared to look bewildered as he listened intently to every word that was coming out of my mouth. When I finished the explanations, Fred stated, "Why is he asking me questions? I'm not going to talk to them and I don't know what to say!"

Seeing Fred's uneasiness, I calmly told him, "Fred, I will dial the social security office and will connect you to a representative, but they require that the individual who is filing for benefits speak to them directly. If you get nervous or anxious, hand the phone to me and I will explain your situation to the representative, but you have to remain here to confirm certain questions or statements that he asks."

Fred did well for about five minutes talking to the representative, but as soon as he was asked something that he didn't understand, Fred quickly handed me the phone receiver and said, "I don't understand what he's talking about! I don't know about some paper he's talking about!"

In answering the phone, I identified myself to the representative and told him that I was employed at the VA hospital in Leeds, MA and that I was the social worker assigned to Fred and further stated that Fred was an inpatient at this VA facility. This representative was very helpful and pleasant and stated that Fred's checks for the past year and three quarters have been returned to social security because he failed to fill out the annual paper stating that he is still disabled. He could no longer receive these checks in the direct mail. Social Security requires the payee to have a direct deposit account. I inquired about the annual questionnaire form for extending his disability benefits and the representative asked me if it was possible to come to the office because there were other forms that he needed Fred to sign before his checks could be re-issued. I confirmed with this gentleman that I could have Fred there at the earliest date he gave me and I was pleased that he gave me a date that was two days away and the first appointment in the morning. Placing the receiver back in the cradle of the phone, I turned my attention to Fred and explained to him that he has to go to the social security office in person. In order to reinstate his checks, there were several forms that he had to sign and that I would escort him there and back. I also told Fred that I thought we should make a morning of this because we also had to go to a bank so that he could open a direct-deposit account as social security no longer mails checks to personal addresses. Fred had an expression of non-comprehension on his face about the phone call and the explanation of the process that he had to do, but he was also pleased of the fact that he would be getting the benefit checks issued to him again that he missed for the past two years.

When Thursday arrived, I requisitioned a government vehicle from the garage to drive Fred to his appointment in Holyoke at the Social Security office. Fred was a little anxious, but manageable and cooperated with everything that was asked of him in the office. He looked in my direction several times when he didn't understand the question or the papers he was signing. I would assist in the answers and explain to Fred in terminology that he would better understand. When the papers were all signed and the reinstatement process was complete, the social security representative informed Fred that he had to get a direct-deposit account. As soon as he got a direct deposit account, he had to call this representative back and give him the numbers of the account and the banking institution. The representative further stated to Fred that he had returned social security checks in the amount of a little over \$25,000 and these checks will be deposited into his account as soon as the account is established.

As we exited the social security building and returned to the car, I informed Fred that he had to choose a bank in Northampton to which he can establish a direct-deposit account because the bank was going to be our next stop. Fred selected a bank in the Florence section of Northampton which was very close to the VA and he felt that this bank would be convenient for him. We entered the side door of the bank, walked up four steps and approached a teller for information about direct deposit accounts. The Teller was pleasant and directed us to take a seat in the waiting area while she tried to contact someone in the accounts department. Fred was nervous and turning to me he said, "Linda, could you please talk for me because I don't know what to say!"

I assured Fred that I would do the bulk of speaking, but if he/she asks for personal information then he would have to answer himself. Fred began to get relaxed after I told him that I would talk for him and he also felt that the time in the waiting area was beneficial to him and eased his mind for ten minutes before we were called into the bank representative's office. Things were going smoothly and Fred was doing well through the process in obtaining a direct-deposit account and the only time that he froze on the spot was when the account representative stated that he needed a \$10.00 deposit to open the account. Fred's eyes were the size of half-dollars and he moved to the front of the chair ready to bolt out the door because he didn't have any money to open the account. Seeing his potential reaction and terminating it before it began, I turned to the representative and stated, "Sir, Fred has no money and this is the reason that he has to get this account so that his social security checks can be re-instated. I will give you the \$10.00 to open his account because he needs to contact social security to give them the numbers for the account so the disability checks are issued to him as soon as possible!"

The account representative applied the money to opening Fred's account and he wrote down all the information that Fred would need to inform the social security office that he had acquired/opened a direct-deposit account at that bank in Florence.

As we left the bank and finished all the business of the morning, we got in the car and headed back to the VA Medical Center. I thought that Fred's behavior was exceptional for all the stops that we made. So, I pulled into a convenience store and I told Fred to follow me into the store and when I reached the counter, I turned and asked Fred, "What kind of cigarettes do you smoke?"

Looking at me with a blank expression on his face he stated, "I have been smoking generics because I couldn't afford the name brands. I can't even afford the generics!"

Letting out a soft sigh, I said, "When you could afford the name brands…what brand did you smoke?"

"I smoked Winstons!"

I turned back around to the clerk and directed him to take two packs of Winstons from the rack which I purchased for Fred. I handed Fred the packs as he stood there in disbelief that an employee bought him cigarettes, but I assured him that he deserved an award for his full cooperation and participation in getting his finances back in play. We returned to the VA and I told Fred to smoke a cigarette outside and then meet me in my office to make the phone call to social security to give them the numbers of his account. I further informed Fred that I wanted him to make a call to the bank every other day just to check on any deposits to his account. Fred was like clockwork in making these calls and a week later when he called from my office to the bank, he was told that $25,000 had been deposited into the account. He was walking on air and I told him to ask for a pass to go into town and withdraw money for things that he needed. He informed me that he was going to ask for a pass for tomorrow and as he opened the door he said, "Thank you very much, Linda! There is nobody else in this hospital that would have helped me get my social security back… but you!"

I wanted to reassure him that there were many who would have done the same, but I knew that Fred was a man of few words and I didn't want to burst his bubble of feeling happiness and contentment. So, I accepted his compliment, shook his hand and smiled as he exited my office.

Chapter Sixteen

I was more off the ward than on it because there wasn't a day that went by that I wasn't taking a Veteran for some sort of interview such as housing, Social Security, Veterans benefits, residential homes and nursing homes. I also had a few trips to courthouses in Northampton, North Adams and Chicopee to clear up some minor infractions that the Veterans had pending. Then again, there were the more serious cases when the Veteran violated a restraining order not once, but three times or breaking and entering with a potential threat of harm to an individual and these Veterans were scoffed off to jail directly from the court. I wasn't surprised when I was informed that many of the crimes that these Veterans committed were under the influence of alcohol and drugs.

Dry periods also occurred when I had no one scheduled for a trip and it was these times that I enjoyed being on the ward and getting to know the new admissions to the unit. Some days I was overwhelmed by the number of Veterans that wanted to talk to me and for the most part, talking with Veterans that were assigned to me by the MSW because she felt uneasy with these particular Veterans. I had heard that some of the Veterans would storm into the MSW office and demand that she write a letter in their defense for court or for housing and in a few cases, a letter to the benefits representative in their town/city. Several times when a Veteran was transferred to our ward from another ward, no information about the Veteran was forwarded with him. It was as if everything had to be started over and this was highly irritating to the Veteran and to me! One would think that all paperwork would be complete and in order along with a list of medications, admitting diagnosis, prognosis at the time of transfer, bio-psychosocial and any precautionary behaviors that the staff needed to know. In the beginning, everything was in order when a patient was transferred to another ward, but then things started to slowly slack off on a continuum of less and less information presented to the staff of the ward that the patient was being transferred. Thus, the staff of the new ward had to acquire the information from the patient. Many times the patient would become irate and state, "I already answered these questions on the other ward!"

Seeing their disappointment at the repetitious questions and the irritating expression on their faces, I remarked, "I'm sure you did answer these questions, but there is no record that was sent over to this ward concerning your intake interview. So, apparently I have to ask you these same questions again because this unit needs this information about you so that we can give you the proper treatment you deserve. I'm sorry for this inconvenience!"

Many times I thought it was impossible for anyone working in the VA system to not do their job because everyone from the director to the kitchen worker was employed to work and care for the Veterans; not to do as they darn well please, but to do it for the Veterans. My boss and supervisor was always the Veteran. I didn't work for the director, I didn't work for the supervisor, I worked, at all times, for the Veteran. I cringed many times over the years when I would hear an employee make statements such as, "I came to the VA because of the benefits and the great pay!"

"I like the pay and the work isn't that hard even though these people are crazy, just ignore them and they will go away!"

If looks could kill, there would be several employees who wouldn't have known what hit them. I am fortunate that my stare could not pulverize individuals, although there have been several who have backed off when they saw my unblinking stare over the top of my glasses and instinctively knew not to approach me. The issue with employees showing total disregard for the Veterans was something that occurred within the last fifteen years. Many psychologists and social workers who had just graduated from college apply at the Veterans Administration Medical Centers because they were told that the best job you can get is with the government. I understand that they have student loans that they have to pay back, but if they are only there for the money and are not comfortable working with the Veterans then they shouldn't apply at the VA! I always hated it when I would slip into this thinking mode of judging new employees by the statements that come out of their mouths because I don't really know them on a personal basis, therefore what right do I have to establish a mental opinion about them. Then again, they have no right to make the degrading statements about the Veterans and a few times I have nonchalantly approached these sarcastic employees and stated, "You wouldn't have a job if it wasn't for the Veteran! Think about that…and think about who you are working for!"

With this point being stated, I would retreat to my office to continue seeing Veterans and assist them in their needs, knowing the worker whom I had just spoken to was mulling over the statements I just made to them.

Jane La Croix was the physician's assistant assigned to 4Upper. She worked all over the medical center from the admissions ward to the PTSD unit and chronic psychiatry. Now, she was working the same unit as I and by working with her, I became more familiar with her than just greeting her on a stairwell or passing her in the canteen. Jane was a phenomenal PA who invested her entire attention into her job. She was very thorough with each Veteran she treated. She took every symptom from a runny nose to a sharp abdominal pain very seriously. I respected and enjoyed working with Jane because we developed a system of discharging Veterans that could not be matched by any other unit in the medical center. The discharge process went as follows, #1 In staff meetings, I would be given a name/names of Veterans who were ready to be discharged and asked to place them in the community as soon as possible. After scribbling the names on my note pad and waiting for the meeting to conclude, I would write the perspective names in Jane's weekly log book that was in the nurse's station.

#2 Jane would view her log every morning and look for upcoming discharges so that she had all appointments and medications ordered for the Veteran. I would call for their psychiatry appointments in the mental health clinic if they were returning to their home or apartment or remaining in the area at the shelter or a boarding house. Everything was done so that the Veteran's discharge proceeded as smoothly as possible, thus preventing any delays that would tend to increase any anxiety for the Veteran. Not often, but periodically, Jane would approach me and inform me that a Veteran could not be discharged because they had not finished all the testing that needed to be completed before they could be discharged. Changing someone's discharge date was never a problem because all the information was collected a week in advance, so if the date needed to be changed to two or three weeks away as a result of further testing, it was easily done.

#3 The Veteran was the last individual to be notified of his/her discharge which usually occurred within a week of their discharge date because of the possible changes that could take place that could cause them frustration, disappointment or anxiety.

#4 The discharging Veteran was asked to pack his bags the night before his discharge so that everything could be carted to the van in one trip.

This process was highly successful for patient and staff alike and it made for a smooth transition from the VA to placement in the community or back to their residences. Prior to all discharges, Veterans that needed placement in the community were given a tour of area boarding houses, halfway houses, residential care homes and shelters so that they were able to choose where they would like to reside.

When assigned to a ward, one is part of a team that consists of several different staff members whose total interest and concern is focused on the care and treatment of the Veterans. It is absolutely impossible for any single staff member to function alone on a ward because the views and suggestions of every team member are required to care for the Veteran. That is the reason there are staff meetings so that all members can participate in the care of ALL Veterans. I mentioned all because some team members only wished to work with patients that were compliant and cooperative and when there was a Veteran whom they felt was the most miserable individual on the east side of the Mississippi River, all heads would turn to me and ask if I would handle this Veteran. It was one of these moments in a staff meeting that I made the following statement, "Yes, I will work with this individual, but I want to tell you all a story that I have used in anger management and when I finish the story I will direct one question to all of you!"

"It was a very hot and sultry Sunday morning in a small town in Arizona. An elderly couple exited their

air conditioned apartment to walk five-hundred yards across some desert to attend their church. The couple entered the church and walked down the aisle to the front pew. The church had no air conditioning and the elderly woman was fanning herself with the missal when she fell asleep and was dreaming about the French Revolution and she was in a cart on her way to the guillotine, sitting side by side with Marie Antoinette. The cart stopped at the stairs of the guillotine and the old woman was escorted up the stairs by two French soldiers as her hands were bound behind her. She was told to kneel down and place her head on the yoke and as the executioner pulled the peg to drop the blade, the old woman filled with fear, had a heart attack and slumped forward in church and died instantly!

What is wrong with this story? There is something very wrong and the only clue I'm going to give you is that the only ones that correctly figured out what was wrong with this story were these difficult Veterans that you feel you cannot deal with or treat or even give advice!"

I had to snicker inside myself as I observed the blank expressions on the faces of these professionals as they turned left and right to inquire with each other if they had an answer to what they thought was wrong with the story. As each attempted to figure out the problem and to arrive at a solution in their group discussion, I stated, "This is how it is supposed to be with every Veteran in this meeting! Every Veteran regardless of their problems, behaviors or personalities should be discussed by the group and not pushed off to a single employee! If we are professionals, then let us function as professionals and provide equal care and treatment to every Veteran that crosses the threshold in the VA! You are all trying to figure out the story and what is wrong with it as if the story symbolically represents the Veterans that are compliant and cooperative and the storyteller appears to represent the difficult patient because no one approached me with any questions!"

Barry looked at me and stated, "You said you were only giving us one clue!"

"That is true; I never said that you could not ask me any questions! You assumed that yourselves!"

After saying this, a barrage of questions headed my way from the staff and I knew that the difficult Veteran would be treated equally by this staff from this point on, but in no way was I going to freely give them the answer to the story. It was up to them to figure it out! About a week later, one of the nurses that was in the meeting approached me and very quietly whispered the correct answer to me and also informed me that she didn't voice her answer to anyone else on the ward. After congratulating her in figuring out the correct answer, I walked to my office and as I sat in my chair I gazed down the hallway and observed several staff members that were caring for the Veterans with total understanding and concern for their welfare. These are the moments that make me proud to be working with individuals that truly care about our Veterans. These thoughts quickly vanished when a Veteran knocked on my door and requested if he could speak with me. I beckoned for him to enter and take a seat and as he did he asked if he could close the door because he didn't want anyone else to hear the conversation. I obliged his request and knew that this was going to be a serious conversation that would be taking place.

In January 2009, it seemed as if the admissions were professional or semi-professional individuals coming in for treatment. Many of them had substance abuse problems and were on a list to enter the substance abuse treatment program that was downstairs. The substance abuse program was an outpatient program and being that these patients came from out of State, they had to be housed on the ward because they could not travel daily to a program that was 21 days duration to complete. These professional and semi-professional patients were from the fields of fire fighters, policemen, executives, nurses and deep sea fishermen. Thus, they had homes to return to after their treatment which eliminated me from seeking housing for them in the community. Jesse hailed from Vermont and having an alcohol problem which he had trouble controlling, resulted in his first admission to the Northampton Veterans Administration. He transferred to 4U from 7U exhibiting an interest to do anything in handling his alcohol problem. Jesse was assigned to my caseload and was awaiting admission to the substance abuse program in which the application was sent to them from the social worker on 7U. In his interview with me, Jesse stated that he was a deep-sea fisherman and his last employment was in Florida, where he fished for marlin and halibut. He expressed interest in returning to this line of work and told me that there was an opening in the harbor in New York City. I sat there puzzled because when I think of NYC harbor, the only thought is a tugboat captain guiding the big ships into port. Jesse started to laugh and stated, "The fishing is done off the extreme end of Long Island, but the catch is brought into the main wharfs in the city, but I'm only thinking of applying, it's not a done deal!"

"Is Florida the only place that you fished?"

"Oh no…I worked off of Nantucket Island, Martha's Vineyard and Gloucester!"

Slowly turning my head and dropping the pen and looking at Jesse, I inquired, "You worked out of Gloucester, MA! By chance, did you function as a sword boat fisherman?"

Jesse looked at me with a smirk on his face and he could tell by my inquiry the information that I was interested in hearing from him, so he remarked, "Linda, I was a sword boat captain and I knew every crew member on the Andrea Gail and also the crew on the Hannah Boden!"

I couldn't believe that I was sitting next to someone who knew the crew of the Andrea Gail that sank in the North Atlantic in 1993. Hollywood produced the picture, "The Perfect Storm" which was one of my favorite pictures depicting this tragic event. Jesse stated that he had also seen the movie and further stated that no one knows what happened on the boat because there was no communication from the Andrea Gail once the storms collided. The filling of the story was Hollywood's version of what they thought occurred when the sword boat was out at sea. Jesse further stated, "I remembered that crew being very responsible and dedicated to sword fishing and many times we told stories of our fishing trips over a shot of booze and a beer in one of the dock pubs! I was working in Florida when I heard that the Andrea Gail went down with the crew and that there was nothing that was found of her ever existing. The ocean is unpredictable…if you respect her than she'll respect you!"

Jesse and I talked for two hours when an aide knocked on my door to inform Jesse that it was time for lunch. He rose from the chair and stated that he enjoyed the discussion and that he was pleased that there was interest in him as an individual and in his line of work. He also stated to me that he would like to further the discussion at a later date and time that would be convenient for both of us.

Jesse was only one of several Veterans that I encountered that were employed in high-risk jobs that could honestly be listed as life-threatening. Many Veterans are attracted to jobs that put their lives at risk. They are still in the combat mode that they experienced during war in Vietnam, Desert Storm or Iraq. If they were asked to go back to war, they would all volunteer in a heartbeat as a result of this combat mode where they were instructed to "kill or be killed". There was no middle of the road, it was either one or the other. I saw this change in my own brother when he returned from serving eighteen months in Vietnam. He wouldn't smile and always had an expression of being suspicious and untrusting of everyone and everything including many family members. It seemed that the only one he trusted or talked to was me. Maybe because we were very close growing up and I respected his requests. I remember he sent a huge crate from Vietnam and addressed it to me and told me to put it in my closet and he would open it when he got home. So, when the crate arrived, I did exactly as he instructed me to do. My parents and younger brother were curious when the crate arrived and asked me to open it since it was addressed to me. I smiled and told them that it was going to be placed in my closet because it belonged to Kevin and even though it was addressed to me…it was not mine!

Kevin was hired on the Holyoke Fire Department when he was still in Vietnam and had one more month to go before his tour ended and would be returning home. I remember he had his picture on the front page of the Holyoke Transcript when he started his job at the fire department. The heading over his picture was "Navy Veteran dons new uniform" as he stood there holding the boots and fire helmet in his hands with not even a grin on his face. Changes were happening too quickly for Kevin. The expressions on his face spoke loudly of his inability to re-adjust back to the American society and home life. Kevin informed me, several months later, that he was irate at his country because he was not allowed to wear his Seabee uniform home because civilians were throwing garbage and rotten vegetables at the returning soldiers as they disembarked from the planes in California. This was during the hippie movement that had swept across the country like a wild fire. They preached peace not war, and were known as "flower children" because they wore flowers in their hair and believed in free love living freely in nature. This movement created several problems with the residents of these cities and towns in this country because they were taking over public parks and picnic areas where the common working people were taking their families for outings on the weekends. The hippies prevented families from this enjoyment because they were high on drugs, particularly LSD and openly engaging in sex in the middle of the day. This organization were the ones that threw garbage at returning soldiers if they disembarked from the planes wearing their uniforms or displayed any military symbols that associated them to having been in the service. My brother felt that he had worn that uniform which represented this country and now his country was telling him to take it off and dress in his civilian duds because Vietnam Veterans were not welcomed back to their home country. Kevin told me that he wasn't the only one that had hard feelings about this and that there was a great deal of complaining on the plane by every soldier there. He further stated that some of the soldiers didn't have civilian clothes to change into and when they walked from the plane to the concourse, they had to be protected from the screaming, garbage-throwing, disrespectful, draft-dodging jerks that were lying in wait for returning combat soldiers. This was no way for any soldier to be treated when he was returning home from combat or from a foreign country. THEY DID THEIR TIME AND SERVED THEIR COUNTRY PROUDLY AND THIS WAS THE THANKS THEY RECEIVED!

At this time, I was also observing many of my classmates from high school seeking help from the VA. By chance, I was standing outside my supervisor's office in Building 1, waiting to meet with her when I noticed a gentleman leaning on the opposite wall holding his leather jacket under his arm. He was familiar to me so I inquired, "Are you Jeff Pierre?"

Lifting his head from staring at the floor and making eye contact with me, he gently gave an affirmative nod. Smiling at him and speaking softly, I informed him how I knew him, "Jeff, I graduated with you from Holyoke High School in 1967 and I know we have all changed! Do you know who I am?"

Jeff eyeballed me suspiciously and said that he had no idea who I was and that he lost a great deal of memory about our high school days.

"Jeff, my name is Linda Leary and I remember a million things about our classmates from High school!"

I had Jeff's full attention as I told him about how he would tease the heck out of Elena Petrowski in our freshman year and of the time that he found a garter and tied it to the window shade in the English class and asked Elena if it was hers! Jeff started to cock his head around and I knew that I had triggered his memory banks because he was slowly smiling and I knew that he was picturing the whole thing in his mind. His stance was a little more relaxed and he gestured that he now knows who I am and inquired if I was a Veteran being that I was in the VA!

"Jeff, I guess you can say that I am a Veteran of the VA since I have been employed here for thirty-two years and I still live in the homestead in Holyoke!"

Jeff looked at me with a surprised expression on his face when he heard the length of time that I was working at the VA and he commented, "You are more of a Veteran than I am if you have been working that long in the VA! You have had a daily diet of Veterans from all services, wars and conflicts! I was only in the Army for roughly three years and one of those years was spent in Vietnam!"

I couldn't help smiling at him as he shook his head and wondered how I could work with Veterans and their problems for so long a time and not exhibit any war scars emotionally, psychologically or physically. I remarked, "Jeff, I'm not invincible! I have heard every war story that any Veteran could tell, from the loss of a good buddy who was shot by enemy fire to the intricate removal of an ear and stringing it on a necklace and proudly wearing it around the neck to be displayed like a trophy of conquest."

Jeff knew exactly what I was referring to and he informed me that he was a "tunnel rat" over in Vietnam and stated that it was the scariest thing he ever did in his life because there were booby traps in the entrances of these tunnels. The booby traps were usually snakes or poison spiders that when they bit you, you were dead in two steps. The snakes were bush vipers (2-steppers), cobras and pythons and they also had rats that were as big as a small dog. They had pongee sticks that were dipped in poison. Even a scratch from it would kill you. They usually had two or three booby traps at each entrance so that if you made it past one, they counted on one of the next two to do you in. It was at this point that Jeff was summoned into his therapist's office and I told him where my office was located and to come and have coffee there any time he was in the vicinity. I continued to remain in the hallway waiting for my appointment with my supervisor when Molly Pasak, who was now the secretary to one of the directors' of the mental health service line, came out of her office and informed me that my appointment was cancelled because my supervisor was on the road and couldn't make it back in time to see me. After penciling me in to a new appointment scheduled for next week, I slowly walked down the hallway shaking my head and thinking of the time that was wasted by standing in the hallway, waiting for a supervisor who wasn't even in her office. This sort of thing went on frequently and it is one of the major reasons that employees cannot finish their work on time, resulting in completing the notes the following day.

I guess when one works in a facility for over twenty years they learn the ins and outs of everything. You also learn which patients are coming in for treatment and the ones that are there to get monies. It seemed that after the year 2000, the increase of service-connected disabilities hit an all-time high and has continued to the present day. The VA was now receiving Veterans from Operation Desert Storm and Operation Iraqi Freedom and Enduring Freedom. These Veterans were very different from other war Veterans because they wanted to utilize outpatient treatment. They wanted nothing to do with inpatient treatment, although there was a speckling of war Veterans who needed to be inpatient as the result of the severity of their depression and suicidal ideation. These Veterans were high-priority and well that they should be because their behaviors of isolating in their rooms or homes, not eating or sleeping because the intrusive thoughts of war continue to plague and control their psyche to the point that they will harm themselves. These Veterans were very nervous on a ward and the first question they asked was, "When do I get out of here? I really don't like being here!"

They would also sit in a chair that was closest to the exit door of the ward or pace the hallways and several times a staff member would approach them and would talk to them and calm them down. Sometimes the conversations were beneficial and other times it didn't make any difference at all.

The patients who came in to the VA solely for the purpose of obtaining money were a different breed and they made their reason for admission very obvious. They wanted to be admitted to the hospital and when they arrived they were cocky, loud, impatient and demanding and had no respect for the other Veterans or the staff. They demanded admission because they were smart enough to know that they needed a paper trail in order to even apply for a service-connected disability and had heard from their friends that you have to be an inpatient because the process will go much quicker as a result of daily notes from the medical and psychology staff. Not all, but many of the admissions for solely obtaining money had the diagnosis of substance or alcohol abuse. This diagnosis does not warrant a service connected disability. It is at this point, that they start to self-diagnose and say that they were raped in the service, they have PTSD from being in a war area or from saying that they were in a hurricane or some other natural disaster. When in fact, there are no recordings of these mishaps in any of their records. These are the hard cases that usually would be given to me to find out the facts because in several instances, the doctor did not have the time to get this information. It didn't take me too long to get this information because if the patient stated that they were in a hurricane and had PTSD from it, I would ask them what the name of the hurricane was and where were you when it hit? After asking this question, I would lean back in my chair anticipating a long drawn-out fictitious story concerning their reasoning for needing to be service-connected. I would allow these individuals to ramble on about something that they were never involved in or experienced, particularly if they were attempting to make a service-connected claim for PTSD because they were in Vietnam. But, realistically they were never there. I would always catch them as being deceptive with one single question, "What corps (military division) were you stationed in Vietnam?"

When I was given the answer to my question by these presumed war Veterans as, "Oh! I wasn't in the Marine Corps, I was in the Army!"

Smiling, I put my pen down on my desk and turning my eyes in the Veteran's direction, I stated, "I want you to be completely honest with me. What Vietnam Veteran did you over hear tell the story you just recited?"

He stared at me in shock and his mouth dropped open as he said, "What do you mean?"

"You see, Vietnam was divided into four military divisions called corps (I, II, III, and IV) and these corps are written in Roman numeral form so that if someone was in I corps, they referred to it as (eye) corps which was up by the border of North Vietnam and IV (four) corps was down in the Mekong Delta area. Anyone who served in Vietnam would know what I meant when I asked what corps they were in and that it has nothing to do with the Marine Corps! Your answer just informed me that you were never in Vietnam, were you?"

I watched as this Veteran slowly slumped back in the chair and with a bowed head and his eyes focused on the floor, sat there shaking his head back and forth and emitting low audible sighs, admitted to me that he was never in Vietnam. I didn't say anything to him because I wanted him to process the wrong that he tried to make me believe along with the fact that he was caught in a lie. He appeared to have difficulty getting out of the chair because the shame and embarrassment seemed to weigh very heavily on him. He looked at me and uttered, "Linda, are you going to write this in my record?"

I assured him that the only thing that would be stated in his chart is that he does not have PTSD and that he did not meet the criteria for PTSD and does not qualify to submit papers for service-connected disability for PTSD. Before he exited my office, I asked him "why" he would falsify a diagnosis and the only response I received from him was a shrugging of his shoulders. He put his hands in his jean pockets and with his head still bent towards the floor, I watched him as he slowly walked down the hallway to the dayroom and wondering how I ever discovered his little game of "tell a lie and shame yourself".

In the four years that I have worked on 4Upper, there were several changes in staff from the nursing assistants to the doctors and even the janitors. Even I was a change to the staff from the social worker who was previously there. Now that my office was upstairs on the ward, the staff and Veterans no longer had to look for me downstairs. They just had to walk down the hallway and knock on my door or call me on the phone and know that I was at their disposal.

Dr. Gina Lester was the new psychiatrist assigned to 4Upper, arriving about a year and a half before my retirement. She was a big asset to the ward because she was pleasant and easily approachable to staff and patients alike. In staff meetings, she would always lend a listening ear to everyone who made suggestions about a patient that they were having difficulty with. She would take careful consideration of everyone's opinions before she made a decision about the treatment and care that a patient should receive under her leadership. Gina was there about two weeks when I decided to approach her in the same way that I was approached when I first was assigned to 4Upper. She was walking down the hall when I stopped her and said, "You know Gina; it is customary for everyone newly assigned to 4Upper, regardless if they are the doctor or the janitor, they have to buy bagels for the entire staff!"

She smiled back at me and stated, "Is tomorrow too soon?"

I assured her that the staff would be thrilled and that I gave her that informational request so that she would have time to plan it. If she wanted to change her mind and buy them for next week, she could certainly do so. The following morning when I walked into the meeting room, I noticed bags of bagels and different types of cream cheeses in the middle of the table. The staff started to file into the room and noticing the fine treats on the table, selected and enjoyed the bagel of their choice accompanied with a cup of coffee.

The biggest task that Gina had to learn was getting to know the staff and the job connected with each member. She didn't want to step on anyone's toes, but at the same time, she didn't want any Veteran to be ignored. She was getting overwhelmed with paperwork and comp/pen (compensation/pension) exams. So when someone approached her about the need for a progress report, placement referral or a letter to court for one of the Veterans, she would truthfully remark that she didn't have time for it. I was the one who approached her with these requests because these requests had to be signed by the doctor. After my fourth request, Gina turned to me and stated, "Linda, would you please write the letter and I will sign it! You are more familiar with these requests and you know what they want. Therefore, you would assist me greatly if you write the letter and put it in my mail box and I will sign it. I'm sure that they just want to see the doctors' signature and this way I am also informed about the happenings of the patients."

I agreed to write the letters for the doctor and then have her sign them because this wasn't the first time a doctor made this request of me. After thirty-two years of employment in the VA, writing letters for doctors goes all the way back to the PTSD unit when I was the admissions coordinator. This has continued to follow me right up to the present day. When Gina asked me to do this task of letter-writing, I knew that she trusted me to do so. She was new to the VA and wasn't familiar with the other staff. It was at this time that she was getting inundated with paperwork and orders and was also covering other units and admissions. I admired her because she was intelligent, caring and respectful of the Veteran's needs. Gina had a sense of humor and quite often she would laugh at someone's remark in a staff meeting. The remarks were never directed at the Veterans, but rather, they were mostly directed at a supervisor or someone in authority. Sitting in a staff meeting, there was always someone who announced that they were unable to stay for the entire meeting because they had an appointment with some big shot in the main building. Today, a nurse whose name was Greta informed the staff that she had an appointment with Rhoda Monahan who was a nurse supervisor in building 1. When I heard the name, I sat there and shook my head and said, "Oh brother!"

I could hear snickers from others who were sitting in this meeting when Gina inquired about Rhoda Monahan and what was the problem that others had with her. All eyes were glaring in my direction and I assumed they were glaring at me because of the comment that I just made. So I turned to Gina and I said, "Rhoda is not a bad person, as a matter of fact; she constantly walks around smiling at everyone and everything. This too is not a bad thing, but you really have to sit down and converse with her. She's well educated, she knows many things, but she is no teacher or instructor because she doesn't know how to get the point across to anyone! She goes off on tangents and no one understands where she is coming from or where she is going with her instructions. Basically speaking, she can't spell YMCA with three clues!"

Needless to say, Gina was almost falling off her chair from laughter along with everyone else that was sitting around the conference table in the meeting room. Even Greta who was the one who was going to be meeting with Rhoda had to sit down from laughing and turning to me she said, "Linda, I won't be able to keep a straight face when I meet with her. I'll be thinking of what you just said and I'll laugh!"

"Don't worry about that! She's always smiling anyways and she'll probably think that you're delighted to be meeting with her!"

Again, there was another round of laughter in the room and when everyone settled down, we all concentrated on the task of discussing patient care and treatment which was the main reason we were in the meeting room. We picked up our pens and gave all our attention to the staff member who was assigned to be in charge. She started the meeting by introducing the first patient's name who was listed alphabetically on her paper. Some patients had no changes for the better or for the worse, but everyone was mentioned and discussed.

At breaks and lunchtime, I would take a walk around the grounds just to get some fresh air and have a little time for myself. Today appeared to be different from other days that I took a walk because there seemed to be a great deal of people walking on the grounds as well. I thought that there must be a party or a picnic on one of the units, but those gatherings required numerous vehicles parked on the grass and these vehicles were not present, nor were they parked in any direction that I looked. The word had also gotten out that I was seriously thinking about retiring from the VA and this news didn't set well with many of the patients and staff that had known me over the years. Many of the staff would approach me in the canteen or in the clinic area or sometimes on the grounds as I was getting out of my car and ask me directly if my retiring was a rumor or fact. Smiling at them and seeing so much curiosity in their eyes, I couldn't resist inquiring about where they got that information! I was getting stopped many times as I walked around the grounds and asked by patients and employees alike, "Linda, are you really going to retire?"

"I'm only thinking about it. Everybody's walking around and thinks that it is a done deal. It is not, it is only in the thinking stage! I have been employed at this facility for thirty-three years and that is a long time to be working in the same place. I'm starting to get tired and I will retire within the next two years, but I do not have a set date picked out as yet!"

I realized that you have to beware of whom you voice your thoughts to because it will pass faster than   FOX News or a CNN report. When I started to receive calls and visits from patients in the community that I had no contact with in years asking me if it was true that I was going to retire, I couldn't resist saying, "Well, we're all going to retire someday, but as for me, I have no specific date planned as yet!"

It was as if everybody was getting nervous that I would possibly retire, even if my planned time to make my exit was a year or two away. I could only wonder that the reason I was approached by so many was the fact that I worked in this same facility for thirty-three years and patients and staff were used to seeing my face around the campus. I also experienced visits from patients that I had in the past and I mean distant past, that were calling me and inquiring about my so-called impending retirement information that they had received from others. Some of these Veterans were individuals that I worked with in the 1980's and haven't been back to the Northampton VAMC since then. Many of the patient inquiries were from out-of-State such as New York, New Jersey, Connecticut, Rhode Island, Vermont, New Hampshire and North Carolina. I was flabbergasted that so many of my past Veterans knew that I had mentioned the thought of retirement. I guess it stems back to the Veterans grapevine where information passes faster than a bolt of lightning hitting the ground before one drop of rain falls from an impending storm cloud. These inquiries were numerous at first, but like everything else, they slowly faded, but were never forgotten.

The closer I was getting to seriously contemplating retirement, the more noticeable it was that the VA was falling apart. Not literally by bricks falling to the ground and roofs caving in, but rather by an internal caring stance in which the attitude appeared by the administration to be devoid of any care or concern for the Veterans. Everything was functioning like a huge assembly line and the patients that arrived just for minimal treatment or to inquire if the VA could help them with their mental problems, couldn't utter a word of why they were there because they were given a discharge date before their problems were even heard. Many patients waited for hours in the waiting room before being called and then to receive a discharge date before the interviewer even knew why the patient was there! I heard from some other Veterans that there were several patients that just walked out the door and never looked back as a result of this rude and uncaring reception that they had received in the admissions office. Many were not there to be admitted, but rather to see if there was any assistance they could receive for their medical or psychiatric problems on an outpatient basis. There were some exceptional, caring and truly concerned receptionists that sat behind the admissions desk interviewing Veterans who came into the VA seeking help for their problems. Thank God for these caring employees who directed the Veterans to medical doctors and psychiatric experts so that the Veterans' problems were dealt with promptly and to their satisfaction. No Veteran who walks through the door of a VA hospital is there for a runny nose or hangnails and if they are confronted by an angry, rude and disrespectful receptionist who cares less about the Veteran or his/her name by comments such as, "NEXT!"

"What do you expect us to do for you?" or "Can't you see that I'm busy, you'll have to wait in the chair until I call you?"

I witnessed these comments to Veterans when I had to walk through admissions on my way to a meeting in building 1. A few times I had to stop at the receptionist's desk to get an appointment for a Veteran who was being discharged from ward 4U. One time the waiting room was very crowded and there was an elderly Veteran standing by the receptionist's desk because all the chairs were occupied so he decided to stand against the wall near the desk. I entered the automatic doors and stood behind this gentleman thinking that he was in line to be served when suddenly the receptionist stated, "Linda, can I help you?"

I looked at the elderly gentleman and inquired, "Excuse me Sir, but have you been seen at the desk yet?"

He gently raised his head and looked in my eyes and stated in a soft voice, "No!"

I turned to the receptionist and addressed her directly and told her that I was standing behind this Veteran, so he will be served before me because he had been waiting quite some time. She wasn't too pleased with me, but I didn't care because everyone's job in the VA is to serve the Veterans. As this man was being served by the receptionist, I wandered around the waiting room and quietly asked the Veterans how long they were waiting to be called to the admission desk. Some had been sitting there for over two hours, so I approached the desk and told the receptionist that I would have my turn after the four Veterans who had waited over two hours sitting in the waiting room were served. If looks could kill, I would have been dead, but I wanted the Veterans served for their needs and I waited for those four Veterans to be served before I asked her for an appointment for a Veteran that was being discharged tomorrow from Ward 4U. These Veterans have places to go and people to see just like anyone else and when they are given an appointment for 8:30 a.m. and they are still sitting and waiting at 10:30 a.m., it is gross negligence and complete disrespect for the Veteran clientele that we were hired to serve. NO VA EMPLOYEE IS MORE IMPORTANT THAN THE VETERANS THEY SERVE! I wholeheartedly believe this statement and it extends to everyone who is employed in the VA, including the directors and the Secretary of Veterans Affairs in Washington DC.

I had stated earlier that I liked change, but at this time change was occurring on a daily basis and was very chaotic. When some ward was receiving reconstruction in the past, there was total concentration on that ward until the construction was complete. After they located the staff and patients into the newly revamped ward, then another ward came under the gun to be renovated. The construction was no longer on a one-to-one basis; it was all over the hill! There were three or four wards being torn apart and displacing several Veterans who were confused and didn't understand the reason they had to be placed elsewhere. Trees were being cleared to build Veterans apartments, not by the VA, but rather by a private organization on the VA grounds along with roads and parking lots getting ripped up to lay new pipes and electrical equipment for these buildings. It was getting to a point that the employees could not reach their ward destinations because the roads were blocked off as a result of all this construction. It was at this point that I decided to plan my retirement date because I no longer looked forward to going to work. In some cases, just going from ward to ward was like you encountered an obstacle course or a maze that eventually had a light at the end of the tunnel. I knew that if this construction situation was uncomfortable for me, then the discomfort for all the Veterans who were seeking assistance and treatment had to double. Everybody looked puzzled and the only question people seemed to ask was, "Why is this construction taking place at the same time?"

I couldn't begin to comprehend the reason, if there was one, why that entire hill was being ripped apart. Workers were taking their sweet time and didn't seem to care when they completed the building project, so I decided that now would be a good time to notify the retirement board that I had selected my date to retire from the VA.

I notified the retirement board about eighteen months before my target date of retirement. The board that I utilized was located at the Brockton VAMC which is south of Boston in Massachusetts. I had a fervent desire to complete thirty-five years in the VA, but with the decrease of patient admissions and the decrease of staff by attrition, this resulted in doubling and tripling the workload on the remaining staff. This resulted in an overload of work which was not fair to the faithful staff that remained. The VA in Northampton was being overrun with psychologists and MSW's. If this was the military, it would be the hiring of all officers. There was no hiring of the ground troops (janitors, CNA's, kitchen workers and ground workers) which are the individuals who actually do the work that the officers get the credit for! There were more bosses and assistant bosses who seemed to be tripping over each other and this pompous atmosphere was not conducive to my remaining in employment at the VA.

Word passes very quickly when an employee is going to retire or at least has set a date for their retirement and this was true for me as well! No matter where I went or who I encountered, I was greeted with the title, "Short Timer!" Even though my target date was fifteen months away, I was anticipating that some would try to talk me out of leaving and others would be envious because of the length of time that I had worked at the VA. But, I figured that thirty-four years is long enough for anyone to work in the same place and to undertake the many changes that I have experienced, both positive and negative, over the years.

With all the talk of retirement waning, I managed to get myself focused back on the ward and to care for the Veterans and their needs. I was pleased to hear a Veteran knock on my office door and inquire if I could assist him with a small problem he had instead of stating, "Linda, is it true that you are going to retire?"

This question was usually followed with inquiries such as, "Are you going to have a huge party because you've been here over thirty years and there are many patients and staff that would attend a party in your honor because you helped many of us?"

Slowly turning my head in his direction, I uttered, "There will not be any party because I don't want one and personally I think that they are ridiculous! They are ridiculous because nobody gave me a party on my first day of employment. I opened the front door all by myself, so why should my exit be any different from entrance. There are many employees on this hill, who love to make parties for any little thing, but I am not one of them and I will not be the subject or the title of any party! I just want to walk out the door the same way that I walked in, nearly thirty-four years ago! I could never understand why these parties were made for individuals retiring because they did the job that they were hired to do. If they didn't, they were let go and as far as working past thirty-years, that is another decision that the employee makes themselves, not the administration."

I noticed the saddened look on this Veteran's face as he sat there solemn and I knew I had burst his bubble of party excitement. I also had a feeling that he was sent into my office by the ward staff to feel me out about a ward party in my honor. Basically, I didn't want anything to do with the so-called reward system of the VA because they were absolutely ridiculous and farcical. These awards appeared to be limited to individuals that worked the day-shift because this was the shift that the administration worked as well. I felt that the "Employee of the Month" was the most ridiculous of all awards because it was limited to only twelve individuals for the twelve months in the year. In April of the following year, there would be a get-together for "Employee of the year" which would consist only of the twelve candidates chosen "Employee of the Month" from the previous year. There are over five-hundred individuals employed at this VA facility and only the chosen few get selected for this award which consists of a $100 bill and a small plaque. I have also seen the same individual receive this monthly award two and three years in a row. It reminded me too much of a political campaign where the slogan is, "You scratch my back and I'll scratch yours!" It's absurd! The only honor and satisfaction that I ever appreciated came from the Veterans that I served. To see them emotionally comfortable, financially secure and dwelling in an appropriate residence satisfied with the care and medications of their mental and medical problems and to approach me with a simple "Thank you for all you have done for me" is the only honor I will take with me when I retire! The Veterans are also the only ones that I will greatly miss as well and there is no administrative award that can compare with that type of loss and none that can make up for it.

I was not aware of it at the time, but the demands on me were lessening by both staff and patients alike. It was as if they were telling me that I should start to concentrate on what I have to do for myself before I retire. It felt weird because I now had time to complete all the paperwork and notes and nothing was left to complete for the following day as it had been for several years. I started to go through my personal papers which were contained in three very thick folders and in doing so; I managed to have a few laughs over a few papers that I had totally forgotten about from past supervisors who are   deceased. There were several promotion papers stating that I would notice a step-increase in pay and it would be reflected in my paycheck in the next pay period. There were also several education-earned credit papers from in-service meetings both through the VA and from the community. I even came across invitational letters from the court system in Northampton MA. I hadn't thrown away anything and now I had to decide what to keep and what to shred. I had piles of papers all over my office marked as keepers, throw, and maybe keep, questionable and shredder-bound. There were papers on the desk, the floor, the bookcase and the chair and I was thinking that I must look like someone who survived an explosion in a paper factory.

Patients would come to my doorway and would inquire about the papers that appeared to be wall-to-wall covering my office and as they smiled, they started to make remarks and jokes about it. I heard them say such expressions as, "It will do you no good to talk to Linda because I could just about see her among the paper piles!"

"Linda is up to her neck in paperwork!"

"She's from Holyoke and it is known as the paper city!"

I couldn't help but smile and sometimes laughing at some of the remarks because they were correct in stating that my office did look like "paper city". I had one saving-grace as I was sorting out my files that the Nurse Manager and an RN on ward 4U would be retiring one-month before me and this allowed the barrage of questions from the patients and the focus of retirement to be shared among the three of us.

CHAPTER SEVENTEEN

I was amazed to realize that once I had given my target date to retire, it seemed like assignments and details appeared to be less strenuous and not as demanding on me. I was always looking forward to my next vacation, which I planned on an average of every three months and now I didn't have to plan vacations. My calendar that was posted on the side of my file cabinet was numbered in reverse from 24-1, starting in February 2009 and ending with number 1 on January 2011. I wrote these numbers in red magic marker on each month of the calendar and this resulted in many questions concerning the numbers because they were so highly noticeable by anyone who entered my office. Even if they stood in the doorway, the red magic marker was like a neon light that seemed to jump out at you. So everyone always would inquire about the meaning of the bold, red numbers on the calendar.

A year and a half before I retired, Brooke Bergeron, MSW was assigned to the 4 Upper ward as the ward social worker. Brooke was a very nice and pleasant individual and was also delighted to be working in the VA system. Her office was next to mine and she would often remark about the plants and setup of my office stating that it looked very comfy and pleasant. I noticed that she started to bring in plants that she brought in from home or had purchased from the greenhouse on the VA grounds. She brought in this one plant that was absolutely beautiful. It was so full that it appeared to resemble a bush that overflowed from the plastic pot it was in. The leaves reminded me of an elephant ear plant and she placed this plant on the top of her file cabinet and as she did so, I told her that to maintain that plant it had to be tended to every three days. She may even have to transplant it into a bigger pot so that the roots had room to expand. She was very good at attending the plant for about three weeks, but when the work picked up and she started to run around with the rest of the staff caring for the clientele, the poor plant almost became the victim of planticide. I guess the plant was out of sight, out of mind and suffered as a result. I received a call from Brooke stating that she would be late and asked me if I could go into her office and get a certain form and as I opened her office door, I noticed the once beautiful plant drooped over the edge of the pot and dry as a bone. I took the plant and the form into my office, placed the plant in the sink and ran water into it and picking up the phone receiver told Brooke that I had the form and then proceeded to tell her about her limp plant. I explained that I put it in my sink and then stated, "That plant was so dry that if it was a hydrant, it would be chasing a dog!"

She was laughing hysterically on the phone as a result of my comment that when she finally caught her breath, she told me that she would be more aware of the plant and care for it. Brooke was now on her way into work and when she arrived she still was laughing at the comment about the hydrant. She stepped into my office and inquired, "Linda, where do you come up with these expressions? You are hysterical!"

Turning to her I stated, "I just want to make a comparison so that you get a mental picture of the situation!"

It seemed that for the rest of the week, every time Brooke saw me she would start laughing each time she thought about that comment about her plant. She also had some other plants that she was rooting in water that were lined up on her window sill in small glass jars and vases.

When the time was starting to close into my retirement date, I became thoroughly engrossed with transporting patients to various placements and was on the road three-to-four times a week with this assignment. Brooke realized that when I retired, this entire transportation of patients to residential and community placements home would rest entirely upon her. Up to this point, I was the only employee on 4U who did this task. Brooke approached me and inquired about the process of requesting a government vehicle and arranging the time and placement where the patients would reside in the community. I instructed Brooke to start off her transporting of patients between the Northampton/Springfield areas because she would be more familiar with these areas and after she could expand outward to encompass the entire New England area. I had her shadow me in reserving a vehicle, filling out a trip-ticket, confirming the time and date of the patient's community placement, securing the medications and appointments from the doctors and confirm that all the discharge paperwork was complete. Brooke appeared to be a little bewildered at the process and stated, "That seems to be a lot to remember all at once!"

I assured her that she would get used to it and that the more she did it the easier it would become. I also told her that the bulk of the process could be done days ahead so that when the transportation day arrived, everything would be smooth as silk and that there would be little to no distress on her or the patient being discharged into in the community. Brooke stood there looking at me as if I just spoke to her in a foreign language. I could see that she was overwhelmed with this information, so I reassured her that I would be available to assist her in this process.

I was unable to attend the weekly meetings when the status of the patients was discussed because I was more off-the-ward than on it during my last six months of employment. The staff and patients were beginning to get a little edgy because the retirement dates for the three of us was quickly approaching. I also began to hear of others that were retiring at the same time. There were about seven individuals who would be retiring on January 1, 2011 and my date was February 1, 2011 and there was another employee who was also retiring on the same date as I. It seemed as if there was a grand exodus of seasoned employees leaving the Northampton VA Medical Center in the first two months of 2011. I believe that one of the main reasons for the departures was merely the fact that we were tired and just could not keep up the pace anymore, along with fact that many were disenchanted with just waking up early and dragging themselves into work. The older we get, the less motivation exists. In other words, "Our get up and go, got up and went!"

There is truth in the saying, "The busier you are the faster the time goes by!" because now it was December 2010 and I was witnessing the edginess of the staff wondering what it would be like when the nurse manager and staff nurse retire in two weeks and in a month and a half, I exit the premises with a fond farewell. I was feeling badly for the staff and the patients because they must have felt like they were having the rug pulled out from underneath them with three staff members retiring within a month of each other. Many of the medical staff on the ward approached me with concerns about Fred Baganelli and wondered how he would react when I left. One staff nurse inquired, "Linda, what is Fred going to do when you leave? He has grown to trust and respect you and you have done so much for him with his financial problems which resulted in less outbursts of anger on his part. I guess that we are worried that he will revert to his old behaviors after you're gone!"

With serious interest and concern for her question, I answered, "For the past three months I have been thinking and pondering about Fred and I feel that it wouldn't be right just to up and leave him hanging without anyone to talk with about his concerns. My thoughts have been directed to transitioning Fred to someone else, but I needed someone to volunteer for the job!"

"Why do you need a volunteer, can't you just transfer his case to Brooke! After all, she is the other social worker on the unit."

"Easier said than done and the fact that Fred doesn't like Brooke because he finds her very abrupt and he doesn't like that, so that arrangement would never work. That is the entire reason why I need a volunteer and the volunteer has to be a nurse because he knows the nurses; they give him his medications on a daily basis. I need a volunteer because not everyone gets along with Fred and many don't want to work with him, so I need a volunteer who will willingly take on this task."

"Oh! Now I understand the reason you need a volunteer!"

With that said, the staff nurse who was standing in the doorway of my office turned and walked down the hallway to the nurse's station to continue doing her work that she had abandoned to talk to me.

The following morning, this same nurse who I knew as Trixie, approached my office and stated that she would be willing to volunteer for the task of talking to Fred. I was very pleased that she was the one that volunteered because I remember Fred telling me that he liked Trixie and that she was nice. Smiling at Trixie, I stated that I couldn't ask her to be the one that would do case work with Fred because of her nursing responsibilities and that is why I needed a volunteer, someone that would have the time to be there for Fred when he needed someone to be there. I further explained to Trixie that Fred likes to be by himself for the most part and that his requests to talk are infrequent and not time-consuming. For the most part, Fred is looking for a yes or no answer, not an elaborate explanation to a simple question. I assured Trixie that the sooner we could transition Fred over, the sooner he would adjust without any difficulty. I informed her that I would discuss the transition with Fred this afternoon and hopefully she would be able to have time to shadow me in this transition starting tomorrow. Trixie stated that she would check her schedule to see what time she would have available. In order for Fred to build up trust in anyone, he needs to know the days that the individual have off or working off-shift because this information would decrease his anxiety. This would decrease any potential outbursts because he would be able to save his question until the individual returns or he sees them on a different shift. At lunchtime, Trixie called my office and informed me of the times that she'd have available for the rest of the week. She was thrilled to know that there was a good hour every day to shadow me and to make the transition as smooth and easy as possible, both for her and for Fred.

Christmas and New Years were quickly approaching and the staff knows that I always take Christmas week off for vacation. This year was very different because the nurse manager and the staff nurse were retiring, the transition for Fred was complete and this was the last Christmas vacation I would have in this VA. It was January 3, 2011 and my last day of work was January 31st. As I gazed at the calendar that was still hanging on the side of my file cabinet, I found it hard to believe that in less than a month, I would be retired.

Brooke was very busy with her clientele and was slowly taking over my cases and requested that if it was possible, she would greatly appreciate it if she could have my kardex with all the contacts in the communities and all the contacts that were out of State. I handed the roll-a-dex to her as she was standing in my doorway making this request. She appeared shock and stated, "You don't have to give it to me now! I meant at the end of the month just before you left!"

"Brooke, I no longer have to rely on these contacts because they all know that I'm retiring and that you will be taking over all the patients on this unit. I have a few more patients that I will be transporting into the community and all the arrangements have been made and the discharge dates are given, so you see I no longer have need for these contacts."

Brooke left my office with the contact files in her hand and as she turned toward the hallway, she smiled and said, Linda, I will never forget your expressions which made me laugh every time or your personality and the way you get along with everyone throughout this hospital. Most of all, I will never forget the love and dedication that you have for every Veteran that walked through the door of this ward and on the grounds of this VA. You have so much knowledge in your head that I couldn't even hope to gain a quarter of it."

Brooke expressed her feelings and compliments as she stood in the doorway which amazed me because she usually would come and flop in the overstuffed chair that was positioned directly next to my desk. She surprised me because this was another side that I had not seen of her. She was sincere and a private person, in that there was no one around when she expressed herself to me in this manner.

When the second week of January 2011 came around, I no longer had to count months or weeks for my retirement, but instead I was counting days. I was walking down the hallway on Ward 4U when Brooke asked me to wait because she wanted to tell me something. I stood against the railing and waited for her to approach and as she neared me she said, "Linda, your last day of work is January 31, 2011! Is this correct?"

Looking at her with my brow lowered, I assured her that it was my last day of work and wondered why she inquired about that because she knew, as well as everyone else on the ward that January 31, 2011 was my final working day in the VA. Brooke was evasive when I asked her why she wanted to seek an answer to something that she was already very aware of and knew! Smiling at me, she stated firmly and directly, "YOU better show up to work that day! You better not call in sick or for annual leave or anything because if you don't come in, I will be forced to go to Holyoke and get you and bring you in!"

Looking puzzled at her I said, "I have every intention of coming into work on the 31st! What's the big deal?"

Brooke just smiled as she walked away from me and never uttered another word, leaving me to wonder just what she had up her sleeve for the 31st. She was well aware that I disliked any parties because the individuals that you would like to see are always so busy that they are unable to attend. The people that you don't want to see show up in droves and they are more interested in the food then they are of the one who is retiring. At this point, I shook the thought out of my head and continued my walk up the hallway and concentrated on my work that I had remaining which wasn't much, but I didn't want to leave any pending work to Brooke because she already had enough to do with her own assignment.

Sitting in my office, I would periodically gaze out the window and although my eyes were focused on the trees and sky, my thoughts rushed ahead to the day that I would clear and disengage myself from the VA. Having these thoughts didn't seem to make my retiring any easier because for thirty-four years I was conditioned to awake at a certain time, stop for a coffee and a newspaper, proceed up Route 5 along the same winding road to Northampton and then turn on to Route 9 to the VA. I found it hard to believe that this daily process that I did for thirty-four years would be terminated on February 1, 2011 when I would have my computer dismantled from my identification in IRM (Information Resource Management), turning in my employee badge and keys which were literally part of my dress code and other various departments listed on the clearing slip. My thoughts were interrupted by a knock on my door from a Veteran requesting to talk to me and I was grateful that he did so because I felt that I would most likely get depressed if I remained in that train of thought.

The days seemed to be flying by and the date was now January 24, 2011 and I'm sitting in my office knowing that today, I have officially completed thirty-four years of government service. A week from today would be my last day of employment at the VA. I could feel the butterflies in my stomach realizing that when someone retires it appears to be instantaneous. That the employee has to clear, say goodbye and then trek off the premises, but it is the readjustment of being unemployed and no longer having the focus of going to work that takes a long time to change. I was dwelling on these thoughts when a Veteran stopped in my doorway and stated,

"Linda, you look like you're lost! You look like you don't know what to do! I can understand that because your office is empty and no longer looks like your office! By chance are you getting second thoughts?"

"No, I'm not getting second thoughts because I'm just thinking about several things that I have to do and wondering how I am going to do them! I think these are referred to as waning thoughts!"

The Veteran just stood there smiling at me and I could tell by the expression on his face that he was hoping that I would change my mind and not retire. I watched him as he walked down the hallway and noticed one of the nurses beckoning me to come to her. I rose from my chair and walked down the hall to meet her and when I stopped in front of her she stated, "Linda, your presence is requested at the morning meeting!"

I was a little surprised to hear this request being that there haven't been many meetings that I had attended over the past three years because I was usually transporting patients to various placements in the community. Nonchalantly, I accompanied this nurse to the waiting patients and staff in the dayroom which is where the morning meeting was held. This meeting incorporates the daily schedule of events and appointments for the patients such as: recreational activities, medical and psychiatry appointments, groups and patient detail assignments. These announcements are followed by a question and answer period in which any patient can address any staff member with a question. Heather Dean, RT (Recreation Therapist) was the staff member who was conducting this meeting and she is the recreational therapist who is assigned to ward 4U. Heather made the introduction of the question and answer period to the patients and surprisingly about eight hands went up when the usual amount was no more than three. Heather pointed to one of the raised hands who happened to be one of my cases who rarely raises his hand and stated, "I would like to ask Linda Leary a question! Are you truly retiring next week and is there any way that you will change your mind and decide to stay before next week?"

I didn't expect this kind of question which took a little wind out of my sails, so I hesitated for a second, looked at the floor and then lifted my gaze to the Veteran who asked the question and said, "Well, you hit me with more than one question so I'll do my best to answer! Yes! I am retiring next week. All the paperwork and arrangements are completed, but I have known some employees that have changed their minds to continue work the day before they were to retire, but that will not occur with me. When I started my employment at this VA, I was twenty-seven years old. I am now sixty-one years old and thirty-four years have tired me out. I feel that I can no longer keep the pace that I had maintained in the past with all of you. I will also give my farewell speech next week because my desire is to speak with all of you, patients and staff on an individual basis for the remainder of this week so that it is more personal and not a generalized soap-box speech."

Heather turned her attention back to the patient clientele and inquired about the other hands that she saw raised and calmly and quietly no hand went up. She specified that there were about seven other hands raised and now no one is raising their hands! I directed my attention to Heather and stated, "Maybe the others had the same question for me that Buddy just asked me!"

Heather smiled at me and ended the meeting and as everyone dispersed in their own directions, Heather approached me and whispered, "Is there any chance that you will change your mind and stay?"

For the remainder of the week I was pleased that I was able to meet with various patients and staff on a personal basis to tell each one that it was a pleasure and respect to have had the opportunity to care and work with them and I expressed it with sincere admiration. I also expressed to each one that I hate public speeches because you have to maintain your speech in a generalized form. Generalized speech is not specific to individuals, but rather it is like a blanket that touches a tiny bit of each person and in some cases, doesn't even come close to touching others. There always seems to be someone excluded in generalized speech and that was the main reason that I wished to meet with them on an individual, personal basis so that specific compliments targeted each patient and co-worker.

It was 8 a.m. on January 31st when I walked onto the ward on my final day of employment at the Northampton VAMC and I had a myriad of emotions going through me. I felt sad that I would no longer see the patients and co-workers that I assisted over the years with housing, financial needs, family contacts and judicial problems. I felt a little numb for the same reasons that I was feeling sad because when I walk out the door this afternoon, it will be my final exit from work. I was excited because I would be stepping into the realm of retirement and my daily plan of action would be new and intriguing to me and I found this to be a little confusing because I had no idea what I had planned for my retirement other than an occasional thought of perhaps to write a book.

I was hanging out for the most part around the nurse's station on 4U because my office was empty of all my personal things. My plants were gone, the Red Sox schedule and pictures of the players no longer were posted on the side of the file cabinet and all my family pictures were removed by me and taken home. My computer and phone were still working, but I had no need for them on my last day of work so I decided that I would talk to the patients in the dayroom and to the ward secretary and nurses who would periodically take a break from their work to converse with me about my retirement. Brooke came into work on time, but then I didn't see much of her and assumed that she had to transport a patient to a community placement. Dr. Gina Lister greeted me when she arrived and quickly stepped into her office to do her work. Heather came and announced that there would be a bingo on the ward on Wednesday evening and as she passed me, she quickly wished me good luck and happiness in my retirement. This was a typical Monday and was one of the busiest days in the VA, so it was understandable that employees were flying all over the place and doing what needed to be done.

At about 11 a.m., Guy Gilbert who scheduled appointments and answered the phones for the VA Homeless program and Substance Abuse program which were on 4Lower, came walking up the hallway on 4U. I was surprised to see him upstairs because he had no connection of duties on 4U. Guy approached me as I stood at the nurse's station and said, "Linda, could you please accompany me downstairs; there is someone who wants to see you in the kitchen area?"

Shrugging my shoulders, I walked with Guy down the hallway and then down the back staircase which was situated next to the kitchen door on 4L. Guy opened the door for me and to my total surprise there stood a gathering of employees with food and a cake to celebrate my retirement. I stood in disbelief because I gazed around the room and saw Brooke, Heather, Dr. Gina, Penny, Paige and several other faces that I had not seen in years, but had worked with in the distant past. There was only one thought in my mind and that was the remark that Brooke expressed two weeks ago about my last day of work. I visually surveyed the room for her and before I could point my finger at her, she put her arm around my neck and gave me a big hug. Everyone else started to fall in line and approached me with a hug and congratulations. This gathering lasted about two hours and there was a constant traffic of employees coming in when they had time. At roughly 12:30 p.m., Dr. Kendall who was my immediate supervisor, entered the room carrying a large framed object. Dr. Kendall approached me and shook my hand and extended congratulations to me for my retirement. I instructed him to help himself to the display of food on the tables and thanked him for coming. I returned to the small plate of food that I was eating when Paige insisted that my attention was required by her. Paige had written a very nice letter and wanted to read it to all who were present and before she started she stated that this letter describes the attributes that she saw in me. Her letter was very nice and very complimentary and I also know that it was sincere and right from her heart, but my experience in the VA especially during the last ten years of my employment in the Northampton VAMC, was that I have never been the recipient of anything complimentary from any supervisor concerning my own capabilities. This was strange for me because I received many high-quality performances in the first twenty-four years of employment. When Paige had finished reading her letter and the applause ceased, Dr. Kendall stepped forward and requested that I stand at his side. There was complete silence and everybody's attention was on him. He lifted the framed item that he had in his hands and looking at me he stated, "Linda, I would like to present to you in recognition of your retirement from the Department of Veterans Affairs, following 34 years of dedicated service to the Government of the United States of America, this Certificate of Retirement."

I stood there in awe, reading the certificate and being thanked for a job that I loved doing. The clapping had subsided and I was asked to give a speech, but I was speechless and tried to digest something that I did not expect which was a complimentary acknowledgment from the Northampton VAMC. After a minute or two, I was able to express the benefits that I received from working in the VA.

"My greatest VA education was taught to me from the Veterans through their memory, pain, experience and losses. Anyone can go to college and take a psychology course involving schizophrenia, obsessive/compulsive behavior, borderline personality, post-traumatic stress disorder and various other psychological diagnosis, but if you really want to learn about PTSD, talk to the war Veteran who has the disorder or the schizophrenic Veteran with that diagnosis and I guarantee that you will learn more from them than you will learn in any book."

I was given an acknowledgement when I finished from the individuals who were present that heard me. The gathering was winding down and several were cleaning up while I collected the gifts I was given and carried them out to my car. I returned back to 4Upper for about thirty minutes before I made my final exodus from the ward, the patients and staff. At 2:30 p.m., I bid a fond farewell to the staff and the patients who were in the dayroom and addressed the patients to have good health and a speedy discharge and to find a comfort zone in the community. To the staff I stated, "It has been a pleasure and an honor to have worked shoulder to shoulder with you. Although we have had some ups and downs, there were much more ups than downs, I feel that if we always agreed with each other, it would have made for a very boring ward. Stay in good health, be happy, be content and I will try to stay in touch with you!"

As I turned and walked down the back staircase, I knew that this would be the final time I had to walk up or down this staircase. Getting in my car and driving down the hill, I knew that I would make one more trip up and down the VA road when I came back tomorrow morning to clear.

The morning of February 1, 2011 had arrived and making myself a cup of coffee, I was looking out my kitchen window at the darkness that still prevailed at 6 a.m. The sky appeared to be white and the temperature was 22 degrees. I turned the TV on to the weather channel to catch what the weather was predicted for the day. I wasn't surprised when the weatherman stated that there was a snowstorm predicted because I knew snow was in the air when I noticed the white sky earlier. I hoped that the snow would not start until I was done clearing because I had to wait until 8 a.m. before I could get my clearing slip from the secretary in mental health because she didn't arrive until 8 a.m.

At 7:30 a.m., I left my house and started my final trek to the VA to clear. I drove my usual route along Rte. 5 and just before I entered Northampton, I noticed that it started to snow. Small flakes were falling on my windshield, but not enough that I had to turn the wipers on. When I reached the entrance to the VA, I parked my car behind the eastside of building 1. The time was 7:55 a.m., so I entered the building and walked down the hallway of the mental health service and found the secretary sitting in her office. I pleasantly greeted her and she returned the greeting and then handed me a piece of paper and stated, "Linda, you have to have all of these departments signed off before you turn it back in to me! You have to go to everyone and they will check their records to see if you have anything outstanding. Good luck and happy clearing!"

I figured that I should start my clearing in the building that I was already in because I thought it would save some time, which it did, until I hit a glitch in another building when an employee didn't arrive at work because of the falling snow which was falling heavier and was now covering the ground and the roadways. I was informed by her co-workers that she would be coming into work, but she will be late because she lives up in the hills and the snowfall is much worse up there. Hearing this information, I decided to continue and clear with the rest of the departments and save this one for last. I managed to clear everyone except the last by 9:30 a.m., so I decided to have some breakfast in the canteen and wait for the employee to arrive. I met Scrappy Lindstrom in the canteen and informed her that I was clearing and asked her to join me at a table for breakfast. Scrappy quickly accepted my invitation and as we took a seat at a table, she looked at me and said, "I can't believe that you are actually leaving!"

Looking at Scrappy and shaking my head, I showed her the paper that I had for clearing and told her that I had only one more stop to make and then I leave the hill never to return again. She never noticed that I was no longer wearing my ID tag because I had already turned it in along with my VA keys. She appeared to be sad. So, in trying to prevent her from being depressed, I started to talk about some of our past escapades when we worked together at the community care center and ward 8. At about 11

293

a.m., I received a call in the canteen that informed me that the individual for my last stop had reported into work. I traveled from the canteen to the second floor of building 12 where I met with a very pleasant woman who apologized profusely for being late and holding up my clearing process. We talked for a little bit after she signed the paper and informed me that the snow was about six inches deep and continued to come down heavily. I thanked her and excused myself because I had a long trip back to Holyoke after I handed this paper back to the secretary in mental health. She bid me good luck in my retirement and as I exited building 12, I noticed that the snow was deeper than it was before I left the canteen. Walking across the parking lot while the snow was blowing hard and quickly piling up, I entered building 1, walked down the hallway to mental health and handed the clearing paper to the secretary. She bid me good luck and after saying "Thank you" I walked out the door and cleared my car of the snow that had piled up on it. Driving my car down the hill of the VA for the last time, I knew that my connections with the VA were now done. Any identity with the VA that I had was turned in and my name was cleared off of the computer, the phone and any electronic devices that were assigned to me. The door to my VA life that lasted thirty-four years was finally closed today.

Conclusion

This book was written for a number of reasons, but primarily to give the Veteran a voice that could be heard above and beyond Washington DC. The American Veteran is the one who has preserved our rights of freedom of speech, press, religion, to bear arms etc., not the Senate or Congress. Congress takes a vote on whether the United States should or should not enter a war, but they are not the ones who go to war. The Veterans are mechanics, farmers, plumbers, artists, doctors, nurses, carpenters and multiple other tradesmen and professionals who love and strongly believe that our Constitution is worth upholding and protecting. There is no hesitation when our country and citizens are under attack for the principles of which this country was founded and that any man or woman would proudly fight to defend and preserve these principles and freedoms.

Over the years, I have pondered expressions and sayings that Veterans have uttered during some speeches or addresses to some grand assembly like a college, university or a military academy. Gen. Douglas MacArthur was the main speaker for a graduating class of West Point Cadets in years past and in his speech he stated that, "Old soldiers never die, they just fade away". I have rolled this statement around in my brain trying to make some sense of it and being the concrete thinker that I am, this was not an easy task to do. I recalled every prominent Veteran I could think of starting with the Revolutionary War right up to the Iraqi War. I thought of Washington, Andrew Jackson, Robert E. Lee, Ulysses S. Grant, Thomas "Stonewall" Jackson, Theodore Roosevelt, Audie Murphy, The Five Sullivan's and countless others who fought to preserve our right to be and remain a free nation. I also thought about the city and town commons that have monuments with names of the Veterans who proudly served and died in the various wars. The smallest hamlet and village has displayed pride in recognition of any Veteran who hailed from their area. This past June, I was on a bus trip to the Amish Country in Pennsylvania and on my way back, the bus rode through the town of New Holland, PA. As we traveled through the town, I noticed that there wasn't a vacant light post that was not displaying a banner with the picture of a Veteran along with his/her name, branch of service and the date of death and the war that they fought in. I was filled with such pride that I thought that my heart was going to leap out of my chest in that this town showed an enormous respect and admiration for their fallen Veterans. If there is any reward for towns or cities that display pride and respect for their Veterans, New Holland, PA would be at the top of my list as a recipient because of the true love they have for their Veterans and for the United States. The banners and monuments in the town commons and the flags that are displayed in cemeteries on Memorial Day, throughout this country are recognized to respect all of our deceased Veterans. I also think of the 58,000 names on a wall in Washington DC who lost their lives in Vietnam. These are all soldiers who have died, but are not forgotten. It is in this thinking that I feel that Gen. MacArthur's statement was said in reverse and should have been stated as, "Old soldiers do die, and they never fade away!"

In some of my research, I discovered that there were 26 of the 44 presidents who were Veterans, with 20 being combat Veterans. We Americans are aware of Washington, Andrew Jackson, U.S. Grant, Theodore Roosevelt, Eisenhower and Kennedy as being war heroes, but many have no idea that James Monroe was an officer in the Revolutionary War or that William Henry Harrison and Zachary Taylor fought in the War of 1812. A. Johnson, Hayes, Garfield, Arthur, B. Harrison and McKinley all fought in the Civil War. Harry Truman was a Veteran of WWI and L. Johnson, Nixon, Ford, Reagan and G.H.W. Bush served in WWII. Many never would think of Abraham Lincoln as being a Veteran, but he was a Veteran of the Black Hawk War and is listed in the military Army records as being a Veteran.

A Veteran, by definition, is a person who has served in the armed forces of a country. They do not specify that they have had to be involved in combat or that they have to be men only, but rather anyone who enlists into the armed forces is considered a Veteran when their tour of duty is complete. I firmly believe that our greatest export is the United States military being that our country has established military bases all over the world. Our military has fought for the rights of people who were unable to fight for themselves and many American soldiers have perished in doing this assignment by sacrificing their lives to a people and a country they don't even know. This has been true for every war that American soldiers have fought in foreign countries, which is inclusive of all wars from the Spanish American War to the Iraqi/Afghanistan War of today.

A soldier's mind is pliable in that he enlisted into the military for the excitement and the glory that he viewed in the war movies and he was looking for this same experience for himself. He soon realized that his/her introduction to basic training was a far cry from anything he ever anticipated. Disillusionment was now occupying their thoughts and it is not to say that they made a mistake by enlisting, rather the mistake was made in believing in the movies. One has to learn to be a soldier, it doesn't happen just by putting on a uniform. Soldiers are trained physically and mentally up to the limits of their endurance and sometimes beyond and I have heard many parents make the statement, "The boy that left my house to join the military is not the same son that returned home!"

Many mothers have expressed changes that they have seen in their sons when they have completed their basic training. Along with these changes, the majority of mothers have exhibited enormous pride in their soldier sons and upon seeing these regimented men in full uniform, they became so excited that they would shed tears of joy while hugging them. These young soldiers have completed the first hurdle of their military life and are aware that they no longer belong to their civilian family, but rather are a full member of the family of the military of the United States of America.

When I first started working in the VA, there were several Veterans in the system that were drafted into the armed forces and it was only after they were in boot camp that many of these draftees were recognized as having some form of mental illness. Many were discharged immediately with a

Service-connected pension and remained permanent residents in various VA facilities. There were a few combat Veterans that were drafted and sent to Vietnam, but they were truly few and far between the men who enlisted and chose to fight in combat. My exposure with combat Veterans were soldiers who fought in the Vietnam War. They were a tough bunch of guys and they didn't trust anyone or anything, particularly anything that was connected with the Federal Government. There were several grievances that these combat Veterans uttered to a few employees that they felt comfortable to communicate with and I was honored to be one of them. The grievances that were mentioned are as follows:

"I can't understand that a country that sent me over to fight a war will not accept me back home! I have been called Baby-killer, hooch burner and had garbage thrown at my uniform and some or should I say many, have been told to take their uniform off before the plane lands. None of this makes sense to me because when I left the USA in full combat dress to go to Vietnam, there was no one at the airports throwing garbage at us. As a matter of fact, it was very quiet leaving. I would even accept a quiet reception on my return to my country rather than having shouts of nasty name-calling and rotten fruit and vegetables thrown at me!"

I have heard several complaints by combat soldiers about the government and the manner in which the government is run. They feel that all senators and congressmen should have served time in the military because you have to be part of something in order to understand it. The President is "Commander and Chief" of the armed forces, but if he has never been in the military, how can he be in charge of something he knows nothing about? How can he make a military decision that concerns the lives of a hundred thousand men and women serving in the military? I was amazed to hear combat Veterans discuss their political views so openly and to express a basic requirement for anyone to run for the Senate, Congress and President of the United States, in that anyone applying for these offices should have some experience in the military. The more they talked, the more I had to agree with their suggestions and requirements for the governing administrative leaders of this country. Everything these Veterans said made perfect sense to me and as I sat back in my chair in the dayroom, I was making a mental comparison of a non-military President as Commander-in-Chief of the armed services to be equivalent of a Park Ranger being head of the American Medical Association. A Park Ranger hasn't the slightest notion or experience of being a doctor and is now in a position of telling them what to do and directing them in areas that are not familiar to the doctors. A doctor's job is to save lives, a soldier's job is to defend lives and principles. Thus, when there is someone who is placed in charge with no knowledge of the field they are in charge of results in mistakes and loss of lives. More than half of the Presidents of this country have been Veterans and I am sure that many of the Senate and Congress were also Veterans who served during the many wars that occurred on our own soil and abroad. A Veteran knows how to be Commander-in-Chief of the armed forces as a result of his/her experience in the military and would make a logical decision concerning every uniformed soldier or sailor and would protect, to the best of his ability, the citizens of the United States from foreign and domestic foes. Therefore, I firmly believe that for anyone to run for the Senate, Congress or the President of the United States he/she should be required to have served time in the military prior to their application to those positions.

The respect and admiration that I have for Veterans goes deep into my very cells. I learned to sing the Star Spangled Banner as a child and I still continue to belt it out when I hear it. There is one difference though, today when I sing our national anthem my eyes well up with tears as I stare at the most beautiful flag in the world. I think of those men and women who sacrificed their lives to preserve our freedom to continue to live in accordance with our Constitution and the American way of life.

When I worked the PTSD unit, I recall so many combat Veterans that died; not from a trip-wire, a grenade or a bullet from an enemy's rifle, but rather from their own hand. There were well over three hundred Veterans that took their own lives because of flashbacks that occurred on a daily basis that would trigger a horrific memory or experience in Vietnam. Many were fearful to go to sleep for fear that they would be back in the jungle or the rice paddy completely surrounded by Viet Cong who were bombarding our soldiers with everything they had. Many squads would go out consisting of five to seven men for a search and destroy mission and often there would be four or six men returning. When another squad was sent out the following day, they would come across the missing soldier impaled on a tree with his castrated genitals stuffed in his mouth. Another combat Veteran told me of an incident that involved a small Vietnamese child of about four years of age. The soldier was part of a small combat group that was resting in a small clearing in the jungle. The clearing was just outside of a village that they presumed was friendly. They heard some rustling of leaves and noticed at the far end of the clearing a small Vietnamese boy who was harnessed with grenades and this boy was walking in their direction. Upon realizing that they were live grenades, the soldier stood up and motioned the boy to go back to the village with his hand, but the little boy continued to walk toward them. He knew that he had no choice and he picked up his rifle and shot the little boy thus preventing his group from being blown to smithereens. I noticed that this Veteran had tears that were welling up in his eyes as he told me this horrific experience that he endured. He appeared to be in an emotional limbo somewhere because he wasn't proud that he saved his men from being killed and he wasn't ashamed that he killed the little boy. He had an expression of bewilderment on his face and the only word he stated was, "Why?" Sitting silently beside this Veteran, I wondered about the question he just asked and my only response was, "Why? What?"

"Why do things happen in ways that you don't expect? I was trained to fight combat man-to-man, but Vietnam was so different from other wars! None of the Viet Cong had uniforms and many were women and children. In the United States we are raised to protect women and children and respect the elderly, but in Vietnam they put live explosives on women and children and these individuals are instructed to go into a group of American soldiers and wound or kill them. The children have no idea that their lives will be sacrificed, but the women are well aware because the women lure the soldiers to brothels where the prostitutes or the beds are fixed to trigger an explosion during the sex act. I can't get these memories or thoughts out of my mind and I think I'm crazy!"

I listened intently to the two Veterans that were conversing about their experiences in Vietnam and now understood more than I had in the past about the combat Vietnam Veteran. I knew why so many were alcoholics and drug addicts because this was the only way that they could wipe the thoughts and memories out of their heads, even if it was only for an hour. I understood that they were taught to be top-notch soldiers, but they were never instructed as to the culture of the country they were fighting in. The Vietnamese have a high respect for the afterlife and they also believe that the body has to be whole when they die or else the spirit will wander forever and never rest. This is the reason that they castrated soldiers, removed their ears, fingers or toes and in some cases, a decapitation, but most of the time it was having the body impaled on a tree with his castrated genitals stuffed in his mouth because this was an insult after the killing by the Viet Cong to have the spirit of the American soldier to wander and never rest.

I enjoyed working with Veterans and I grew particularly close to the Vietnam Veterans because of the manner in which they were treated in our own United States. These were the forgotten soldiers that were taken prisoners of war in their own country, who had garbage greeting them instead of a ticker tape parade as was had in other wars for our returning soldiers. There were no hugs and kisses of greeting for the Vietnam Veterans returning home or a "thank you" for serving in the armed forces. They came home to a country that they no longer knew and were treated like they were the enemy and a stranger on their own soil. The Vietnam Veterans fought in the longest war in American history which involved fifteen years of constant combat and for these combat Veterans in which 58,000 died and had their names chiseled on a wall in Washington DC, had finally received the recognition they deserved. What about the survivors of that war? These are the ones that returned with multiple mental and emotional problems. These are the ones that were so numb and full of distrust even for their own families. They rarely smiled because there was nothing that pleased them or comforted them in any way. They were not allowed to join any VFW's, American Legions or any military club because they were told by WWII and Korean War Veterans that Vietnam was no war, so they were not allowed to join. Not to put the blame on the media because I'm sure that their intentions were beneficial, but they appeared to be one-sided in their reports and pictures. I recall seeing pictures of mass graves of dead Viet Cong covered with lime and the universal picture of the little girl running down the road, burnt by napalm at the My Lai massacre. These pictures were published in newspapers and magazines all across the United States and my fellow Americans believed these dead to be civilians because they wore no uniforms. The little girl was an innocent victim and a tragic site, but she survived and I believe she is living very contently in Canada. I never saw a picture of American soldiers in body bags, piled five feet high on a loading dock at the airport or being loaded on the planes to return to the United States and their final resting place. Never saw a picture of a slaughtered American squad and one of the members impaled on a tree or a soldier holding the mortally wounded body of his friend in his arms attempting to comfort him as he takes his last breath of life. These are the pictures that remain in the minds of the surviving combat Veterans who were exposed and experienced these travesties and that the American people never saw in any paper or magazine. I firmly believe that if both sides were represented equally by the media, the American public would have had a better understanding of the combat Veteran and would have given him the respect and gratitude that he deserved.

As I stated at the beginning, I am writing this book to give a voice to the Veteran who has difficulty explaining his feelings, continues to be numb after thirty and forty years. These Veterans experienced divorce, loss of a job, loss of children because the divorce awarded the children to the mother, siblings and parents that don't understand what the Veteran is going through and finding it hard to relate to them. The Veteran has been kicked to the curb for a long time and I am pleased that the Iraqi/Afghanistan Veterans are recognized and there are many program and projects that are available to assist them and their families. The voices of the Veterans that I would like to have heard throughout this country are the Veterans from Operation Desert Storm, Bosnia, Lebanon and the Vietnam War. I ask God's blessing on every American Veteran because no one, not peasant or president would be living in the greatest country in the world and experiencing the freedoms that those Veterans fought to keep.

God bless the United States Veterans and God bless the United States of America and God grant that Old Glory will forever wave over the land of the free and the home of the brave.

Relatives in the military

Brothers

David J. Leary – US Army

David entered the service on 4/19/59 and did his basic training at Ft. Dix, NJ. His MOS was heavy equipment operator along with a secondary MOS as guided missile instillation electronic maintenance. Dave did his advanced training at Ft. Leonard Wood, Missouri. Spent eighteen months in Korea and was discharged on 5/7/62 at the rank of SF4. Sadly, David passed away on 8/16/13, a month shy of his 73rd birthday.

Kevin M. Leary – US Navy (Seabees)

Kevin entered the Seabees on 8/4/66 and did his basic training in Davisville, RI. His MOS was equipment operator and he had advanced equipment training in Gulfport, Mississippi. Kevin belonged to mobile construction battalion 40 (MCB-40) which was commonly referred to as "Fighting Forty". His entire battalion was sent to Camp Lejeune, NC for combat training. Kevin had two nine-month tours of Vietnam with three months off between tours. His first tour was from 10/67 – 7/68 and his second was from 10/68 – 7/69. He was discharged from the Naval Seabees on 7/31/69 at the rank of EO2/E5.

William C Leary Jr. – US Navy

William enlisted into the Navy on 7/21/61 and basic training was done at the Great Lakes Naval Training Center in Illinois. Bill's MOS was seaman and he was assigned to the USS Courtney (DE-121). His ship was on alert for the Cuban Missile Crisis. Bill stated that when they were at sea, there were many unusual sights that he witnessed such as: water spouts, St. Elmo's fire, and the eeriness of the Bermuda Triangle when there were no stars in the sky and total quiet. He was discharged on 12/12/64 at the rank of E-3.

Dennis R. Benson – US Air Force

Dennis is my brother- in-law and an important member of my family because he is my one-and-only brother-in-law. Dennis enlisted into the United States Air Force on June 7, 1966 and his MOS was base supply (64550). He worked several jobs under this MOS and was even lent out to the US Marine Corps. Dennis did his basic training in Lackland AFB in Texas and attended tech school in Amarillo, Texas. He spent three years in Italy at Aviano AFB as part of NATO and was transferred to Luke AFB in Arizona for his final year of enlistment. Dennis was honorably discharged on April 1 1970 and the highest rank he achieved was Staff Sergeant (E-5). He stated that he was released two months early because the military was downsizing and was allowing several military branches to release potential discharges, two to three months early.

Nephews

Scott M. Leary – US Air Force

Scott enlisted on 8/20/90 and completed his basic training at Lackland AFB in Texas. He completed his advanced training at Chanute AFB in Illinois and his MOS was (45426) Electro-environmental systems technician for flight lines. Scott always worked his MOS for his entire time in the service. He was indirectly involved in Desert Shield and Desert Storm. He was transferred to McCord AFB in Tacoma, Washington for the last two and a half years of his enlistment. He was discharged on 12/18/93 under the Palace/Chase program as a result of the drawback of troops from Desert Storm and was needed in AMC (Air Mobile Command) and was stationed at Westover AFB in Chicopee, MA until 1996. Scott was discharged at the rank of staff sergeant (E-5).

Christopher R. Leary – US Navy

Chris enlisted into the Navy in May of 1990 and attended basic training in San Diego CA. His MOS was aviation electricians mate (AE). He was in the service during the Gulf War but was never directly involved in it. Chris always worked his MOS on helicopters aboard ship. He was assigned HM-14 which was helicopter mine-countermeasures squadron 14 in Norfolk Naval Air Station. He was aboard ship only once and stated that he did many land assignments and in 1992 was in Cherry Point NC showing Marines our mission capabilities for getting aircraft up. In 1993, Chris was involved in Operation Joint Venture aboard the USS Inchon (LPH-12) in which he flew out and met the ship and spent two months in the North Sea and his duty was to locate old German mines in the North Sea. Chris discharged from the Navy in December of 1994 at the rank of E-4 (3rd class petty officer).

Sean B. Leary – US Navy

Sean enlisted on 6/6/86 into the US Navy and his basic training was done at the Great Lakes Naval Training Center in Illinois. His MOS was machinist mate and he was never directly involved in any wars or conflicts, although he did state that his assigned ship, The USS Saratoga was stationed in the Gulf of Sidra (pre-Gulf War). Sean worked his MOS for the entire time he was in the service. He was discharged on 12/7/90 at the rank of E-4 (petty officer 3rd class).

Terrance W. Leary – US Navy

Terry enlisted into the Navy on 7/7/87. His MOS was engine mate (EN2) and he also was a sharpshooter for the boat crew. He spent nine months in the Red Sea aboard the USS Saratoga during Operation Desert Storm. He was discharged on 6/6/91 as an EN2 (E-5) upon completing four years in the military.

Timothy J. Leary – US Army

Tim enlisted in October 1985 and his basic training was done at Ft. Benning GA where he also attending airborne training. He was assigned to the 325th airborne and his MOS was 11B (combat soldier). Tim always worked his MOS in the service and he served in the Panama Crisis in 1989. Tim also worked with the border patrol in Texas on the Mexican border. He was activated in 1990 by the individual ready reserves for the Gulf War for two months but was never deployed. Tim discharged from the Army in 1991 at the rank of Sergeant (E-5). He is presently a lieutenant on the Holyoke Fire Department.

Daniel J. Major – US Air Force

Dan enlisted into the Air Force Reserves on 8/10/81. On 9/15/81 he did his basic training at Lackland AFB in Texas. He did his advanced training at Lackland and Bullis AFB for 6 additional weeks where he was trained as a security specialist and received a MOS of 81190 (security specialist). Dan was activated to full active-duty twice during his twenty-three years in the Reserves: 1) 12/3/90 – 7/31/91 – Desert Shield, 2) 11/5/01 – 9/3/03 – Enduring Freedom. Dan's duty during his activation was to guard Air Force weapon systems at bases and on planes. He was discharged on 1/31/04 with the rank of E-8 (Senior master sergeant). He is presently employed at the rank of sergeant on the Chicopee Police Department.

Patrick J. Major – US Air Force

Patrick enlisted into the Air Force on 9/2/86 and did his basic training at Lackland AFB in Texas and his advanced training at Lowry AFB in Aurora, CO. His MOS was precision measurement equipment operator (32450). He was discharged on 3/12/90 at the rank of E-4. Patrick enlisted into the Massachusetts Air National Guard on 6/1990 and was stationed at Barnes ANGB in Westfield, MA. While at Barnes, he was involved in several world conflicts. He spent August and September of 1995 in Bosnia. He was sent to Kuwait in 2000 and was involved in Operation Southern Watch. From 2/2003 – 6/2003 he was involved in Operation Iraqi Freedom. Patrick stated that during his enlistment in the US Air Force Reserves, he had several MOS's such as ITTS, Electrical Warfare Specialist and Maintenance Control Specialist. He was discharged from the USAFR on 10/12/06 with the rank of E-7 (Master Sergeant). Like his brother, Patrick is employed at the Chicopee Police Department at the rank of lieutenant.

John Rasmussen – US Navy

John enlisted into the Navy in August 1983. He did his basic training at the Great Lakes Naval Training Center in Illinois. John's MOS was propulsion plant basic/machinist mate. He completed nuclear power training in Orlando, Florida, where he also had prototype training and his MOS switched to nuclear machinist mate (MM1/SS). He then attended SIC in Windsor Locks CT for six months for training in submarine engine propulsion. John always worked his MOS on submarines while in the service. His longest cruise was 87 days under water in the North Atlantic. He discharged from the Navy in August 1991 as a 1st Class Petty Officer (E-6).

Cousins

Joseph J. (JJ) George – US Navy

JJ completed Navy pilot training in 1975. As an E2C pilot he deployed aboard the USS John F Kennedy, the USS Forrestal and the USS Coral Sea. In 2/15/91 he served aboard the USS Theodore Roosevelt and was stationed in the Northern Arabian Gulf. He took command Of VAW-124 (Bear Aces). He served as comptroller at Naval Station, Norfolk, VA. He also served as Naval Attache' American Embassy Brasilia, Brazil and Executive officer at the Naval Air Station, Oceana. JJ served and dedicated 29 years in the Navy and was discharged at the rank of Captain. Sadly, JJ passed away on 12-21-11, two months after his 60th birthday.

Susan (Leary) George – US Navy

Susan was commissioned as an Ensign USNR in December 1974. She entered Officer Indoctrination School (OIS) in Newport RI in January 1975. 1975 – 1978, she served as a staff nurse at Naval Hospital, Corpus Christi, TX. Completed the Navy Operating Nurses Program at Camp Pendleton, CA and finished her tour as an operating room nurse. From 1978 – 1982 – served as OR nurse at Naval Medical Center, Portsmouth, VA. 1982 – 1986 stationed at Lafayette River Naval Medical Clinic as a clinic nurse; completed assignment as the Officer in Charge. 1986 – 1987 was Division Officer at Naval Hospital, Keflavik, Iceland. 1987 – 1990 served as Division Officer General Surgery & Plastic Surgery Clinics at National Naval Medical Center Bethesda, MD. 1990 – 1993 served as Division Officer and Assistant Officer in charge of Sewell's Point Clinic, Naval Base Norfolk, VA. 1993 – 1995 served as Department head ambulatory surgery unit, post-anesthesia care unit and Pediatrics & Oral Surgery Clinic. Susan served Stateside during Operation Desert Storm and Desert Shield. She retired in 1995 after serving twenty years in the military. She retired at the rank of Commander USN.

Albert Laprise – US Army

Al joined ROTC in college and entered the Army on 10/6/55 and was immediately promoted to an officer's rank. He served in peacetime and from July 1956 – September 4, 1957 served thirteen months in Germany where he was head of the 2nd platoon, 3rd Army. He was discharged on 9/4/1957 at the rank of 1st lieutenant.

Christine Leary – US Air National Guard

Chris entered the Guards in August 1992. She did her officer training at Ft. Sam Houston, TX. In 1994 she was stationed at Brooks AFB for flight nurse training for six months in Texas. In October 1997, Chris was stationed in Panama for three months to bring injured back to Brooks. In December 1999, she was stationed in Germany at Ramstief AFB. In January 2000, she left for Kosovo for three months. In 2003, Chris was stationed back in Germany for three months in support of the injured troops from Afghanistan and in 2005 did the same for the injured troops in Iraq. Chris was discharged in August 2013 as a major.

John T Leary Jr. – US Army

John enlisted into the Army on August 25, 1972. He did his basic training at Ft. Dix, NJ and his MOS was 76D – Divisional logistics. John was never involved in any wars. He was stationed in Germany for six years and was assigned to an anti-terrorist team which was basically a domestic deal. John did his AIT at Ft. Leonard Wood, Missouri. In Germany he was stationed at Ramstief AFB and his job was to protect planes. John was discharged in May 1980 at the rank of E-5.

Rebecca I. Leary – US Coast Guard

Becky enlisted in the United States Coast Guard in July 2000. Her basic training was done at Cape May, NJ. Her MOS was a boatswain. Her first duty station was in Newport, RI and then she was stationed in Sandy Hook, NJ. Becky was discharged at the rank of petty officer 3rd Class in 2004. She is presently an FBI agent in Portland, Oregon.

Mark D. Waterhouse – US Army

Mark enlisted into the Army in May 1981. He served as a Captain in the US Army for 7 ½ years. Mark served 51 months in the armored division located in Nurnburg, Germany. In his last assignment, he had the distinction to serve as Company Commander of more than 300 soldiers in Ft. Jackson SC. Mark was a paratrooper and was awarded the Meritorious Service Medal for his services to our country. Mark discharged in December 1988 at the rank of Captain.

<u>Close friend and neighbor</u>
Thomas M. Chirgwin – US Coast Guard

Tom served in the US Coast Guard from 1965 – 1969. His basic training was in Cape May NJ and his advanced training as a radar man was for eight weeks training in Groton CT. Tom served as radar man on the USS Half Moon and served one year in Vietnam when he was stationed in Tonkin Bay. Tom was discharged in September 1969 at the rank of 3rd Class Radar man. I mentioned Tom as part of the family because I grew up with him and he is still my next door neighbor. I couldn't be any closer to him if he was my brother

Acknowledgements

Brooke Heisler-Leary

Brooke is my great niece and she has been highly beneficial in assisting with the copying, spacing and grammatical corrections in the writing of this book. She has been my right-arm assistant in her computer knowledge and has saved my sanity and fear of possibly erasing this book, if by chance, by pressing the wrong key. She makes up for my lack of computer knowledge. Brooke is a senior at Holyoke High School and is a member of the National Honor Society, the school marching band and an active member of the Holyoke Crew Club. She is enrolled in all advance classes at school and is interested in furthering her education in the Engineering field when she graduates from high school in June 2014. She is also interested in attending the United States Coast Guard Academy in Groton CT. Brooke informed the family that she has been accepted to the Coast Guard Academy and is expected to start her studies there on July 21, 2014. I am very proud of her.

Douglas P. Major

Doug is my nephew and a very talented artist and actor. He had been drawing free-hand since around the age of 4 years. I have an oil painting that he painted for me when he was fourteen years old and proudly display it on the wall in my game room. Doug is the designer of the cover of this book and I am grateful and proud that he accepted this task. Doug lives in New York City across from Central Park and is frequently seen in the park taking his dog Ivy for a walk when he is not busy working in the back street theater district. He has performed in many theaters in Western Massachusetts and in October 2012, Doug was requested, by popular demand, to return to the Majestic Theater in West Springfield, MA to star as Mickey in "Blood Brothers", which he performed in over fifteen years ago in that same theater. Doug was born in Northampton, MA and raised in Chicopee, MA where he graduated from Chicopee Comprehensive High School in 1983. He became interested in the acting field when he was hired to paint the background setting for a play in South Hadley MA. He has played many major roles in several theaters throughout the Pioneer Valley and also had a bit part as the warden in the movie "Sleepers" which was filmed in Connecticut. There is no doubt that Douglas is extremely talented in the

Field of Art and the main reason I approached him for the cover of this book.

Paula M. Mogelinski

Paula is my dear and close friend with top-notch computer and editing skills. She is the primary editor of this book and has done an outstanding job in editing this book and making this book uniform and in proper format. Paula attended Greenfield Community College and received her Associates degree in Executive Secretarial in 1976. She is the oldest of six children and has lived in Sunderland, MA her entire life. Paula has a talent to multi-task, in that she cared for her mother until her mother's passing in October of 2004 and is presently caring for her father and an elderly uncle (father's brother). She is also the family member that her siblings approach when they are seeking an opinion or advice about family situations that are problematic to them. Paula is one of those individuals who possess a heart of gold that is seen by her family and friends through her loyalty, understanding, sincere and compassionate behaviors that she freely gives to them. She is unique and special and I feel privileged to have her as my friend.

Donna Fountain

Donna was a high school classmate of mine and she is responsible for the picture of me on the back cover of this book. I had not seen Donna since graduating high school in 1967 because we all went our separate ways and approached life's goals in different ways. Strangely, we reconnected with each other at my niece's funeral (Brooke's mother) and it was there that I was informed that Brooke's boyfriend was Donna's grandson. Donna had photographed several weddings and senior class pictures for the student yearbook and when she learned that I was writing a book, she inquired if I would allow her to take my picture for the back cover of the book. I was pleased she had mentioned having my picture on the back cover because the thought never crossed my mind. She did a terrific job since I haven't had a picture done of me in over forty years. It really is a small world after all!

All Veterans

The United States Veterans have to be acknowledged because we would not even have a country if it was not for the love, dedication and efforts of our veterans. Veterans have protected and defended our freedoms and thousands of lives have been lost in accomplishing the task in keeping America free. Veterans are the alpha and omega of this book and it doesn't matter if the veterans were from the Revolutionary War or the Afghanistan War of today. Administrations do not win wars, but they continually take the credit for it. These administrations are not just limited to Washington D.C., but rather to include any administration that deals with veterans such as all VA facilities (hospitals, clinics, outreach centers, domiciliaries and outpatient clinics). Veterans have protected our homelands and shores for centuries and even

George Washington, when he was President, wanted to isolate our country because he felt that the United States was highly vulnerable and needed to build up the strength and morale of this new country. The people of the United States owe the veterans the utmost gratitude for serving instead of having negative marches and unpatriotic aggression towards them. When I would read or view these negative behaviors, I am sure that these agitators never thought of the veteran that defended their right to demonstrate, the right to free speech and the right to express their feelings. These agitators would be shot on the streets if they were in China or Russia or any country that is under oppression. Veterans are the strength of this country and I will continue to respect and honor them, right to the time that I take my last breath of life. The veteran took care of us, why is this country not caring for them with respect and acknowledgement in making them as comfortable as they have made us. We were able to sleep at night while they stood watch and made sure we were safe. The Veterans are the ones who should be receiving entitlements, not the illegal aliens or any other foreigner who has entered the United States looking for a free handout. The Veteran has been the first one cut from their benefits and their care and treatment. The illegal can walk into an emergency room and get 100% care within an hour, the veteran has to wait nine to ten months to be seen in a VA facility and many times they have had their appointments cancelled and were never called back with a rescheduled appointment. There is nothing fair in this country in its treatment of our veterans. I seriously feel that there should be some new amendments to our constitution that protects, supports and cares for our Veterans because they are the defenders of our country and they keep us safe. May God Always Bless Our Veterans!